D0847190

WITHDRAWN

3 0700 10914 8584

MANAGEMENT EDUCATION IN THE NETWORK ECONOMY

MANAGEMENT EDUCATION IN THE NETWORK ECONOMY

ITS CONTEXT, CONTENT, AND ORGANIZATION

by

P.J. van Baalen

and

L.T. Moratis

Erasmus University Rotterdam, The Netherlands

KLUWER ACADEMIC PUBLISHERS

BOSTON / DORDRECHT / LONDON

A C.I.P. Catalogue record for this book is available from the Library of Congress.

ISBN 0-7923-7595-5

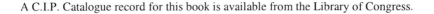

Published by Kluwer Academic Publishers,
P.O. Box 17, 3300 AA Dordrecht, The Netherlands.

Sold and distributed in North, Central and South America
by Kluwer Academic Publishers,
101 Philip Drive, Norwell, MA 02061, U.S.A.

In all other countries, sold and distributed
by Kluwer Academic Publishers,
P.O. Box 322, 3300 AH Dordrecht, The Netherlands.

Printed on acid-free paper

All Rights Reserved
© 2001 Kluwer Academic Publishers, Boston
No part of the material protected by this copyright notice may be reproduced or
utilized in any form or by any means, electronic or mechanical,
including photocopying, recording, or by any information storage and
retrieval system, without written permission from the copyright owner.

Printed in the Netherlands

Table of contents

**Chapter 6   The institutional perspective: Business schools'
markets, organization, and strategy**

Preface

This year 2001, The Rotterdam School of Management/Faculteit Bedrijfskunde is celebrating its sixth lustrum. In the thirty years of its existence, the School has evolved into an international business school, focused on the acquisition, transfer and application of knowledge, with respect to entrepreneurship and management. Research driven, because we want to pre-act on economical, technological and societal developments and their impact on management, interdisciplinary and guided by the future needs of international business. The School has preserved its distinctive pragmatic identity and has been able to build a solid reputation over the years. In fact, the School has been among the thirty best business schools worldwide the past few years.

Our School is very much aware of the power of contemporary developments in its environment and their possible far-reaching consequences for management education, ways of learning, composition of faculty and students, and the organization of business schools. The reality of the network economy is that it is causing landslide changes in the organization and management of enterprises. More and more, traditional monolithic firms have become flexible networks of international outsourcing and comakership. But these changes have their impact also on management research and education, and for business schools there is an excellent opportunity to reconfigure organizational arrangements following the same network logic. That is, why the School took, on the occasion of its thirtiest anniversary, the initiative to write this book. To show, that we recognize the changes and the consequences they have for our future activities and organization.

This book reflects on these encompassing developments. It tries to grasp the essential characteristics and dynamism of what nowadays is called "the new economy" and introduces the network perspective, in order to integrate the different characteristics of the new economy into one concept. Furthermore, it presents a particular vision on the organization of management education and business schools. On the basis of this vision, the School is actively (re)designing its strategy and preparing its future programs and activities, in order to play its role in management research and education in the coming decades.

I am proud to present this book to you. I hope that you will find enjoyment in reading it and that it will elicit new and innovative thinking regarding the organization of management education and strategy in business schools.

Prof.dr. P.H.A.M. Verhaegen
Dean Rotterdam School of Management/Faculteit Bedrijfskunde

Acknowledgments

More than a year ago, we started to write this book about the implications of the emerging 'new economy' for management education. At that time, there were hardly any signs that the new economy would collapse into just a 'normal' economy with increasing inflation, decreasing economic growth, downsizing of firms, and large-scale lay-offs. The word 'new' covered a wide range of developments and it appeared to be hard to study these from a single clear perspective. Moreover, what's new, becomes old.

After a lot of reading and our discussions with experts in the field of management education and people from business, we found that the network concept fitted the things we wanted to describe best. We therefore tried to think through the implications of the rise of an emerging network economy for the demand for new management knowledge, competencies and managerial roles, the implications for existing pedagogical views, the use of ICT and network concepts for learning, and organizational structures of business schools. We have tried to support our view by empirical research done by leading researchers and institutes, by collecting examples and cases, by combining innovative ideas we found in literature, and by discussing with visionary people in the field of management education.

However, this book would not have been written without the support of a number of people that should be rendered thanks to. We are indebted to Peter Lorange and Annie Tobias (IMD), Eric Cornuel, Liliana Petrella, Nicola Hijlkema, Gordon Shenton, and Veronique Roumans (efmd), Walter Baets (Nyenrode), and the Department of Management Learning at Lancaster University, in particular Stephen Fox, Mark Easterby-Smith, Vivien Hodgson, and Anthony Hesketh, for their willingness to contribute and exchange ideas. Paul Verhaegen (Dean Rotterdam School of Management/Faculteit Bedrijfskunde) and Han van Dissel (Rotterdam School of Management/Faculteit Bedrijfskunde and director of Erasmus Executive Development) are rendered thanks to for creating the opportunity to write this book. A word of thanks is also directed towards Jeroen Hoff, Edwin Lau, and Maurits van der Linde (&Partners Research), for continuous support and for helping to develop the final manuscript.

Peter van Baalen
Lars Moratis
August 2001

CHAPTER 1

Introduction

WHY THIS BOOK?

"It is change, continuing change, inevitable change, that is the dominant factor in society today. No sensible decision can be made any longer without taking into account not only the world as it is, but the world as it will be (...). This, in turn, means that our statesmen, our businessmen, our everyman must take on a science fictional way of thinking", Russian born US-author Isaac Asimov (1920–1992) was once quoted. Over time, many things that have been labeled as science fiction have turned out to become reality – or at least pretty close to reality.

Call it science fictional thinking, scenario planning, or anticipation, what is important for organizations is to develop a vision on the future – what it may look like, what its consequences may be, and what the organization's role in this future may be or should be. Many organizations are faced with this challenge, educational institutions not in the least. Contemporary economic realities are threatening the subsistence of education as society has known it hitherto. These challenges apply all the more to institutions of management education.

This book is about changes and the consequences of these changes in the field of management education and current realities facing business schools. Business schools are encountering a lot of changes, challenges, and new demands in both their internal and their external environment. This book contains both a description of important trends and developments that are taking place within the context of management education and a particular vision on these trends, developments, consequences, and realities: a network vision.

This book takes a broad view on developments in the field of management education and the (need for) progression of business schools in the network economy. By means of a network perspective it aims at exploring future directions and roles for the business school and its activities in order to survive new economic and competitive realities. As the British philosopher Bertrand Russell proclaimed (1872–1970): "change is one thing, progress is another."

MANAGING AND LEARNING IN THE 21ST CENTURY

In times of change, it is a soothing and convenient thought to capture the essence of reality into a single encompassing notion. What, then, is that one feature, concept, or term that concisely describes what the 21st century (social-)economic landscape is

1

about? Is it the 'new economy'? Is it the digital economy? Perhaps it is technology? Or, in more general terms, is it about paradigmatic change?

Economies develop over time and different economic eras are characterized by different dynamics. The transformation from a society based on agriculture to an industrial society invoked fundamental changes, as well as the transformation from the industrial society to a society based on knowledge. Some have labeled this contemporary knowledge society in terms of a new economy, while others have demonstrated a one-sided preoccupation with globalization or information and communication technologies (ICT). What is generally agreed upon is that the transformation to this era of new economic realities brings truly fundamental changes inducing fundamental new dynamics, a new landscape, and new players competing within this landscape.

This book views these changes, dynamics, and the new landscape particularly from a network perspective, since the idea of the network perspective seems to provide the opportunity to integrate different important developments and features into one single concept. The creation of networks, for instance, is facilitated by the application of ICT and the process of globalization. Knowledge, then, becomes crucial in the network economy and can be seen as the glue that holds the network together.

When knowledge becomes of crucial importance, there is a prominent role for education and learning. Transferring knowledge and developing the right competencies and skills are prerequisites for organizational and individual maneuvering. Terms like smart products, the knowledge worker, the learning organization, and the intelligent enterprise have become established parts of today's business vocabulary. The way of conducting business has changed and so have approaches to organizing: today's enterprise is flexible and adaptive to changing market and environmental circumstances. Management has changed accordingly and the present-day manager is confronted with different and fast-changing competitive and organizational realities.

In addition, the boundary between work and learning is blurring; ICT has penetrated both business processes and educational processes; management knowledge is changing; skills, competencies, and experience have become integral parts of the learning process,

Concerning educational institutions, and universities in particular, it should be observed that they have manifested themselves as truly enduring institutions. They have existed in the course of many centuries. Though what can be described as their core competencies becomes a crucial ingredient for surviving in the network economy, the seemingly paradoxical question raised by different scholars is if these institutions will be able to endure. It is not so much the transformational process itself that seems a cause for concern – in fact, universities have witnessed and survived different periods of drastic change – it's the scale and the scope of the consequences that contemporary changes bring about that pose serious questions to the viability of traditional educational institutions.

Sir John Daniel, Vice-Chancellor of the Open University and author of 'Mega-universities and knowledge media' (1996), summarizes some of the most important challenges that traditional universities are to encounter:

−   Emphasis on learning productivity is the route to more effective teaching. This will require institutional redesign in order to provide each learner with an experience that integrates, at a personal level, a range of interactions with the rich resources of the university;
−   As the habit of lifelong learning spreads, students will become increasingly diverse. The majority will combine study and employment. Students, who will have a wide variety of academic backgrounds, will expect to choose from an extensive curriculum delivered in a convenient and affordable manner;
−   The notion of an academic community will have to be conceived with less emphasis on physical campus as a common focal point. This paradigm shift may strengthen awareness of the core functions of a university and create a new basis for a sense of institutional belonging among students and staff;
−   Universities will need to become increasingly adept at managing collaborative ventures with a wide variety of bodies, including other universities. Such collaboration will be required in order to offer students work-related courses and to make the investments necessary for the preparation and distribution of high quality intellectual assets such as learning materials;
−   Public funds will constitute a decreasing proportion of the financial support for higher education, demanding a more entrepreneurial attitude from universities to explore other financial resources. Direct grants to institutions are likely to be replaced by mechanisms that channel support through individual students. Governments will, however, continue to develop explicit procedures to ensure accountability and quality assurance in universities.

These challenges also apply to most business schools. In a sense, business schools have been closer to some of the developments that are at the basis of these challenges, since they have had contacts with industry for a long time, have been serving a more varied student body than traditional universities, and have been using a more varied set of learning methods and techniques. This doesn't mean, however, that business schools are, by definition, more adaptive to changes and well-positioned to cope with these challenges. In the 21st century, many strategic challenges are facing higher education in general and business schools in particular: new entrants, new competitive dynamics, institutional change, and a highly differentiated demand for education are posing additional threatening forces. Indeed, a whole new playing field has emerged in the area of management education and business schools, often requiring non-traditional market approaches and new organizational arrangements.

AIMS OF THIS BOOK AND TARGET AUDIENCES

This book doesn't invite the reader to join a purely academic or theoretical journey, nor is it a mere enumeration of remarkable facts or important trends. What, then, is this book aiming for? The objective is threefold.

First of all, the objective of this book is to dig into some of the dynamics of the contemporary developments and the newly emerging playing field of management education and business schools. This means that the reader must have some understanding of some important current macroeconomic developments and the consequences of these developments for society as a whole, the field of management knowledge, management learning, and management education, as well as the logic of organization.

The second aim is to explore the changing nature of education and learning in more general terms. This includes topics like paradigmatic changes in attitudes and opinions about learning and the (consequences of) the use of ICT in creating learning environments.

Thirdly, this book aims for an exploration of the network perspective, especially from an organizational and managerial viewpoint, and to describe a vision on the consequences of the network concept for management knowledge, skills, competencies, learning, and business school organization.

This book takes on the challenge of exploring reality from a network perspective. It's not the first book that takes this concept as a central point for elaborating on and explaining dynamics in different parts of society's realm. Many publications – some quite renowned – have preceded. For example, Manuel Castells, author of a comprehensive trilogy on the Network Society, has produced seminal work from an economic and sociologic view on this theme. From a business perspective, Raymond Miles (former dean of the Haas School of Business at Berkeley) and Charles Snow (Professor of Business Administration at the Smeal College of Business Administration at Penn State University) have written several influential articles about network organization. Ronald Burt's writing on structural holes and the social structure of competition (1992) has been deemed one of the most fertile theories regarding the functioning of networks. However, as Salancik (1995) notes, scholars are still in need of a solid network theory of organization.

Though this book will not contribute significantly to extensive theory-building on this topic, it certainly does explore different topics that are relevant from the perspective of the organization of contemporary management education, management learning, and business schools from a network perspective. Conceptual understanding and exploration of this perspective in the field of management education is perhaps what best fits the idea of this book. Therefore, this book is of a more conceptual nature, trying to get a grip on environmental dynamics and organizational logics that are in force by looking at things from a specific angle. Therefore, a number of concepts and ideas from the perspective of management education and business schools will come to the fore that provide some insights into the central subjects.

Hence, a broad range of topics is covered in this book, ranging from explorations into the dynamics of the 'new economy', the content of the management curriculum, new ways of management learning, and the role of ICT in creating learning environments to the developing playing field and emerging organizational modes of management education.

This book will therefore be of interest to a relatively wide range of audiences. It should first and foremost appeal to business schools and their stakeholders – including administrators, faculty, staff, students, industry and government. Educational administrators in general may also want to read this book, as well as every person interested in (the future of) management education and learning.

Still, there is more to the transformation in management education and business schools than the topics will touch upon. This book may not do justice to the variety of different institutions of management education, nor will it exhaustively elaborate on every subject. Nonetheless, it is a description of some of the most important developments and challenges in this particular field and provides a vision on how management education and business school organization may look like in the network economy.

COMPOSITION OF THIS BOOK

The writing of this book was seen as an opportunity to discuss an encompassing set of topics concerning management education and business schools in the 21st century's network economy. To a certain extent, the book deals with its title's different constituting topics.

In Chapter 2, the book takes off broadly by examining some of the essential characteristics and dynamics of what has been called the new economy. In this chapter, a picture is portrayed including definitions of the new economy, macroeconomic perspectives, future outlooks, and, at the end of this chapter, different views on the new economy which have in common the assumption that the new economy is largely about the importance of intangibles in common. It shows that ICT as well as knowledge are central defining elements in the new economy, as opposed to the agricultural and industrial era, causing learning and education to move centre stage as a way of economic development. Finally, the idea of conceptualizing the new economy in terms of a network economy and network dynamics is incepted, serving as an outset of Chapter 3.

Chapter 3 introduces a network perspective, since such a perspective allows for integrating different views on and defining characteristics of the new economy into one concept. Though a lot of literature approaches the network perspective from an ICT-dominated viewpoint, this chapter explores the topic from a conceptual viewpoint regarding network organization. It starts with 'informationalism', a term coined by Castells (1996), indicating that the network economy is the outcome of the processes of globalization and developments in ICT. Consequently, it elaborates on the dynamics of the network economy, using contributions from contemporary literature. Next, the basics of network organization, as a way of structuring organizations, are dealt with, exploring definitions, typologies, firm structures, the network organization of a firm's operations, and challenges firms encounter in the network economy. Ultimately, some challenges for business schools in the new economy are explored, which forms the building blocks for later chapters.

In a sense, Chapter 4 is a little jaunt, or sidetrack, compared to the previous chapters, though still relevant from the central topic of this book. It discusses management knowledge, the nature of managerial work, and consequences for management curricula from the perspective of the 21st century's network economy. It briefly reviews literature, research, and ideas about the complex nature of the managerial job and describes what management knowledge, skills, and competencies will be needed in the network economy as well as what the managerial job will look like in the future. In the 21st century network economy, the manager has to be technologically savvy, knowledgeable about interpersonal relationships, able to develop and maintain partnerships, and sensitive towards the firm's stakeholders. In essence, the 21st century manager is a network manager. Chapter 4 will also touch upon the developments in the transformation of management knowledge for the 21st century in accordance with the paradigms as discussed by Clarke & Clegg (1998) as well as the composition of the management curriculum, curricular critics, and (sub)topics that are deemed most important.

Chapter 5, especially, integrates a wide range of topics regarding contemporary transformations in education related to both (higher) education in general as management education in particular. This set of quite revolutionary developments are catchphrased in the term 'the new learning'. This encompassing chapter can be divided into two comparatively separate parts. The first part ferrets about current developments within education and learning. By now, learning has become a lifelong undertaking, since the average shelf life of knowledge has decreased dramatically over the decades. In addition, procedural knowledge and conditional knowledge are seen as equivalents of declarative knowledge in terms of value. The blurring boundary between work and learning brings about the need for just-in-time learning and just-in-place learning as opposed to traditional just-in-case learning. Hence, new approaches to education have emerged, bringing new roles for teachers and learners and putting new demands on the development of curricula. This part of the chapter is rounded off with an exploration into the area of network learning and networked learning environments, since this provides an interesting perspective on contemporary management learning.

The second part of Chapter 5 relates to the integration of ICT into the venue of education, exploring the efficiency and effectiveness of educational technology as well as characteristics of technologically-enabled learning environments and the interface of pedagogy and technology in educational settings. The chapter ends with discussing the role and some of the possibilities ICT provides to be integrated into management education. The idea of virtual communities as a form of networked learning environments is seen as one of the promising applications of ICT in management education.

Chapter 6 provides an institutional perspective on this book's central theme in two ways. It starts by investigating some of the most important trends and developments within the broader institutional context of (management) education and business schools. Themes like the internationalization of higher education, accreditation, and the pivotal role of branding will come to the fore. Next, the chapter looks at current developments in the organization of management education, which seems to be characterized in the future by the forming of partnerships between universities, business schools, content providers, publishers, corporations, and e-learning firms. Different examples within a typology of partnerships are briefly elaborated.

The chapter's second conception of the term 'institutional' relates to the organization of institutions higher education in general and business schools in particular. A number of visions on the organization of universities and business schools are expatiated upon, including the distributed (virtual) university, the business school as a learning centre, and the hybrid business school. The concept of the networked business school will especially draw the attention of the reader as a descendant of network organization. The concept of the networked business school is illustrated with a case study.

Chapter 7 contains an epilogue, which construction has been mainly infused by an interview with the President of the International Institute for Management Development (IMD), Peter Lorange, and a recent article written by him. In particular, this final chapter explores strategic direction setting within business schools and the role of the business school's dean, and relates this to the concept of the networked business school.

BOOKMARK

Since this book encompasses a wide variety of topics relating the new and network economy, network organization, managerial knowledge and roles, management learning, education in general, educational technology, and the organization of management education and business schools, readers stemming from particular audiences may benefit from a bookmark.

Those readers who are interested in views on the new and network economy and network organization, may want to limit their reading efforts to Chapters 2 and 3, as well as – if interested in the network organization of (management) education and business schools – Chapter 6, in particular its second part.

Readers that are looking for topics related to current developments in higher education are referred to Chapter 5 and the first couple of sections of Chapter 6.

A combination of Chapters 3, 4, 6, and 7 is recommended to readers taking an interest in the current state and future of the organization of management education and business schools.

CHAPTER 2

THE NEW ECONOMY

INTRODUCTION

Generally when speaking of the new economy, reference is made to the role information and communications technologies (ICT) play in society. In fact, there has been a tendency to relate much of contemporary economic successes to the contribution of ICT. Indeed, ICT has led to what is called the compression or even the collapse of space and time, meaning that it enables continuous information exchange and the development of global economic structures. Space and time do not matter as much as they did in the 'old economy'.

It is clear that we have entered a new era of economic development that is accompanied by the emergence of a new economic landscape. But it seems a landscape full of paradoxes, not in the last place due to the prominent place technology and knowledge capture. According to Alan Webber, former editorial director of the Harvard Business Review, the whole logic of the new economy is founded on paradoxes. He says:

> "[The] process of technological transformation is a curious paradox. Think of it as the 'self-canceling technological advantage'. As technology transforms the logic of competition, technology disappears as a sustainable source of competitive advantage" (Webber, 1993: 26-27).

So, what is this new economy about, really? Is it as 'new' as it has been claimed to be? Is it about globalization? Is it the emergence of the information era and the impact of ICT? Or is the new economy a mix of interdependent features that is to complex to be unraveled?

In order to explore the central characteristics of the current economic landscape, to round out the dynamics of contemporary competitive structures, to discuss the influence on the way companies behave and (re)structure themselves, and to explicate the role of ICT, knowledge and global economic structures, some essential insights on the new economy are provided in this chapter. In fact, this chapter will scout what this phenomenon called the new economy actually seems to comprise, how it can be defined, and what it's main drivers are. After having briefly defined the major characteristics, the focus will first be on a macroeconomic perspective and some implications of the main drivers behind the economy. More detailed information is provided on the role ICT plays in the new economy, so as to establish its true importance, which still seems a rather controversial issue.

9

Next, the issue of value creation in the new economy will be dealt with from a number of specific and challenging point of views. Since the new economy will prove to be about intangibles, too, the focus of the ways of value creation will be on perspectives that include the importance of knowledge, experience, and attention.

THE NEW ECONOMY AND INDUSTRIAL REVOLUTION

In recent years, much has been said and written about the so-called new economy. Though very different conceptions of this new economy have surfaced, it has appeared that it refers to an economic era characterized by a whole new set of economic activities, economic turbulence, new organizational forms, and paradoxes. Corporate activity, including huge mergers and acquisitions, numerous internet start-ups and restructuring processes like downsizing, have become high and global, while at the same time ICT has deeply penetrated all layers of society without apparent productivity gains. In this era, change seems to be the only feature that comes close to safe ceteris paribus conditions.

This new economy has brought about economic industriousness of a totally different nature and of completely distinct dimensions. Just as the second industrial revolution moved society from local to national economies, by entering the third industrial revolution the global economy will be the scope that matters. Illustrative for this is the observation that the emerging global companies are larger than any national companies ever seen. The market value of the world's largest company in 1990 (a national company, Nippon Telephone from Japan) isn't even close to make it to the 1998 list of the ten largest companies in the world (Martin, 1998). The scope, reach and power of business has become global, and has – especially relative to governments – immensely increased.

For about eight thousand years, wealth was created by agricultural activity. With the world's first industrial revolution at the end of the eighteenth century and the beginning of the nineteenth century, this source of wealth creation came to a large extent to its end. While, in retrospect, the end of the nineteenth century and the steam engine can be considered to be the hallmarks of the second industrial revolution, we already speak of current structural economic transitions to be the third industrial revolution, which is commonly described as the information or knowledge revolution. Boisot (1998) speaks in terms of the transition from an energy-based to an information-based society. In the old economy, the traditional production function shows a trade-off between labor and capital. Capital, represented by new technologies, replaces labor-intensive production, while in the knowledge or information economy there's a trade-off between data and physical production factors. The knowledge or information society arises as a consequence of the gradual substitution of physical production factors by data.

As was the case in the second industrial revolution, corporations that are positioned to take advantage of this third industrial revolution can achieve high rates of returns and growth, even though the economy's growth rate is lagging compared to previous decades. New big firms, and new big fortunes, can virtually grow as if by magic. In contrast to struggling giants, threatened by the pace at which technological developments take place, new firms have the advantage of not having to destroy (parts of) themselves in order to remain competitively viable, let alone save themselves from total downfall. The new economy demands industrial restructuring, instigates to rethinking value creation, and puts pressure on traditional sectors.

Oil is a revealing example of the impact of the information or knowledge revolution on an traditional industry. The oil industry used to be an industry of luck and brawn, but now leans heavily on brainpower. Supercomputers permit three- and four-dimensional acoustical soundings, which has resulted in a factor ten increase in hit rates for finding new oil and doubled extraction rates. Norway has now become the second largest exporter of oil in the world – instead of the prediction two decades ago that it would be out of oil by now – due to the possibility of drilling two miles deep into the water. On the offshore oilrigs, yesterday's well-paid muscular workmen have been replaced by well-paid knowledge workers. The industry is still producing oil, but in such profound different ways that it can be characterized as a knowledge industry. As a result of these technologies, reachable oil supplies have expanded much faster than demand, and real prices have fallen to the lowest levels in human history (Thurow, 1999: 27).

With rapid changes and advanced developments in technology, it is far from sure where future profits will be made. The question, therefore, is where and how wealth is created in the new economy and where value-adding activities take place. It's not just a matter of technology, nor is it solely a matter of information or knowledge. One should not take for granted the euphoric voices and noises that hail only a preoccupation with ICT, though this is undoubtedly one of the most important drivers of the new economic landscape.

DEFINING THE NEW ECONOMY

The use of the term 'new economy' is by now more than widespread, though managers, policy-makers, scholars, and business magazines that are referring to it, seem to have different perceptions, or even models, in mind. One prominent conception of the new economy is the view that it is merely about information and communications technologies (and young entrepreneurs starting internet companies). Though it's an understandable view, and also a partly true one, this seems to be only a small part of what the new economy actually comprises. Besides, several prominent scholars and new economy gurus, like Donald Tapscott, actually do, in fact, place ICT at the center of anything that pertains to the new economy. Important here is to keep in mind that ICT is a central element in the new economic order as a driver in the sense that ICT has an enabling role. Therefore, it's the central aim of this section and the following sections to acquaint the reader with a broad range of (macro)economic topics related, and often directly assigned, to the concept of the new economy. In order to do this, however, it's necessary to get a definition of this new economy. A good starting point and a rather encompassing definition of the new economy is provided by Wired's Encyclopedia of the New Economy:

> *"When we talk about the new economy, we're talking about a world in which people work with their brains instead of their hands. A world in which communications technology creates global competition – not just for running shoes and laptop computers, but also for bank loans and other services that can't be packed into a crate and shipped. A world in which innovation is more important than mass production. A world in which investment buys new concepts or the means to create them, rather than new machines. A world in which rapid change is a constant. A world at least as different from what came before it as the industrial age was from its agricultural predecessor. A world so different its emergence can only be described as a revolution"* (Wired's Encyclopedia of the New Economy).

A quote originating from Davis & Meyer complements this definition, by saying that the new economy is governed by new rules, since it encompasses a whole new business reality and economic landscape:

> *"It's a whole new economy. It's a new business reality resulting from the convergence of three huge forces. You can't get a bead on it because it's a moving target – today's business is marked by unprecedented speed. You can't get your arms around it because it's intangible – the assets that create the most value are not on the balance sheet. And you can't sort it out because it's a rat's nest. The interconnectedness of computers, workers, firms, and economies has reached a point where the famous 'six degrees of separation' is starting to feel more like three"* (Davis & Meyer, 1997: 17).

The new economy, following these descriptions, is a knowledge and idea-based economy where the keys to job creation and higher standards of living are innovative ideas and technology embedded in services and manufactured products; it is an economy where risk, uncertainty, and constant change are not the exception but the main rule (The New Economy Index website). Looking at these definitions, one could draw the conclusion that new economy adherents say it really is a new economic era, while, on the other side, new economy adversaries say it definitely isn't: there are no new rules to survive in this economy. Old economic rules still apply, skeptics and adversaries say.

Different scholars assert that this new economy is characterized by fundamental economic transformations. With these transformations, some say, new economic rules are coming into force. But it is the strong and blatant presence of such proclaimers of the new economy, especially those who have been labeled new economy gurus and fad-chasers, that has triggered criticism: this period of disinflationary growth (continuing rapid economic growth, without a stronger than proportional rise in the level of inflation) will end, critics say, and they predict that growth will eventually decline. In a more fundamental and general sense, some authors say there's not that much new to this new economy or even that there's no such thing like a new economy. The influential economist Paul Krugman, for example, is one of these authors. He contends that there is in fact nothing new about technological change and that productivity measures do not measure all productivity in 'any new economy'. Moreover, economic change always seems more dramatic to the people living in such an era of change than mankind, in retrospect, tries to believe when people encounter economic change.

However, there is something new about the economy, as tends to happen about every fifty years (defined as Kondratieff cycles). In fact, it's not the first new economy. From a different point of view, and depicted in table 2.1, global development unfolds through the succession of new economies, underpinned by Schumpeter's concept of creative destruction. The new economy about which people are talking now is, in a sense, an economy that's somewhat reborn, meaning it has successfully weathered what could be termed as a maturity crisis and has challenged relatively recent predictions of economic decline (Norton, 1999).

	Also known as	**Period**	**Main symbols**
New Economy #1	The Industrial Revolution	1787-1842	Cotton textiles, iron, steam power
New Economy #2	The Bourgeois Kondratieff	1842-1897	Railroadization
New Economy #3	The New-Mercantilist Kondratieff	1897-1939	Electricity, automobile
New Economy #4	The Cold-War Kondratieff	1939-1989	Defense, TV mainframes
New Economy #5	The Information Age	1989-????	PCs, telecommunications, entertainment

Table 2.1. Five 'new economies'.
Source: Norton (1999)

When taking a broader and more profound economic perspective, some unique elements and developments that constitute the new economy can be discovered. In the next sections a macroeconomic perspective and a focus on the contribution of ICT is taken to illustrate this.

THE MACROECONOMIC VIEW: STRUCTURAL FEATURES OF THE NEW ECONOMY

Looking from a macroeconomic perspective, Norton (1999) states that the idea central to the new economy is that ICT is creating higher productivity growth, which in turn accounts for faster growth in output without a rise in the rate of inflation. Though it can be argued that some of the skepticism of people seems very legitimate ("Everywhere I see computers, but in productivity statistics", Robert Solow once said), others state that in the new economy measurements of productivity are simply useless. After all, the only ones who should worry about productivity are in fact not human beings, but robots, as Kevin Kelly's argument reads. And the areas of the economy that has shown a rise in productivity have been US and Japanese manufacturing sectors, which have seen an annual increase of 3% to 5% in the 1980s and the 1990s. It's these kinds of sectors where the measure of productivity can be a useful one (Kelly, 1998).[1]

---

[1] In later sections of this chapter, a more profound look into the interplay (and discrepancies) between ICT contributions and productivity measures is taken.

Taking such a perspective allows different particular features of the new economy to be distinguished. Weinstein (1997) attributes some specific macroeconomic traits to a new economy. He states that a new economy is an economy:

-    that grows without apparent threats of recession;
-    that continues to expand without a pickup in inflation;
-    constantly restructuring itself for greater efficiency and productivity;
-    replenishing and revitalizing itself through new technology and capital investment;
-    that functions without excessive debt, either public or private;
-    that maintains a balanced budget;
-    that is increasingly globalized and export-driven.

According to this enumeration, the new economy has particularly strong economic fundamentals upon which successful economic life can be build. The New Economy Index mentions thirteen indicators, illustrating the emergence of these structural roots of the new economy (The New Economy Index website). These indicators are divided into four themes: (1) industrial and occupational change, (2) globalization, (3) dynamism and competition, and (4) the information technology revolution.

Industrial and occupational change

Within the first theme, several trends can be witnessed. First of all, more people work in offices and provide services. Decreasing amounts of time are spent on physical labor, whereas knowledge-intensive work, requiring analytical and interpretive skills is increasing. This is linked with the rising importance of the service sector in Western economies. For instance, in the United States 80% of the workforce does not spend their days making things: they work in jobs that require them to move things, process or generate information, or they provide services to people. Secondly, high-wage and high-skill jobs have grown, as well as low-wage and low-skill jobs have grown. Knowledge-based jobs (requiring post-secondary, vocational or higher education) are growing as a share of total employment both in the US and Europe. In the US, managerial and professional jobs increased as a share of total employment from 22% in 1979 to 28.4% in 1995.

Globalization

Concerning the globalization theme, first of all, trade is an increasing share of the new economy, which means more intense competitive structures. As a consequence, firms have to innovate on a constant rate in order to be successful. The value of the world economy that is 'globally contestable' – meaning open to global competition – will rise from approximately 4 trillion US dollars in 1995 (which equals about one-seventh of the world's output) to over 21 trillion US dollars by the year 2000 (half of the world's output) (Frazer & Oppenheim, 1997). To illustrate globalizing tendencies, foreign direct investments (FDI) are usually a revealing indicator. FDI is a conditio sine qua non for business not to become outperformed by future competition in this globalizing world. Developments in FDI relating to OECD countries are shown in table 2.2.

	Inflows			Outflows		
	1993	**1994**	**1995**	**1993**	**1994**	**1995**
France	12142	10995	12156	12167	10895	9582
Germany	240	3003	9012	19557	14587	34890
Japan	86	888	37	13714	17938	22262
Netherlands	6507	4371	5889	10993	11502	7929
UK	14536	11066	29910	25697	29721	37839
US	41107	49442	74701	72601	49370	96897
Total all OECD countries	126661	138517	189788	189532	187550	242890

Table 2.2. FDI.
Source: Clarke & Clegg (1998: 79), derived from OECD (1996: 38)

Dynamism and competition

The theme of dynamism and competition poses six trends in the observation of a new economy. First, there is the spawning of new, fast-growing entrepreneurial companies, which is an indicator of the degree of the economy's innovative capacity. Especially the so-called 'gazelles' (companies with a sales growth of at least 20% per year for four straight years) are an important indicator within this. In addition, one can observe an increasing embracement of entrepreneurial dynamism by investors, especially in the sector of ICT. Second, there is a general increase in and intensification of competition. For example, in 1965, IBM faced 2,500 competitors for all its markets. By 1992, it faced 50,000. Stable industries have become dynamic and global, while at the same time there are the numerous mergers and acquisitions, of which the former does not only take place between corporate giants, but the latter also takes place in the form of acquiring the most innovative small- and medium-sized enterprises. Third, just as merging and acquiring are ways of coordinating corporate activity, cooperation among competitors has become ubiquitous. The dynamics of organizing through network structures and 'co-opetition' have been labeled the prominent organizing principle in the new economy (see for example Drucker, 1999). Firms are looking for opportunities to establish partnerships with suppliers, consumers and universities to enhance product and service development and technological innovation. Fourth, the new economy is constantly churning, indicating the balance between job creation and job destruction (this is called 'flux'). Though this constant churning poses workers with insecurity, instability and, thus, economic risk, it is also a major driver of innovation and growth. Fifth, consumer choices are exploding and consumer needs are more specifically addressed. Due to the fact that mass customization and flexible production have replaced mass production and standard products ('one-size-fits-all'), customers now can choose, and order at a price level a fraction of before, tailor-made products and services ('one-size-fits-(n)one'). Variety and diversity at low cost are conjoint in the new economy. Sixth, and last within the theme of dynamism and competition, speed is becoming the standard. Competition-induced time-to-market considerations and short product life cycles are characteristic of the new economic order. A well-known example is Moore's Law: every 18 months, the processing speed of microchips is doubled, while prices are cut into half. Business has to run, just to stay in place in an economy where people talk about technological development in 'web years', which is a quarter of a normal year. Greater consumer choice and the sophisticated nature of interaction between business and customers are just two examples of the possibilities the increase in speed brings.

The information technology revolution

Finally, the fourth theme concerning the rise of the new economy relates to the aforementioned information technology revolution, which entails three trends. First, there's the omnipresence of microchips, which is the foremost characteristic of the digital era. In 1984, worldwide shipments of semiconductors totaled 88 billion units, and by 1997 world shipments were close to a tripling of this number. By 2003, the number is expected to pass the 400 billion unit mark. Second, the costs of computing are dramatically decreasing. Computing costs are dropping nearly 25% per year. Since information technology is expected to increase efficiencies, enables cost-cutting, driving customization of products and services and increasing the speed of commerce, all sectors of business are investing in ICT. Therefore, this trend is important as it enables the transformation of business and even whole industries. The third trend is co-depending on the previous trend: data costs are plummeting. Global communications is, undoubtedly, one of the major enablers of the economy.

The impacts of this information technology revolution and the fact that ICT can be seen as one of the major driving forces of the new economy, have caused authors to coin the term 'digital economy'. This digitization version of the new economy comprises the observation that the relatively smooth transition from the old economy to the current new economy, has been caused by the emergence of information goods, which can be digitized. The prominence of the information commodities entails three landmark events: the invention of the microprocessor in 1971, the introduction of the IBM PC in 1981 and the commercialization of internet in 1994 (Norton, 1999). The microprocessor carried the world from an analog to a digital mode in which "due in large part to that one significant product introduction in 1981, virtually every person, company, and government is a customer for technology products. The definition of technology industries has expanded from large computers to include personal computers, software, semiconductors, semiconductor equipment, communications (both telecommunications and data communications), and medical technology (biotechnology and medical devices)" (Murphy, 1998). The coming of the PC thus rendered anything and everything subject to the power of the computer, while retaining the crucial dimensions of human scale, decentralized decision making, customized design, and creativity.

In the next section, the role and the importance of ICT is elaborated more extensively.

THE ROLE AND CONTRIBUTION OF ICT: SOME EVIDENCE

Macroeconomic insights thus seem to indicate that a constant and enduring rate of economic upswing is central is this new economic climate: continuous growth, no or modest inflation, self-reinforcement and balanced budgets. With this list of fundamental economic transformations it appears that, indeed, ICT plays an important enabling role, though not all economic transformations and successes can be attributed to technological developments. Though many authors account for a positive answer to the question if ICT contributes significantly to economic prosperity, there's a lot of discussion if ICT is really paying of.

The real value of ICT's contributions to output growth and productivity measures, therefore, is at stake when discussing the new economy, and it is necessary to assess these contributions. At least three complementary approaches for assessing the role of ICT in output growth: (1) looking at the importance of ICT production in the economy, (2) taking into account ICT's role as a capital good, and (3) looking at benefits which go beyond those accruing to investors and owners, for example through network externalities (spillovers) (OECD, 2000: 52). Regardless of issues relating to measurement methodology, some studies have concluded that ICT has no positive economic contribution, while other studies certainly have provided seemingly conclusive results indicating the opposite.

Recent OECD research (OECD, 2000) shows that investments in ICT are making an important contribution to growth and labor productivity growth across the OECD. Over the past two decades ICT investment progressed at two-digit figures and it accounted for 10 to 20% of total non-residential investment in the business sector. Schreyer (2000) notes a contribution of ICT producing sectors to output growth across seven OECD countries for the period to 1996. Technical progress has led to rapid improvement in the price-performance ratio of ICT capital goods and reduced the user cost of ICT capital goods relative to other types of assets. Consequently, significant substitution of ICT capital for other types of capital and sustained growth in the volume of ICT investment has occurred, outpacing investments in other types of capital goods. These developments are depicted in table 2.3.

	Canada	France	Germany	Italy	Japan	UK	US
Growth of output							
1980-85	2.8	1.7	1.4	1.4	3.5	2.1	3.4
1985-90	2.9	3.2	3.6	3.0	4.9	3.9	3.2
1990-96	1.7	0.9	1.8	1.2	1.8	2.1	3.0
Contributions (percentage points) from							
ICT 1980-85	0.25	0.17	0.12	0.13	0.11	0.16	0.28
equip- 1985-90	0.31	0.23	0.17	0.18	0.17	0.27	0.34
ment 1990-96	0.28	0.17	0.19	0.21	0.19	0.29	0.42
Total 1980-85	1.3	1.0	1.0	0.9	0.8	0.8	1.1
capital 1985-90	1.1	1.3	1.2	0.9	1.3	1.1	1.0
1990-96	0.7	1.0	1.0	0.7	0.1	0.8	0.9

Table 2.3. The contribution of ICT to output growth.
Source: Schreyer (2000), derived from OECD (2000: 50)

After 1995, the diffusion of ICT accelerated, based on applications such as the World Wide Web and email. At relatively low cost, these technologies are linking existing capital stock of computers and communications systems in open networks that significantly increase their utility, according to the OECD. This rapid diffusion exemplifies the shift in the relationship of innovation, science, technology and the economy. The OECD states that:

> "ICT's contribution to labor productivity is rising, along with its contribution to innovation, as increased patenting indicates. The advent of the internet and e-commerce has created a potential for further innovation, largely thank to low-cost, open access, lowering potential barriers. However, the internet's most profound economic impact may in fact be its effect on existing industries that are adopting ICT and restructuring to exploit the new technology. While technology diffusion and investment in ICT offer the potential for stronger growth, organizational change is indispensable. ICT seems to offer the greatest benefits when ICT investment is combined with other organizational assets, such as new strategies, new business processes, new organizational structures and better worker skills" (OECD, 2000: 10-12).

Since organizational restructuring tends to be firm-specific, conclusions relating to this last observation show huge variation across organizations (Brynjolfsson & Hitt, 1997). Nonetheless, in table 2.4 an overview of six different studies is depicted, showing the role of ICT in individual firm performance.

Study	Sample	Issue addressed	Main findings
Lichtenberg (1995)	US firms, 1988-1991	Output contribution of capital and labor deployed in information systems	One information systems employee can be substituted for six non-information systems employees without affecting output
Hitt & Brynjolfsson (1997); Brynjolfsson & Hitt (1997)	More than 600 large US firms, 1987-1994	The impact of the adoption of IT and organizational decentralization on productivity	Firms that both adopt IT and organizational decentralization are on average 5% more productive than those that adopt only one of these
Black & Lynch (1997 and 2000)	US firms, 1987-1993, 1993, and 1996	The impact of workplace practices, IT and human capital on productivity	The adoption of certain newer work practices, higher educational levels, and the use of computers by production workers have a positive impact on plant productivity
Brynjolfsson & Yang (1998)	Fortune 1000 US forms, 1987-1994	The impact of IT and intangible assets on firm performance	The market value of $1 of IT capital is the same as $10 of capital stock. This may reflect the value of intangible investment associated with ICT
Brynjolfsson, Hitt & Yang (1998)		The impact of the adoption of IT and organizational decentralization on productivity	The market value of $1 of IT capital is higher by $2-5 in decentralized firms
Bresnahan, Brynjolfsson & Hitt (1999)	400 large firms, 1987-1996	Complementarity between IT investment, human capital and decentralized organizational structure	IT combined with work practices such as higher skills, greater educational attainment, greater use of delegated decision-making lead to a higher value of IT investment

Table 2.4. Firm-level research on ICT, productivity, and organizational transformation.
Source: OECD (2000: 56)

TECHNOLOGY, INFORMATION, AND NEW ECONOMICS

It has been widely argued that, until recently, huge investments in ICT did not show any increases in productivity, contrasting high expectations. Moreover, during the 1970-1990 period, in which significant developments and investments in ICT have taken place, productivity in most countries even decreased. This phenomenon has been called the Productivity Paradox. Regarding ICT investments the abovementioned OECD study has already provided some answers to this question, namely that ICT investments require different organizational arrangements (firm structure, business strategies) to be really effective and result in productivity gains. Oxford University economist Paul David provides a second – more general – explanation. A critical mass, or penetration rate, of 50% has to be realized in order for new technologies to yield increases in productivity. He states that, historically speaking, productivity has accelerated only for 40 years after the introduction of electricity in 1880. The transformation of industrial processes by the new electric power technology didn't acquire real momentum until after 1914-1917, when the charged rates fell considerably. Major investments and the realization of economies of scale also contributed to the use of electricity, since they engendered efficiency gains (David, 1991). David & Wright note, however, that:

> *"[I]t would be a mistake to attribute the protracted delay in electrification exclusively to problems on the supply side. The slow pace of adoption prior to the 1920s was largely attributable to the unprofitability of replacing still serviceable manufacturing plants embodying production technologies adapted to the old regime of mechanical power derived from water and steam. Coexistence of older and newer forms of capital often restricted the scope for exploiting electricity's potential"* (David & Wright, 1999: 7).

In accordance with the OECD findings, companies had to reorganize themselves to exploit the advantages of a breakthrough technology like electricity. It is not surprising, therefore, that economic effects attributable to ICT are coming to the fore only since recently. The Dutch Central Bureau of Planning (CPB, 2000) provides some additional general arguments for the fact that these breakthrough technologies do not yield macroeconomic effects until after a long period. Complementary innovations, structural changes and learning processes take time before producing any results and firms are hesitant to invest considering uncertainties in technological development. Moreover, adoption externalities occur between the sector producing a breakthrough technology and sectors applying it. The producing sector has an incentive to innovate when there are sufficient applications, while the applying sector has an incentive to innovate when the technology has been developed to an adequate extent (ibid.).

Robert Shapiro, former Under Secretary for Economic Affairs at the US Commerce Department, says we don't know the answer to the question whether the adoption and spread of new information technologies is creating a new economy in advanced countries, of high growth and productivity, and low inflation and unemployment, because evidence isn't all in (Shapiro, 2000). Information technologies, however, do have certain singular qualities that could well make a difference in how fast an economy grows, as we have seen. Among them are the facts that, compared to refrigeration or jet propulsion, information technology as a class is a 'general purpose' innovation that can be applied to every sector and aspect of business. As a result, productivity gains directly associated with an expanded or improved capacity to obtain, process, store and transmit information can mount up. As an additional distinctive feature, applying information technologies to business induces 'cascading innovation' (ibid.). Productivity gains don't just appear from deploying new technologies enabling faster information processing. In order to really exploit advantages of these technologies, businesses usually have to rethink their operations and organization, which calls for organizational innovations. Recent research, like the OECD's, shows that investments in information technologies are most effective in businesses that also undertake organizational changes, but not very effective at all without those kind of changes.

ICT AND ECONOMICS

Next to the already mentioned particular features of ICT, network externalities and network effects are also distinctive features of information technologies. Network effects comprise the logic of the more broadly they are used, the more value they generate. Obvious examples of this feature are the use of telephones and fax machines, which hold increasing value with an increasing number of users. If you're the only one around using a mobile WAP telephone, there's no value in it for you. Once products that account for these kind of network effects become the standard or a technology becomes a platform technology, value is created through selling products or services to markets that build or operate on these standards. From this perspective, Kevin Kelly's Law of Generosity – 'follow the free' – can be explained: if services become more valuable the more plentiful they are, and if they cost less the better and the valuable they become, then the extension of this logic says that the most valuable things of all should be those that are given away.

The new economy, therefore, is an economy of increasing returns, rather than one of traditional diminishing returns. For certain categories of goods, value actually increases as the market becomes more saturated with them (Arthur, 1996). Initial development costs may be high, and therefore initial returns low. However, marginal costs to make additional copies of, for example, a software program or data transfers over the internet are very low. Consequently, marginal costs can rapidly approach zero.

The central question remains: do economic rules change with the omnipresence of computers and the dynamics of networks? One of the most authoritative answers to the question has come from Shapiro & Varian with their book 'Information Rules' (1999). Not only does this title refer to economic rules that are governing this new economy, in their view it also means that information is the one 'thing' the new economy is about. At the heart of their argument, there's the 'Casablanca rule': the fundamental things apply when times goes by, or, as Shapiro & Varian nicely express it: technology changes, economic laws do not. The fundamental economic principles still determine success and failure. To understand what's going on in this 'non-revolutionary revolution' one should just have to look at technological changes that occurred in the past. The key to grasp the information rules lies in understanding just three simple economic principles:

1.   Information goods are experience goods. Consequently consumer value varies widely, which lies perhaps at the very heart of the problem businesses are being faced with: "[t]he tension between giving away your information – to let people know what you have to offer – and charging them for it to recover your costs" (ibid., p. 6). Segmenting markets and charging those customers who are willing to pay a higher price a lot then is the key strategic imperative;

2.   Information goods have an unusual structure of costs. Fixed costs are high and fixed costs are sunk and marginal costs are near zero and capacity

constraints are absent. Either businesses have to differentiate their products, achieve cost leadership, or disappear (DeLong, 1998);

3.   Networks are sources of powerful externalities on both demand and supply side. On the supply side economies of scale occur by producing high-volume products, while at the demand side network externalities occur: value will increase when more people buy the same product, as has been illustrated with the mobile WAP telephone example.

These characteristics account for the assumption that traditional economic rules are still in force in a new economy. However, they also account for a recomposition of playing fields, different dynamics, and some consequences from a managerial viewpoint. Both at the end of this chapter and in the next chapter the dynamics and consequences are portrayed from a number of particular perspectives relating to these characteristics.

THREE OPINIONS ON THE FUTURE OF THE NEW ECONOMY

By now, it may be clear that the economy has found itself in an upswing due to a technological revolution that has made ICT a major driver of economic development. The information age will only be a technological revolution like previous ones, and, hence, of a temporary nature. More radical critics state that the new economy is an 'internet bubble', an unstable situation of economic growth that, once brought out of balance by a certain trigger, will lead to an economic recession. They speak of an internet boom, or internet hype, and warn for an internet depression that will follow this boom (Mandel, 2000). Hence, three perspectives on the new economy can be distinguished, namely the vision of the new economy as (1) a 'real' new economy, (2) a technological revolution, and (3) an internet bubble. These views are depicted in figure 2.1 and elaborated consecutively (derived from De Moor, 2000, pp. 18-23).

Opinion 1: A 'real' new economy

The first opinion, in fact, holds new, unbounded economic growth without inflation and structural increases in productivity driven by ICT. The wave of innovation – and, therefore, an increase in productivity – can endure, according to advocates of this view. A first argument for this premise are the positive predictions for the IT sector by research companies. Datacorp, for example, predicts that global IT investments will have passed the 975 billion US dollar mark in the first years of the new century, meaning a minimal increase of 10.4% compared to 1999. IDC forecasted a 119 billion US dollar corporate investment in internet initiatives for the year 2000, while this number will grow to an amount of 284 billion US dollar by 2003. A second argument contends the advantages of ICT. These advantages are so obvious to companies that they will keep investing, which has become a prerequisite for staying competitive. Even in the case of an occurring recession, companies will continue their investments in order not to lose the competitive struggle: do what your competitors do, or die. A third argument points at the large amount of financial capital that is present in the market which will be available for investments (Reinhart & Burrows, 1999).

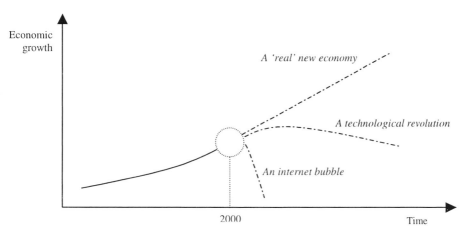

Figure 2.1. Three views on the new economy.
Source: De Moor (2001)

Paul Saffo, director of the Institute for the Future in California, also is convinced of lasting technological developments and continuing increases in productivity. In addition to the previous arguments, he reasons that (in Woodall, 2000):

–   The current penetration rate of internet is low: only 6% of the world's population and only 35% of the West is connected to the internet, therefore contending an enormous growth potential;

–   The percentage of firms using internet for purchases and sales is still relatively low. Even in the US, which has a lead over Europe, this percentage is only 33% among production companies;

–   Currently, multiple technological revolutions are taking place. The sectors of fuel-cell technology, genetic technology, and biotechnology are tremendously advancing. The combination of all technological developments could induce a long-lasting wave of development;

–   The US is the first country the new economy flourishes in. Europe, Japan, and other emerging economies may be able to generate even higher returns than the US.

Paul Romer's 'New growth theory' poses that the wave of innovative activity can indeed be enduring. The traditional theory of growth was developed in the 1950s, concentrating on inputs by means of capital and labor. Technological innovation was seen as an autonomous factor. The 'New growth theory', however, contends an endogenous nature of knowledge creation, which can be influenced by both the public and the private sector. Romer states that if conditions for innovative activity are being optimally met, innovation can continue. Among those conditions are stable fiscal and monetary policies, deregulation, and free trade (Het Financieele Dagblad, 2000a). Additionally, Gartner poses that conditions concerning education, a competitive telecom industry, cheap access to the internet and a well-functioning and reliable digital pay system have to be met (Het Financieele Dagblad, 2000b).

Opinion 2: A technological revolution

Proclaimers of the second perspective, the new economy being a technological revolution, argue that there will be bounded economic growth and limits to increases in productivity: after a boom there will always be a bust, they say. There is a lower boundary to the decrease of unemployment and an upper boundary to productivity increase. First, the economy will meet a point in time when wages will get so high due to labor-market shortages, which will lead to inflation when the increase in wages will outpace productivity. Secondly, labor productivity cannot keep climbing due to the point of saturation of new technologies. This saturation occurs, for example, because penetration rates will get to a high and stable level. Historically speaking, parallels with technological revolutions induced by the invention of steam power, the rise of railroads, the invention of electricity and the rise of the automobile seem apparent. During these past revolutions, one could, in retrospect, also speak of a peak in economic growth and even 'bubble' symptoms like those ascribed to the current new economy. Perhaps, it is better to indicate the economic tendency not in terms of a new economy in this view, but rather in terms of an elevation of the potential economic growth path, driven by ICT developments.

Opinion 3: An internet bubble

In his book 'The coming internet depression', Michael Mandel (2001) cautiously points at the risks of a depression the new economy holds. Multiple chain reactions taking the entire economy into vicious circle will occur in case of a recession. He notes:

> *"An Internet Depression, if and when it comes, will not be centered in the automobile and steel factories that led the economy into the Great Depression [of the 1930s]. Rather, the Internet Depression will hit hardest at the new information technology and communications industries that drove growth in the 1990s. And just as the hallmark of the New Economy has been an accelerated rate of technological innovation, so the pain of the Internet Depression will be felt as a dramatic and pervasive lowering of our expectations for future growth"* (Mandel, 2001: 85-86).

Instead of taking the apocalyptic perspective of an internet bubble, Christopher Farrell (2000) states that companies will keep investing in internet technologies, even in case of a recession, because of the by now widely recognized improvements in efficiency the internet brings. Furthermore, he takes the edge off of Mandel's argument on the risk of a recession by saying that the new economy is remarkably resilient, referring to past global economic and monetary crises, like the Asia crisis. The new economy's increased capacity to absorb these kinds of irregularities is caused by the growth of efficiency and flexibility within the economy. Labor can be deployed much more flexible, since companies have been able to turn labor costs into variable costs, by means of, for example, hiring temps, using freelance structures, and establishing performance-based wages. Quality management programs like JIT and MRP, in addition, enable companies to react in a flexible and efficient way to developments in the business environment.

VALUE CREATION IN THE NEW ECONOMY: THE IMPORTANCE OF INTANGIBLES AS COMPETITIVE RESOURCES

Sofar, the (macro)economic features of the so-called new economy have been explored in order to draw a picture of what the new economy seems to comprise. The question now is: what are the implications of this new economy from a perspective of value creation? Or: how to make managerial sense of the new economy? As has become clear sofar, the new economy is to a large extent about ideas, information, knowledge, skills, and concepts instead of machines. Put another way: the new economy is largely about intangibles.

The importance of this intangibility is touched upon in the following sections by looking at several specific perspectives on value creation are presented in the following sections. First, the focus will be on a knowledge perspective. The idea of the knowledge-based economy knowledge moves center stage as the particular feature of the new economy. In an era economic prosperity depends on brains rather than brawn, value creation is realized by means of employing knowledge workers and continuous learning. The ideas of the experience economy, and the attention economy, represent the importance of intangibility in particular. Though these views on value creation are somewhat more controversial, they offer an adequate view on value creation from managerial perspective.

The knowledge-based economy

Besides technology, the one thing in particular everyone seems to agree on is the fact that this era will differ to the extent to which it will be dominated by (recently acquired) knowledge and skills. Some even say that knowledge is *the* defining characteristic of the new economy, or that among the different factors causing change in the economy, no one is more important than the changing role of knowledge. Knowledge is a product in itself and increasingly more industries are built upon this intangible and attribute managing information to their core competencies. This importance of intangibility has led to the terminology of 'weightless things and industries'. One of the indicating signs of the importance of knowledge is the rapid emergence of academic chairs that are being funded in knowledge's name, illustrated by the Distinguished Professorship in Knowledge recently funded by Xerox at Berkeley (its first holder, Ikujiro Nonaka, is jokingly referred to as Dr. Know) (Davis & Meyer, 1997).

In the nineteenth century capital equipment was seen as the decisive factor determining economic growth. Skills weren't that important. Adam Smith, for example, barely mentions education in his 'Wealth of nations' (Thurow, 1999: 135), and when he does, he talks about it only as an antidote to the mind-numbing boredom of factory work. According to Lester Thurow, MIT economist, a knowledge economy requires two interlocking, though very different skill sets, in contrast. Knowledge creation requires highly educated creative skills at the very top of the skill distribution. Knowledge deployment requires widespread high-quality skills and education in the middle and bottom of the skill distribution. But, on the other hand, knowledge has been important throughout history. 'Pure' knowledge production has always existed in, for example, art, literature, scientific knowledge and philosophy. In the most basic sense, labor can be viewed as human creativity, mediated by knowledge, finding applications in the material world. What has, however, changed is the quantity and the density of knowledge and information, the speed in which it moves and changes, and the amount of it which is embodied in the design, production, and marketing of products (Curry, 1997).

The ICT revolution makes knowledge the key competitive resource, but knowledge only flows through the technology. It actually resides in people, in knowledge workers and the organization they inhabit. In the new economy, then, the job of the manager is to create an environment that allows knowledge workers to learn from their own experience, from each other, and from customers, suppliers, and business partners. Facilitating conversation, therefore, is the main goal of management. However, focusing conversation poses another paradox: traditionally seen of as a waste of time, conversation is in fact the key resource for competing on time. Knowledge creation and diffusion take place in conversations between knowledge workers, and relationships are created that define the organization and its identity (Webber, 1993). Burton-Jones states that:

> "Future wealth and power will be derived mainly from intangible, intellectual resources. This transformation from a world largely dominated by physical resources, to a world dominated by knowledge, implies a shift in the locus of economic power as profound as that which occurred at the time of the Industrial Revolution. We are in the early stages of a 'Knowledge Revolution', the initial impact of which is becoming apparent in the volatility of markets, uncertainty over future direction within governments and businesses, and the insecurity over future career and job prospects felt by individuals" (Burton-Jones, 1999: 3).

In fact, it's an economy of knowledge, skills and ideas; an economy of brainpower. Intangibles and the unexplored can bring great value. Being curious, wondering why things work, wanting to explore, being willing to learn, getting new knowledge from others, wishing to build knowledge, using new knowledge to make something different. While these characteristics are embedded in human nature, they only become evident when combined with other ingredients in the right environment (Thurow, 1999: 101). In a knowledge economy, both capital and knowledge as production factors gain importance. As Curry contends:

"While a certain number of functions, particularly service jobs (particularly many service jobs) possess relatively low compositions of capital, more and more other jobs require workers with higher levels of training and education. On a general level, the increased composition of capital can be conceived of as an increased density, velocity, and complexity of the social relationships and processes which make up social production under capitalism. This is what we are talking about, in the most basic terms, when we say that we are in an age of information, an information society, or a knowledge economy" (Curry, 1997).

Or, speaking with Drucker, knowledge is not just another resource next to the traditional factors of production; it is the only meaningful resource today. Consequently, the most valuable resource residing in their heads, knowledge workers have become employees with considerable power in the organization.

On a critical note, however, according to critics Drucker takes the power of the knowledge worker perhaps a little too far, as does Gilder in his book 'Microcosm' (Gilder, 1989). By stating that the knowledge worker controls his own means of production and consequently one could speak from a power shift from the corporation to the employee, they seem to ignore the fundamental relation between labor and capital, which – according to Curry – is the same as before. The knowledge component of variable capital today may be far more sophisticated than that in the past, but knowledge embodied in the fixed capital that it confronts in the production process is itself vastly more sophisticated. Without the knowledge possessed and controlled by the firm, and embodied in the organization of the firm, the knowledge possessed by most knowledge workers is useless (Curry, 1997).

However, it is undeniable that labor has transformed from a physical nature to a more non-physical nature, non-physical covering intangibles, like knowledge and information. Also, it cannot be denied that education and learning have gained importance over the past century. An economy that is based on brain rather than brawn places knowledge work center stage. It remains a truth that capital is a key asset, but is a fleeting one. In the new economy, capital will more and more become a function of knowledge, meaning a shift in the means of production from something physical to something human (Huey, 1994). Levi Strauss's Robert Haas says: "The most visible differences between the corporation of the future and its present-day counterpart will be not the products they make or the equipment they use, but who will be working, how they will be working, why they will be working, and what work will mean to them" (in Webber, 1993).

Several additional observations can be made, proving that knowledge, indeed, is one of the defining characteristics of the new economy. Consider the significantly growing knowledge content of products and services. Consumer information, suppliers' ideas and technology are becoming integral parts of all products and services. Smart products (like smart tires, smart cards and smart phones) are revolutionizing every aspect of society, not the least day-to-day life. Moreover, whereas in the old economy labor was an interchangeable commodity, in the new economy it isn't. The knowledge and creative minds of product strategists, developers and marketers are the keys to success. The organization's ability to attract, retain, and continually grow the capabilities of knowledge workers and creativity is what matters (Huey, 1994).

Burton-Jones states that signs of the emerging knowledge economy are apparent in the increasing use of symbolic rather than physical goods, the lessening need for physically massed/allocated resources, and the declining importance of traditional boundaries defined by business functions, industries, and nations. Most of human knowledge is gained vicariously, or indirect: it is generated without having to visit or inspect realities we are learning about physically. Contemporary business is more and more about exchanging symbolic goods, electronic symbols representing information about the physical goods which we need to know to execute transactions. The faster and cheaper for business to acquire the knowledge it needs, the more efficient it can become. Thus, a continuing incentive to improve how knowledge about the real (physical) world is symbolically represented and communicated, is present, removing physical barriers and boundaries (Burton-Jones, 1999). In addition, the need for physical collocation (or massing) of labor, materials and money in order to achieve production efficiency has decreased. Developments in ICT, as a major enabler influencing the role of the knowledge society, already offer numerous ways in which 'demassification' can manifest itself: JIT inventory systems, virtual workspaces, self-paced learning, and personalized, on-site education are just a few examples the collapse of space and time entails. As Burton-Jones notes, it can be expected that activities that depend on the transfer of knowledge will be most easily demassed and distributed. Conversely, activities that depend on frequent and informal sharing of tacit knowledge between people will – at least for the short term – tend to remain physically collocated.

The experience economy

Two more extreme and controversial conceptions of the new economy are the views expressed by Pine & Gilmore (1999) and Goldhaber (1997a and 1997b). These authors respectively proclaim the new economy to be foremost an experience and attention economy. Though different, these views more or less resemble and complement each other and adhere to the prevalence of intangibles and the internet.

> *"What captivates us now is special stuff, stuff that only a few of us can get, stuff that stands for something or symbolizes something. And, more compelling thans tuff, are experiences – events, trips, places, sights, sounds, tastes that are out of the ordinary, memorable in their own right, precious in their uniqueness and fulfilling in a way that seems to make us more than we were"* (Barlow, 2000).

The experience economy is the result of the progression of value creation over time and is based on offering consumers memorable experiences. These memorable experiences are realized by sensory interaction with customers, through which business adds value. In the experience economy, therefore, every business is a stage, and work is theatre.

The progression of economic value can be explained when looking at the history of the evolution of economic offering. Experiences are the fourth economic offering, distinguished from services like services from goods, and goods from commodities. In order to keep adding value in the new economy, Pine & Gilmore argue, manufacturers need to experientialize goods, or "ing the thing": the focus of quality shifts to the consumer, i.e., how the individual performs while using the good.

Several reasons can be observed why the experience economy has emerged. Not in the least, technology has played a major role, enabling a myriad of experiences. The increasing intensity of competition has driven business far into searching for strategies to differentiate products and services from those competitors are offering. This need for differentiation, combined with rising affluence, is a great impetus for the natural progression of economic value. Within the experience economy economic offerings have transformed from delivering to staging, from providing benefits to sensations, and by seeing customers as guests rather than clients. The nature of economic value progression has evolved through a process of customisation.

But what, then, will be next? The most intense experience business can offer their customers is changing or transforming the individual him- or herself (or, rather, letting customers experience personal transformations). Business takes on the role of guiding customers into and through transformations, inducing a change that is sustained over time instead of being memorable. Hence, the customer now becomes the product, being the ultimate way of differentiation. The full progression of economic value is graphically displayed in figure 2.2.

Higher education, in particular, is a sector with the potential to move into value-adding activities through transformation. The tremendous intellectual resources of, for instance, Harvard Business School consists of their top-class faculty with globally recognized professors, classes for (under)graduate degrees, executive education programs, the Harvard Business Review, the Harvard Business School Press, and various newsletters, videotapes, CD-ROMs, websites, and other training resources. These resources can enable Harvard Business School to being a perfect business transforming individuals into corporate executives prepared to face whatever strategic challenges. "To do so", Pine & Gilmore (1999: 168) state, "Harvard Business School would have to extend itself beyond selling book and magazine goods, information services, and educational experiences to viewing its business as changing customers. And for all those colleges and universities jostling to reach the top of the various rankings now promulgated in the press, this is the route to take."

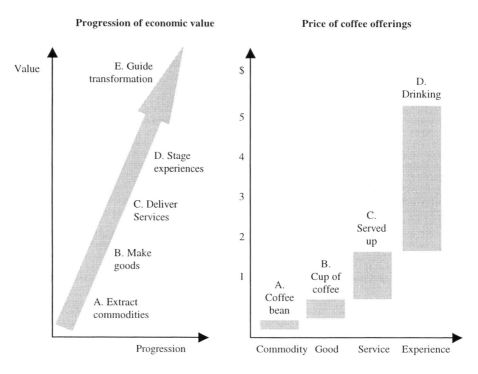

Figure 2.2. The progression of economic value.
Source: Pine & Gilmore (1999)

The attention economy

The concept of the attention economy also relates to the change from producing in the old, routine sense of factory production to performing. In its purest form, the attention economy will have attention as the only meaningful means of exchange, while money remains with no function at all. It involves a radical change in economic life, nullifying the traditional dichotomies between work and home, work and play, and production and consumption. Obtaining and paying attention (the latter referring to a resemblance with the experience economy) will be the main sources of competitive advantage.

The functioning of the attention economy can be best explained by the internet, where attention is the scarcest resource. After all, the abundance of information available dissents the little amount of time people have to look at it. It is this discrepancy between the amount of information produced and the ability to consume, that leads Goldhaber to say that the economic rules that have been in force in the old economy are not applicable to the new attention economy. How can the vast and seemingly irrational growth of the information sector be explained, then?

At the heart of the answer to this question lies the simple observation that it is the need for attention. This intrinsically scarce and desirable 'good' is the clear motivation and principle for contemporary economic functioning. Goldhaber says:

> *"The real promise of the Web and the net and the like, though also a promise it can never completely fulfil, is to help satisfy the ever more pressing desire for attention. To get attention you must emit what is technically identifiable as information; likewise for information to be of any value, it must receive attention. Therefore an information technology is also an attention technology, or in other words, a transfer of information is only completed when there is also a transfer of attention proceeding in the opposite direction"* (Goldhaber, 1997a).

The internet will also contribute to the transparency of economic and entrepreneurial functioning and will eventually leaf to the breakdown of organizational barriers. As a result, organizations will rapidly abate in importance in the attention economy, relative to the importance of the individuals who are temporarily in them. Among these individuals there will be a division between those receiving attention and those paying attention: the so-called stars and fans. Organizations will basically be temporary. They will take community-like forms, where attention is hared around "pretty equally, or, more often, entourages of fans who form around one or a few stars to help them achieve the performances they are attempting" (Goldhaber, 1997b) Capitalizing upon the networks of attention among and around organizational structures will be a major challenge in value creation: attention is property.

The development of Netscape and Linux are two examples illustrating the power of attention. Netscape, a company established by a student called Marc Andreessen, and friends, got lots of attention by giving away its web browser, and then was able to capitalize on its swiftly-established position as the best-known brand on the web. Trying to call the browser didn't work, but companies were keen to buy Netscape we server software because Netscape had become synonymous with the web in the mid-1990s. Linus Torvalds invented Linux, a reliable operating system for computers – an alternative to Microsoft's dominant Windows environment – which is distributed free over the internet. It's 'open source' software, meaning that anyone can use, amend, and improve the code and it's becoming increasingly popular. Bill Gates says he's not feeling threatened by it, but commentators say that shows what a big threat it is. Torvalds wouldn't make any money directly from Linux, then, but he has such a stock of attention that translating it into money (by offering his consultancy services, say) would be easy, if he wanted to (adapted from interview: "Basic web economics: how things work in the attention economy").

FINAL THOUGHTS: TOWARDS A NETWORK VIEW

This chapter has tried to identify the structural characteristics of the new economic era by exploring a wide range of topics. It was shown that the new economy has some particular macroeconomic features, and that it has several drivers behind it. Technology and globalization are two of the drivers that matter most in defining the new economic landscape.

One of the main conclusions from this chapter is that the new economy is not a smooth and calm landscape. Speed (Moore's Law), intangibles (the importance of knowledge and skills amongst others), and connectedness (ICT applications) are prominent characteristics that challenge not only business, but also society as a whole. The new economic landscape isn't perhaps the environment business ideally is looking for – though some, obviously, do and manage to take advantage from this situation. As Robert Shapiro concludes:

> *"New businesses can form and grow to real importance quickly, and then stumble badly. Great established companies can be crippled without seeing it coming, and then reinvent themselves. The values and resources that, for at least a century, made companies prosper and countries strong, still matter. But more is now required for businesses and nations alike – namely, an appetite for change with an appreciation of the present, and the capacity to embrace innovation while retaining sound judgment"*
> (Shapiro, 2000).

The traditional resources that still matter for value creation are increasingly complemented and, indeed, gradually replaced by intangible resources and capabilities. Information, knowledge, the ability to innovate and learn, and the organizational capabilities of being flexible matter now more than ever. As a general conclusion, it can be observed that there are several (and some very profound) differences between what has been called the old economy and the new economy. These differences have been concisely depicted in table 2.5.

From the perspective of this book, however, when searching for an overarching managerial perspective there's one conception of the new economy that entails insights and principles emanating from the previously described views: the network perspective. In fact, looking at the macroeconomic traits and development of the new economy and the previous managerial views, it appears that networks play an important role in the new economy and that they can be seen as the major organizing principle. The principles of the network economy will be elaborated in the next chapter.

Issue	Old Economy	New Economy
Economy-wide characteristics		
Markets	Stable	Dynamic
Scope of competition	National	Global
Organizational form	Hierarchical, bureaucratic	Networked
Industry		
Organization of production	Mass production	Flexible production
Key drivers of growth	Capital/labor	Innovation/knowledge
Key technology driver	Mechanization	Digitization
Source of competitive advantage	Lowering cost through economies of scale	Innovation, quality, time-to-market, and cost
Importance of research/innovation	Low/moderate	High
Relations with other firms	Go it alone	Alliances and collaboration
Workforce		
Policy goal	Full employment	Higher real wages and incomes
Skills	Job-specific skills	Broad skills and cross-training
Requisite education	A skill or degree	Lifelong learning
Labor-management relations	Adversarial	Collaborative
Nature of employment	Stable	Marked by risk and opportunity
Government		
Business-government relations	Impose requirements	Encourage growth opportunities
Regulation	Command and control	Market tools, flexibility

Table 2.5. Differences between the old and the new economy.
Source: The New Economy Index website

CHAPTER 3

THE NETWORK ECONOMY

INTRODUCTION

In this chapter, the concept of the network economy is expounded. The idea of a network economy allows fundamental aspects of the new economy to be integrated into one single (organizational and managerial) concept. The information technology revolution has resulted in the development of advanced infrastructural technological networks. These networks enable and induce global communication and information sharing at decreasing cost and at an increasing speed. Knowledge is being transferred through these interconnected ICT applications and it can be said that, taking into account the prominent place of knowledge in the new economy, it functions as the glue that holds networks together.

Speed, intangibles (knowledge), and connectedness are the three key constituting elements of the new, network economy. As a result of these three factors, one can observe the development of widespread and highly developed social, economic, and technological networks – all interconnected and to an increasing extent interdependent. Both ICT, together with the global scope they create, and knowledge, therefore, are central parts of the network economy. The ongoing process of globalization has resulted in the omnipresence of business in the global marketplace. Many firms now have multiple production sites, regional headquarters, and have access to numerous distribution channels at their disposal.

Next to its encompassing conceptual nature, network organization provides a relatively neutral and sufficiently moldable (and therefore managerially viable) perspective, which has been used in a number of disciplines, like computer sciences and sociology. Network organization, therefore, has the potential to acknowledge and integrate contributions from a range of academic fields, resulting in a holistic perspective. As Van Alstyne notes from this point of view:

> *"In computer science it represents the linked processor: 'networking computers' brings to mind issues of communications, errors, protocols, and control architecture. In economics, networks relate to coalitions and externalities: neither market nor hierarchy, they may still concern vertical integration, scale efficiency, firm boundaries, decentralized incentives, and non-cooperative gaming behavior among agents. And in sociology, the word network calls up connections – lines of interpersonal affiliation and political influence: 'networking' at a social function, for example, recognizes the importance of individual persuasion and non-economic aspects of social pressure as the context for group activity"* (Van Alstyne, 1997: 84).

As has appeared from the previous chapter, different developments leading to and within this new economic landscape have, particularly, influenced the emergence of interlinked business relationships or business networks. The impact of technological developments – especially in the field of ICT – and globalization of both the business, (socio)economic, and the political arena has led to a redefinition of different playing fields, evoking profound changes in competitive forces, corporate behavior, and consumer demands. For instance, deregulation, increased competitive pressure, shorter product lifecycles, the need for mass customization, short time-to-market, lean production, focus on core competencies, and flexibility all have contributed to the genesis of network organization.

This chapter is organized as follows. First, the network perspective is briefly elaborated from a socio-technological point of view by Manuel Castells's informationalism paradigm (Castells, 1996). Subsequently, the focus will be on network technology, network economics, and network dynamics. Next, the network perspective is expounded from an organizational and managerial view. Here, definitions, traits, and appearances of network organization are discussed, followed by looking into the business form of the network mode of organization. Finally, challenges for business schools in the network economy are identified, upon which the following chapters will build.

INFORMATIONALISM: THE NEW SOCIO-ECONOMIC PARADIGM

According to Manuel Castells, the renowned Berkeley socio-geographer, the new economy distinguishes itself from its predecessor by the intertwining of its global and informational features, which has been illustrated in the previous chapter. It is informational because productivity and competitiveness of units or agents fundamentally depend upon their capacity to generate, process, and apply knowledge-based information. It is global because the core activities of production, consumption, and circulation are organized on a global scale (Castells, 1996: 66). At the heart of this transformation towards the new economy lies the information technology revolution, which makes this new economy primarily a network economy or network society. The rapid and pervasive development of information and communication technologies can be seen as the most important enabler for the take-off of the new economy, in his view.

The internet is undoubtedly the most notorious example of a network infrastructure. Besides the abundance of information available, a prominent feature of this complex network architecture is its connectedness: it is made up of numerous computer networks capable of linking up to each other in almost infinite ways. Such a world-encompassing network enables the accumulation of knowledge and is oriented towards higher levels of complexity in information processing (Castells, ibid., p. 17). This lies at the basis of what Castells calls *informationalism*. Informationalism is based on a paradigm of new technologies. The term paradigm refers to the cluster of interrelated technical, organizational, and managerial innovations, which commence new ways of doing business and management. The contemporary change of paradigm can be seen as a shift from a technology based primarily on cheap inputs of energy to one predominantly based on cheap inputs of information derived from advances in microelectronic and telecommunications technology (see Castells,

1996: 60-61). Next to technological structures, it also brings with it new social structures, since it provides an organizational logic of global networks of capital, wealth, power, knowledge, information, and symbols around which important social functions are being organized. Although the shape of this new paradigm is not entirely clear yet, this paradigm is characterized by several features (cf. Boisot, 1998):

–   *Ubiquitous impact*
     As information forms an integral part of all human activity, the new information technologies have impact on all human spheres of life. There is hardly any domain of human activity that will be kept untouched by the pervasive effects of information technologies;

–   *Flexibility*
     Organizations are able to change constantly and become fluid to a large extend. The ontology of the organization becomes unclear as the boundaries are changing and to a large extend are blurring and reshaped;

–   *Convergence*
     A next characteristic is the convergence of specific technologies into a highly integrated, global system. This technological convergence has revolutionized the impact of information technologies during the second half of the 1990s and will continue in the next few years;

–   *Network logic*
     The last characteristic of this paradigm refers to the network logic of information technologies as they become integrated in globally connected information systems like the internet.

The use of new technologies has resulted in the internationalization of core economic activities, such as the functioning of financial markets, multinational enterprises, and the production of highly skilled personnel. No part of the globe has to be isolated from the rest of the world anymore. This global interaction now forms the basis for management, productivity, and competition, which are expressed in more divergent ways than has been the case in former times. As a result, new principles for organizing have emerged. These principles (see Castells, 1996) are being revealed by:

–   A transition from mass-production to flexible production;
–   A crisis for large corporations (traditionally based on vertical integration), and a focus on the vitality and flexibility of (subcontracted) small- and medium-sized enterprises (SMEs);
–   New methods of management (many of which have originated within Japanese firms, such as Kanban, Total Quality Control, just-in-time management, multifunctional labor, worker participation, reduction of uncertainty);

–   Networking between SMEs, i.e., linking up with each other and being licensed/subcontracted by umbrella corporations;
–   The formation of strategic alliances between larger corporations, limited in time and/or by specific markets, products, and processes (not excluding competition in other fields);
–   A shift from vertical bureaucracies to horizontal corporations (forming networks within each firm), where the operating unit is the business project rather than the bureaucratic department.

These changed principles bring about new dynamics in the economic landscape and particularly in the business environment. A different scope, different dynamics, and a different mode of organization come into play.

NETWORK TECHNOLOGY, NETWORK ECONOMICS, AND NETWORK DYNAMICS

The term network society is not merely referring to the new media network that has been developed in recent years but more in general to the successor of the mass society that has grown to full maturity in the 20th century. The mass society has been developed interrelated to the industrial revolution during which large concentrations of people came together in industrial towns, schools, armies, and factories (one place, one time) (Van Dijk, 1999: 23-24).

The process of transformation towards an informational economy is complex and can to a large extent be attributed to the rise of new information and communication technologies. Before ICT could revolutionize business environments a process of technical convergence of different communication networks was needed. Van Dijk (1999) has described this process of technical convergence in three convoluted and interrelated developments.

First, there was the revolution in microelectronics, which led to four generations of computers in 30 years. The miniaturization of components underlies this revolution in computer technology. Through the invention of the integrated semiconductor, the chip, it became possible to concentrate hundreds of thousands connections on a plate of a surface of just a few square millimeters. The capacity of these chips increased exponentially (Moore's law). The real value of this chip technology lies in its multifunctionality, in the sense that this technology could be applied to a whole series of electronic media. It could be applied to central telephone exchanges and micro-electronic updates. It also caused a drastic decentralization of computer processing by which data communication became an important phenomenon. Thirdly, chips and processors were used in audiovisual equipment, which enabled transmission and reception of sound and images on a large scale.

The second main development was, what Van Dijk (1999) calls, the gradual digitalization of all data streams between every piece of hardware used in telecommunication, data communication and mass communication. Until that time telecommunication and mass communication were using natural analogue signals

for text and images. The main problems with analogue signals were the slowness
and the fact that these were subject to interference and therefore to
misinterpretations. With digitalization, signals are chopped in into identical pieces
(zeros and ones) which could be transmitted easily and fast.

The third main technical development concerns the lines of transmission,
transmission capacity and transmission and reception techniques. ICT advancements
account for higher bandwidth, increasing volumes of bytes to be transmitted, and
increasingly compatible technologies. As time goes by, an integration of techniques
and technologies can also be witnessed.

The main implication of this technical convergence was that all sort of intangible
goods can be processed, stored and distributed over the networks in a easy and
cheap way. Like Webster (1995) points out, these information networks routes have
become the highways of the modern age, akin to the railways, roads and canals of
the industrial era. This new ICT based infrastructure can be seen as the physical
foundation for the information or network society. Figure 3.1 pictures the
convergence of different technologies constituting the network economy's physical
foundation.

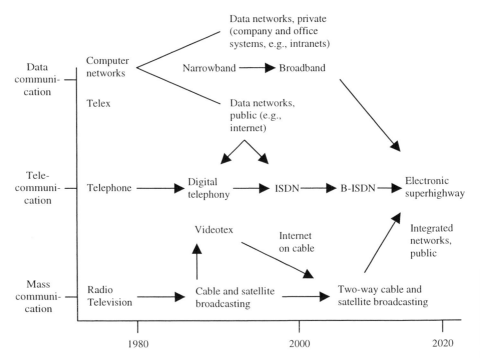

Figure 3.1. Integration of technologies over time.
Source: Van Dijk (1999: 10)

Like Castells explains, the new technological paradigm first changed the scope and dynamics of the industrial economy, creating a global economy and fostering a new wave of competition between existing agents as well as between them and a legion of newcomers. At the same time a process of creative destruction set in which affected large segments of the industrial economy and its institutional attributes. Information and communication technologies have played a crucial role is in reducing our dependency upon material and human co-location. Just-in-time systems, computer-integrated manufacturing, and integrated interfirm networks have contributed highly to the streamlining of production, demassifying factories, inventories, and comprising supply chains.

According to Shapiro and Varian (1999) the central difference between the old and new economies is that the first was driven by *economies of scale* whereas the second is driven by *economics of networks*. The explaining concept here is positive feedback in network dynamics, which are based on the fundamental characteristic that the value of a network depends on the number of other people already, connected to it. This new value proposition is called network externalities.

Network externalities refer the effects that arise when one market participant affects others without being paid. They can be negative as well as positive. The famous example of negative network externalities is pollution; cigarette smoke, for instance, does not only harm the health of the smoker but also the health others who breathe this polluted air. Positive network externalities work in a similar way but with reverse effects. The value of the telephone enhances when more people are connected to this telephone network. This economic network principal is often referred as Metcalfe's Law. During the 1970s Bob Metcalfe, the inventor of a localized networking technology, Ethernet, was selling a combination of Ethernet, Unix and TCP/IP as a way to make large networks out of many small ones. He noticed that if he linked together small local networks, the value of the combined network would multiply exponentially. In 1980 he formulated his law: value = n x (n-1). To put it in words: as the number of nodes in a network increases arithmetically, the value of the network increases exponentially (Kelly, 1998: 23). Each additional member of a network attributes to a disproportionate growth of the value of a network. As was noted earlier in the previous chapter, network externalities and network effects are distinctive features of information technologies. The more broadly they are being used, the more value they will generate. This formed the main legitimization of giving products away for free, or in Kelly's terms, to follow the so-called Law of Generosity (see also Chapter 2).

Shapiro & Varian (1999) point to the fact that these network dynamics are not really that new, but apply to older kinds of networks like the postal service, railroads, airlines, and telephones. However, as Kelly (1998: 24) notes, the latter network's value can only be the grand sum of all possible one-by-one connections. In contrast, the power of online networks multiplies even faster because they provide opportunities for complicated three-way, four-way, or even many-to-many-way connections. The main implication of these network dynamics is 'success breeds success', 'the bigger, the better', or 'the winner takes it all' principle. It also means that it will become almost impossible for smaller networks to survive in a market which is dominated by one big network provider because it is hard to overcome the collective switching cost – the combined switching costs of all users (Shapiro & Varian, 1999: 184). It means that the critical mass that is needed before a new technology can take off and diffuse becomes harder to achieve as long as the standards of different network-based technologies are incompatible.

These new network economics have led some economists to embrace the concept of increasing returns, referring to the tendency for that which is ahead to get further ahead and that which loses advantage to lose further advantage. It fundamentally differs from the Alfred Marshall's 'law of diminishing returns' of industrial economics, which he formulated in the 1920s. The latter law is based on the economies of scale principle: the more products you make, the more efficient the process becomes. Moreover economies of scale stem from the efforts of one organization of single organization to outpace competition by creating value for less. Increasing returns are (though they may be reaped by one dominant network player) created and shared by the entire network (Kelly, 1998: 26). The value of a network is created by producers, users and competitors and therefore cannot be steered by just one player. Or as Kelly (ibid.) puts it: "the value of the gains resides in the greater web of relationships."

NETWORK DYNAMICS: RICHNESS AND REACH

To understand the magnitude of this economic and societal transformation one should take notice of the underlying dynamics of these new information and communication technologies in networks. These dynamics can be best expressed by looking at the opportunities ICT and networks provide for realizing both 'richness' and 'reach' (see Evans & Wurster, 2000).

Recently, Philip Evans & Thomas Wurster have presented the elegantly simple presumption that the new economics of information carries the potential of abrogating the traditional trade-off between richness and reach. The new economics of information is about the prevalence of new technologies, connectivity, and the emergence of shared platforms and common standards and is redefining organizational principles and business practices. When separating information from its physical carrier, the new technologies make it possible not to let richness prevail at the expense of reach and vice versa. The trade-off is being blown-up.

At the core of this idea lies the observation that information and knowledge form the glue that holds together value chains, supply chains, organizations, and society together. Information and knowledge are the flows between (and within) the nodes of networks. Though this idea inclines towards an oversimplified abstraction of reality, it can be used within different contexts. Richness generally refers to the quality of information or knowledge, which includes examples like accuracy, bandwidth, currency, customization, interactivity, relevance, and security. Reach, on the other hand, refers to the number of people participating in the information and knowledge sharing. This blow-up of the traditional trade-off is being driven by both the explosion of connectivity and the dissemination of common information standards. This is depicted in figure 3.2, in which an example is given of the trade-off relating to computer manufacturer Dell.

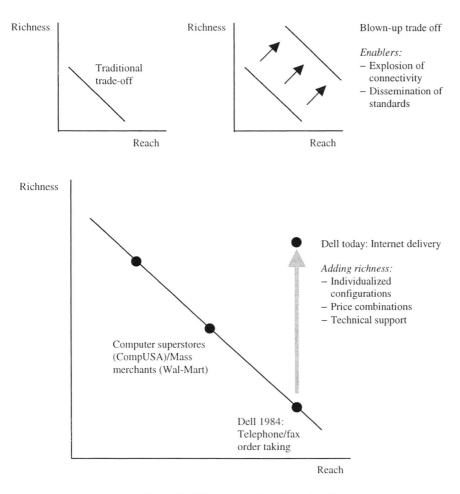

Figure 3.2. The richness/reach trade-off.
Source: adapted from Evans and Wurster (2000)

As a result, the new economics of information and the abrogation of the richness/reach trade-off lead traditional business structures to be redefined. The traditional value chain doesn't have to be fully present in organizations, as was the case with large, vertically integrated enterprises. This deconstruction of value chains results in changing competitive structures. A first illustration of such a change, is that competitive advantage becomes 'de-averaged'. What matters for an integrated value chain is competitive advantage over the entire chain. It is of minor importance where the competitive advantage originates from. However, in a deconstructed value chain averaging competitive advantage is no legitimized way of doing business anymore. Each separate element is confronted with competitors, focusing merely on that one specific element. Survival, therefore, depends on having (a) particular competitive advantage(s).

A second consequence is the escalation of competition, resulting in what has been labeled as hypercompetition. Within each separate and narrowly defined corporate activity, there will be fewer bases of competitive advantage. Evans & Wurster explain:

> "With fewer ways to win, there is less 'netting out' of competitive advantage. With fewer ways to win, there are fewer winners. Where there is only one basis of competitive advantage, monolithic advantage tends to breed monopoly. Where there is none at all, lack of advantage breeds stalemate. In all of the post-deconstruction businesses, their comparative simplicity intensifies competition" (Evans & Wurster, 2000: 59).

So, within this new competitive landscape firms have to reorganize themselves in order to remain competitive or build competitiveness. The question then is, how business organization adapts itself to this changed landscape. The answer to this question lies in flexibility, a concept lying at the core of network organization.

Sofar, the idea of network structures has mainly been viewed from a technological network perspective, pointing at the expanded possibilities, convergence, and economic dynamics these networks engender, which lay at the basis of the informationalism paradigm. Now, for the purpose of explicating the network concept from an organizational and managerial view, a profound view at what this network logic means and implies from these perspectives is presented in the next sections.

DEFINITIONS OF NETWORKS

Organizing by means of using network structures appears to be one of the most dominant contemporary organizational and managerial logics. Since a conception of the abstract idea of a network is important from the viewpoint of the topic of this book, several definitions of a network are provided here. In Castells's view (Castells, 1996: 470-471), a network is a set of interconnected nodes, where a node is the point at which a curve intersects itself. Depending on the kind of network – technological, social, economical, political – a node can be virtually anything. Castells adds to this:

> "Networks are open structures, able to expand without limits, integrating new nodes as long as they are able to communicate within the network, namely as long as they share the same communication codes (for example, values or performance goals). A network-based social structure is a highly dynamic, open system, susceptible to innovating without threatening its balance. Networks are appropriate instruments for a capitalist economy based on innovation, globalization, and decentralized concentration; for work, workers, and firms based on flexibility, and adaptability; for a culture of endless deconstruction and reconstruction; for a polity geared towards the instant processing of new values and public moods; and for a social organization aiming at the supersession of space and the annihilation of time. Yet the network morphology is also a source of dramatic reorganization of power relationships" (Castells, 1996: 470-471).

From a behavioral viewpoint, however, a network is seen as a pattern of social relations over a set of persons, positions, groups, or organizations (Sailer, 1978), while from a technological focus a network is defined as a collection of terminals, computers, servers, and components which allows for the easy flow of data and use of resources between one another. A strategic view of networks considers them "long term arrangements among distinct but related for-profit organizations that allow those firms in them to gain or sustain competitive advantage" (Jarillo, 1988: 70, op.cit. Van Alstyne, 1997).

Within networks, power and resources are normally decentralized, and distributed among the nodes in the network. These nodes add value to the network as a whole and the product, service or experience it engenders. Network organization allows firms to focus on what they are really good at (say, their core competencies) and enables them to subcontract all other activities within the corporation's value chain. By means of complex outsourcing infrastructures and effective supply chain management, (scarce) resources can be allocated wherever and deployed whenever necessary, in order to add value to the final customer. Networks, hence, are synonymous with flexibility.

Principles and key characteristics of network organization

What determines if a specific mode of organization can, in fact, be seen as network organization? To answer this question, it is necessary to explore some of the key principles and characteristics of network organization.

The central principle behind network organization is easy to understand from a resource-based view. When different firms have different sets of (complementary and substitutable) resources at their disposal, they can configure resource packages according to their needs. In a network, firms agree to engage in partnerships on, for instance, R&D efforts or product development, to bring these activities under joint control and to deploy them for the sake of the network as a whole (which can consist of as little as three partners). In other words, the actors in the network become interdependent partners through adherence to the principles of co-specialized assets, joint control, and collective purpose.

Conceptually, networks distinguish themselves from centralized organizations, inflexible hierarchies, casual associations, haphazard societies, and mass markets (Van Alstyne, 1997). The distinctive features of a network – co-specialized assets, joint control, and collective purpose – place this type of organization between markets and hierarchies.[1] In transaction cost economics (TCE), for instance, networks (along with a number of other modes of organization) are seen as hybrid

---

[1] It should be noted, however, that a conceptual distinction between markets, hierarchies, and networks brings some difficulties with it. Networks cannot be placed exactly between market organization and hierarchical organization, since they can include different typical characteristics of both markets and hierarchies at the same time. Making certain distinctions between these organizational forms clear, however, is useful to analyze and compare these archetypes.

forms of coordination. Following TCE, networks should be the proper organizational form in environments in which transactions are typified by moderate asset specificity, moderate uncertainty, and a moderate frequency. From this conceptual view, network organization can be seen as an unstable organizational form, prone to favor either market or hierarchy as the mechanism of coordination. Network organization, therefore, continuously struggles to find an equilibrium between the opposing qualities of stability and flexibility, specialization and generalization, and centralization and decentralization (ibid.). To an increasing extent, however, networks are replacing the dominant coordination mechanisms of markets and hierarchies, since this organizational form integrates these opposing qualities, in a sense that it allows for managing with a certain pliability in choosing which quality or qualities to be the basis of its operations in varying contexts.

Specific characteristics of network organization include the existence of both internal and external organizational boundaries that are highly permeable, facilitating a relatively 'loose' organization. Organizational boundaries become ill-defined and are redrawn from a network perspective. As Baker (1993: 400) illustrates: "The chief structural characteristic of network organization is the high degree of integration across formal boundaries." As a consequence, management is less hierarchical and more democratic, getting its legitimation from expertise rather than from rank. In addition, networks employ more flexible resources, usually with a high degree of intangible, localized, and specialized know-how. The vertical disintegration of the value chain through network organization results in a web of multiple loose associations and allows for specialized and customizable resource deployment. Hence, development cycles can be shortened, lead times can be reduced, and product offerings become more differentiated, addressing local concerns and demands. Next to the advantage of getting (market) information locally, responsibility is usually distributed to lower organizational levels, enabling decision-making in a more efficient and effective way. A higher degree of customization and an inclination towards niche seeking activities are also prominent network advantages. Different stages in product development can be executed simultaneously, implying a project organization rather that a functional organizations; tasks are organized from a market-driven basis instead from of deriving from rationalized corporate functions. As a consequence of all the characteristics, reputations, commitment, and trust become of crucial importance to network success (Van Alstyne (1997), based on different authors).

Flexibility is part of the way of value creation that takes place within networks. In addition, this value creation is underpinned by the effective use of ICT, openness, a win-win orientation, new definitions of market rules, time and standard dependency of labor and competence division, and dynamic problem- and project-related linking of competencies (Wüthrich et al., 1997). This particular way of value creation results in some marked competitive advantages, which can be categorized in advantages related to innovation and know-how, advantages in system competency and flexibility, and advantages concerning time and cost. The more specific advantages are graphically depicted in figure 3.3.

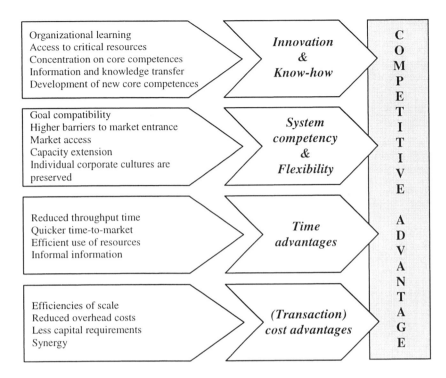

Figure 3.3. Advantages of networks.
Source: based on Wildemann (1996)

ORGANIZING FOR FLEXIBLE VALUE CREATION: THE NETWORK ENTERPRISE

Different new models of business organization are beginning to emerge to capitalize on the new economic and managerial realities in order to create value. Virtual companies have been proliferating as the dividing line between companies disappears with mergers, acquisitions, alliances and partnerships. Outsourcing structures and knowledge-sharing have by now become the rule rather than the exception.

One specific intangible asset is of great value in the network economy, namely knowledge. The creation of knowledge and knowledge sharing – on which innovation is dependent – lie at the heart of the network economy (Tapscott, 1999: vii). Knowledge, as was noted before, can be seen as the glue holding the network together. According to Burton-Jones (1999), tacit knowledge, whether alone or in conjunction with explicit knowledge, can give firms a sustainable competitive advantage. The former kind of knowledge is always associated with people, while the latter is generally capable of being stored, processed, and communicated using (widely available) technologies. This observation has several consequences for managing the firm's critical resources: integration, coordination, and protection of high levels of specialized and tacit knowledge are, then, key aspects of management. Or as Burton-Jones puts it, firms have to understand their role as 'knowledge integrators' not merely 'information processors' (ibid., p. 31).

In a society that is heavily based on the importance of knowledge, which in many ways is powerfully and profoundly facilitated by technological advancements, new business models are being created in order to cope with current and future environmental challenges. A major variety of analogous organizational experiments has resulted in restructuring businesses according to principles of, among others, flattening and downsizing, business process reengineering, subcontracting and outsourcing of non-core activities, creating multifunctional project teams, empowering employees, increasing workforce flexibility (multi-skilled workers), expanding the externalized workforce (temps), replacing highly specialized machinery for flexible manufacturing systems and developing multipurpose information systems. What seems to underlie these experiments (and what seems to be indicated by the consequences for corporations according to figure 3.4) is the development towards a new flexible firm (cf. Volberda (1997), Handy (1995), Kanter (1994), Pasmore (1994), and Peters (1997)). This flexible firm should be able to respond efficiently and effectively to a wide variety of changes in the competitive environment (Volberda, 1997: 1). A whole new vocabulary of flexible organizations has been established by now, which includes concepts of the virtual corporation (Davidow & Malone, 1992), the hollow corporation, the dynamic network form (Miles & Snow, 1986), the hypertext organization (Nonaka & Takeuchi, 1995), the platform organization (Ciborra, 1996), the shamrock organization (Handy, 1995), and the cellular organization (Miles, Snow, Mathews, Miles & Coleman, 1997). Tapscott adds:

> "Throughout most of the nineties, managers worked hard to flatten their organizations, both to control costs and because network structures perform better than hierarchies under most conditions. However, as the Net enables disaggregation of value and a new division of responsibilities among players, there is growing evidence that the integrated firm itself is being replaced as the most effective model of wealth creation" (Tapscott, 1999: xii).

Easily and cheaply allowing businesses to communicate and coordinate with suppliers, customers, employees and competitors and by separating the economics of information from the information of things, complex and flexible networks are created within the hypercompetitive landscape. The business model of flexible networks is increasing the potential scope for specialization and is vastly expanding the size of markets (Shapiro, 2000).

Technological change, and its consequence of business becoming increasingly globalized, has evidently played an important role in the emergence of the network enterprise. This network enterprise has become a rampant structure of the commercial organization of production and reflects the network structure of the modern informational/global economy. The network firm, according to Castells, is able to generate knowledge and process information efficiently, is able to adapt to the demands of the global economy, is flexible enough to deploy resources as quickly as objectives change in a turbulent business environment, and is able to innovate, since innovation has become one of the key competitive weapons in the network economy (Castells, 1996: 171-172). Characteristics ascribed to the network enterprise indicate that it can be seen as a sort of chameleon, able to rapidly adapt to unforeseen changes in the environment, or a 'spider's web'. Dynamic network organizations are spun from small, globally dispersed, ad hoc teams or independent organizational entities performing knowledge or service activities. Faced with changing customer demands and business environments, they reshape or restructure themselves, adding nodes in the network that add value and excluding nodes that do not. (Jarvenpaa & Ives, 1994). In short, table 3.1 summarizes assumptions about future trends and traits of technological developments, organizational structure and management, and the business environment and competition indicating the relevant issues inducing the emergence of network organizations.

Assumptions about future states and trends in...		
Technology	**Organizations**	**Environment and competition**
Information availability (anything): • Terabyte memories Recording and long-term storage of most digital-based transactions • Massive heterogeneous and distributed databases • Worldwide public and private content addressable electronic libraries • "Knowbots" capable of traveling over networks and then searching computer nodes for desired information *Connectivity (anytime, anywhere):* • Worldwide wireless networks capable of sending data, voice, and even full motion video in near real time • One phone number reaches a person regardless where a person is • Open systems and standardization • Worldwide geographical positioning systems *Person-machine interfaces (in any form):* • Personal digital assistants • Speech generation and understanding • Videophone • Pen-based computing • Graphical user interfaces • Virtual reality • Electronic rooms (video walls) • Set of standard productivity tools (electronic mail, calendar systems, intelligent business forms) • Automatic national language translation systems *Economics of computing – at little cost:* • Two orders of magnitude improvement in cost-performance ratios of computer memories, microprocessors, etc., over the next decade	*Structure and control:* • Organic and ad hoc organizational designs • Hierarchies giving way to market and clan structures • Organizations reducing in size • Staff functions absorbed into line functions • Manager role replaced by coordinator and coach roles • Distributed and decentralized decision-making • Outsourcing • Strategic alliances *Resource deployment:* • Human intellect most valuable asset • Cosmopolitan management team • 24-hour window for work day • Virtual work teams and managers • Self-managed work teams • Personalization of human resource management • Mass customization • Core competencies and capabilities	*Environment:* • Increasing environmental uncertainty/turbulence • Information economy: knowledge as the new source of wealth • Work growing independent of workplace • Decreasing economic role of the national government • More diverse work force • Nations will seek competitive advantage by investments in education and knowledge infrastructure *Competition:* • Continued shortening of product life cycles • Economic power from services and service industries • Globalization to reap economies of scale and scope • Reemergence of entrepreneurship/startups

Table 3.4. Assumptions about future states and trends.
Source: based on Jarvenpaa & Ives (1994)

The network enterprise capitalizes on, what has been labeled before, both richness and reach. Not only can it serve a large amount of customers, it is also able to offer these customers their products or services on an individual basis. Another example of such network behavior is the use of resources. The typical network enterprise produces one specific product or service, while 'surrounding' it with the provision of complementary products or services, produced by another company inside the network. Within the network, companies can benefit from the resources that reside somewhere in the network. Dependent on the importance of particular resources, defined by (dependence or uniqueness of) the complementary products or services, the network enterprise can decide to engage in more intensified or longer-lasting cooperation with other firms in the network. Therefore, network organizations differentiate themselves by managing intellectual processes and service processes (intangible flows), instead of managing physical flows. Quinn calls such a network firm the 'intelligent enterprise' (1992), emphasizing the importance of intangible assets, like knowledge and skills. The consequence for the organization is that it, to a more or lesser extent, becomes virtual, implicating a wholly new conception of what is called an organization. It's not easy to figure out where an online grocery store's value-adding activities are, let alone to find out how the value-creating process within the value chain is being managed. What seems to be only one corporation can, in fact, be a large set of independent firms working together, functioning as one.

Types of network organizations

Within the mode of network organization, several different network types can be distinguished. Snow, Miles & Coleman (1992) distinguish between the internal network, the stable network, and the dynamic network. The internal network is located within an individual company. The central aim of this type of network is to capture entrepreneurial and market benefits without having the company engage in much outsourcing (ibid.). They can be seen as loose associations of assets and business units that are enclosed by a single firm. The logic of the internal network is to subject these assets and business units to market forces, and therefore market prices, so that internal units will subject its operations to an attitude of constant innovation to enhance their performance and remain their internal competitiveness. Internal networks are developed, for instance, when a company doesn't want to subject itself to the interdependency a general network entails, but does want to reap (some of) the benefits of network organization, like reduced resource redundancy and decreased response times. Within the stable network, partial outsourcing by the core firm is one of the key features. Typically, a number of suppliers or vendors is to be found around the central core firm. Some of these suppliers may solely depend on the demand by the core firm. Relationships are often long-term, so that flexibility is accompanied by a particular level of certainty, in order to cope with market volatility. Examples of stable networks can be found in the Japanese car manufacturing industry. Within dynamic networks, alliances usually are of a more temporary nature. Firms with particular key skills are centered around a lead firm, which identifies and assembles assets owned largely or even entirely by other companies. These lead firms, which sometimes have merely brokering functions, then rely on a core skill like manufacturing (e.g., Motorola), R&D/design (e.g., Reebok), or design/assembly (e.g., Dell Computer) (ibid.). This model has emerged in highly competitive and volatile business environments. Snow, Miles & Coleman explain:

> *"Each network node practices its particular expertise, and, if brokers are able to package resources quickly, the company achieves maximum responsiveness. (...) The dynamic network operates best in competitive situations where there are myriad players, each guided by market pressures to be reliable and to stay at the leading edge of its specialty. The dynamic network is also appropriate in settings where design and production cycles are short enough to prevent knockoffs or where proprietary rights can be protected by law or by outsourcing only standard parts and assemblies"* (Snow, Miles & Coleman, 1992: 12).

The internal network, the stable network, and the dynamic network are represented in figure 3.4.

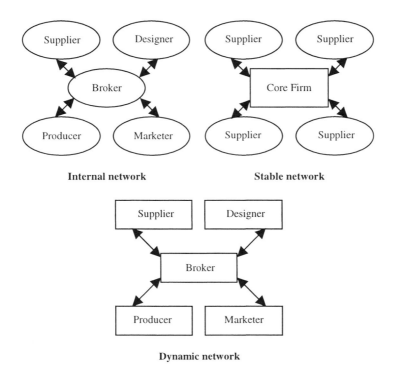

Figure 3.4. Three types of networks.
Source: Snow, Miles & Coleman (1992)

A prototypical business network can be seen as a web consisting of a myriad of relationships, including business partners like suppliers, suppliers' suppliers, competitors, consumers, government agencies, and other non-commercial actors. The nature of the relationships in a network is one of interdependence, pointing at the need for the management of organizational interfaces. Figure 3.5 depicts a prototypical business network.

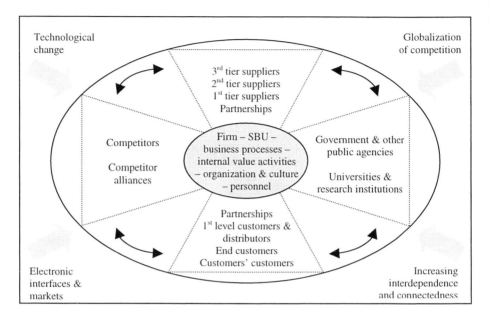

Figure 3.5. A business network with different relationships and environmental forces.
Source: Möller & Halinen (1999: 415)

This independence, however, manifests itself in practice as interdependence and reciprocity, which are important aspects in the conception of network organizations. As a consequence, managing on the basis of intra- and interorganizational network market mechanisms, trust, shared vision and values, common measurement, real-time information, and communication systems (Jarvenpaa & Ives, 1994). Miles & Snow say:

> *"The various components of the network recognize their interdependence and are willing to share information, cooperate with each other, and customize their product or service – all to maintain their position within the network"* (Miles & Snow, 1992: 55).

Typical examples of network organizations include the well-known multinational Asea Brown Boveri (ABB) and the less known Technical Computing & Graphics (TCG), a group of highly innovative information technology firms in Australia. One of the most interesting aspects of TCG is its behavioral protocol, indicating the rules of the game within the network, depicted in table 3.2. These behavioral rules function as a governance mechanism in order to create cohesion, trust and cooperation within the network and contain governance mechanisms that can be implicitly found in other networks in general.

The characteristics of the network enterprise resemble different requirements for survival in the new competitive landscape: strategic flexibility, developing dynamic core competencies, engaging in cooperative strategies, and effective strategic leadership. Strategic flexibility implies the capacity to vary and adjust business objectives according to external demands imposed on the enterprise in order to survive in new competitive landscapes. In addition to building human capital, the development of dynamic core competencies facilitates strategic flexibility. By managing corporate assets in bundles, firms can easily and flexibly reconfigure their assets at any given time. A successful firm is one that creates flexible architectures facilitating continual redesign (Nadler & Tushman (1997), op.cit. Hitt (1997)). By cooperating with other parties, albeit firms, universities or governments, firms get access to different resources and are able to share investments and risks. It's the presence of these features of network firms, that will enable them to counter their competitors in efficient and effective ways.

Mutual independence
The TCG network consists of independent firms whose relations are governed by bilateral commercial contracts. It is open to new entrants who are prepared to abide by the rules. There is no internal hierarchy.

Mutual preference
Member firms give preference to each other in the letting of contracts. Contract may be made outside the group, against a competitive bid from a member firm, when circumstances warrant (e.g., work overloads or a signal to a the member that it has to lift its game)

Mutual non-competition
Member firms do not compete head-to-head with each other. Such self-denial helps to establish trust among member firms.

Mutual non-exploitation
Member firms do not seek to make profits from transactions among themselves.

Flexibility and business autonomy
The flexibility of the network as a whole derives from the capacity of member firms to respond to opportunities they see fit. They do not need to ask for group approval to enter into any transaction or new line of business, provided the proposed innovation does not breach any rules.

Network democracy
There is no overall network owner. Nor is there any central committee or other formal governance structure. However, member firms can hold equity in each other as well as in third-party joint ventures.

Expulsion
A firm may be expelled from the network of it wilfully disobeys the rules. Expulsion can be effected simply by severing all commercial ties with the miscreant member.

Subcontracting
There are no "subcontractor-only" firms within the TCG group. Each member firm has access to the open market, and is indeed expected to bring in work from outside the network.

Entry
New members are welcome to join the network but are not to draw financial resources from the group. New members must obtain capital from banks rather than through equity from other member firms. It is membership in the network that serves as collateral for the bank loan.

Exit
The network places no impediments in the way of a departing firm. However, there is no market for shares held in TCG member firms. Hence, departure arrangements have to be negotiated on a case-by-case basis.

Table 3.2. Governance mechanisms of TCG.
Source: Miles & Snow (1995: 9)

FINAL THOUGHTS: THE NETWORK ECONOMY AND CHALLENGES FOR EDUCATION AND BUSINESS SCHOOLS

In the 'former new economies', distinctive competencies have included (access to) raw materials, natural resources and the presence of, for example, fertile lands. In an era in which knowledge is the important intangible asset, on the contrary, national competitive advantage will increasingly be derived from an educated and empowered workforce, that's able to adapt quickly to the dynamic requirements of a changing world (Ives, 1992). Looking from this point of view, knowledge, learning, and education become ever important matters and move center stage in developing competitive advantage, not only at the level of the nation-state, but increasingly at the firm level and, of course, the personal level.

As the aforementioned quote of Adam Smith implicitly showed, the workforce in the industrial age was viewed as consisting of mindless and numb cogs, required for standard and iterative production. Knowledge workers, as we have seen, will instead be valued for their creativity, ideas, flexibility and adaptability, which requires intelligent and thoughtful human resource management.

Robert D. Atkinson, director of the Technology, Innovation and the New Economy Project at the Progressive Policy Institute (PPI), proposes three main foundations to sustain the growth of the new economy: speeding the transformation to a digital economy, investing in research and innovation, and improving skills and knowledge. The number of engineers, he notes, has grown but not at the rate the new economy requires. In addition, due to intensified competition, the churning of firms and the low employee tenure, companies are spending less on skill training. PPI therefore proposes that companies collaborate, in networks, partnerships and consortia, to invest in training to ensure innovation and growth (Atkinson & Court, 2000).

> *"Sustainable advantage will be enjoyed by those societies (and companies) which best elicit value from human resources. This will require a progressive education system and an approach to human resource management that is predicated on continuous change and human development. (...) Nations that neglect education will wither economically. Domestic business may be compelled, due to a shortage of skilled workers, to improve local education systems. (...) But in a world of dismantled trade barriers, there will be few domestic firms left with the resources required to help reengineer local education systems or to underwrite remedial education programs. (...) Instead of back stopping an inferior national or local education system, these firms may be required by stiff global competition to seek out lower cost sources of expertise from elsewhere in the world. Computer and communications technology will weave these dispersed human resources into an integrated worldwide fabric"* (Ives, 1992).

This quote highlights at least two major challenges the educational system is being confronted with: the role and the importance of business and education and the role and importance of ICT in education. These challenges seem to indicate a (need for a) turnaround of traditional patterns in education, characterized by the lagging rate of investments in ICT in education and the non-existing (even controversial) relationship between education and business. Both subjects will be dealt with extensively in Chapters 5 and 6, as well in general terms as from the perspective of management education and business schools in particular.[2]

So what are these challenges facing business schools in the new, knowledge-intensive, network economy? Since knowledge has moved center stage in the network economy, one of the essential elements of value creation now is (organizational) learning, and, hence, education. Knowledge management systems now are business functions of major importance, linking the right person, in the right place, with the right knowledge, to the right customer. Learning has become one of the most important activities in economic and business development, and education has been labeled as the one major big business for the 21st century. Knowledge turned out to be crucial for achieving competitive advantage. The perception of employee training has shifted from one of being a cost center to one of being a continuously required profit-yielding investment. For instance, Motorola claims every dollar spent on corporate training to result in a productivity growth equaling 30 US dollar within 3 years.

The changed competitive landscape, both in qualitative (the nature of competition) and quantitative (the number of competitors) terms, poses business schools with different opportunities and threats (which will be dealt with in detail in Chapter 6). Their traditional educational environment has ceased to exist and is increasingly penetrated by other providers of education. These providers originate not only from countries all over the world, they also spring from non-traditional educational sectors, like business. In agricultural economies learning often is church-led, supplying knowledge that serves a lifetime's need, while in industrial economies learning has been government-led. In the network economy, knowledge has a relative brief shelf life, has to be updated constantly, and both the nature and locus of providing education is transforming with fast technological developments. The boundary between working and training will increasingly fade. In the network economy, business becomes the main purveyor of education, since knowledge is the glue holding networks together and is the foundation of competitive advantage. "Business, more than government", Davis & Botkin (1994) argue, "is instituting the changes in education that are required for the merging knowledge-based economy. School systems, public and private, are lagging behind the transformation in learning that is evolving outside them, in the private sector at both work and play, with people of all ages. Over the next few decades, the private sector will eclipse the public sector as our predominant educational institution."

Competition in the market for management education will increase, not only between public institutions, but also between public and private initiatives, like corporate universities. The number of corporate universities is still expected to grow, considering their contributions and importance to organizational learning and the criticality of valuable and unique knowledge for competitive advantage (Hitt, 1997: 221). In addition, business schools have to get more customer-oriented,

---

[2] Chapter 5, called 'The new learning', will particularly cope with a variety of new challenges (management) education is faced with.

providing education that is customized and available on-demand, anytime and anywhere, using state-of-the-art educational technology, require an upheaval in educational principles, while at the same time they are being confronted with decreased public funding opportunities. As one result, business schools have to take a more entrepreneurial stance, and engage in commercial teaching, research, and consulting activities.

Also institutional changes with an international scope, like the European transition towards the widely accepted Bachelor/Master structure within higher education, will affect education. This transformation will cause business schools to compete increasingly on quality and reputation, in order to not only attract students, but also to attract and retain faculty.

In short, business schools are challenged to reorganize according to standards that fit the current economic landscape and business environment best and they will also require effective strategic leadership in order to guide them through the opportunities and threats the new competitive landscape. The network paradigm, therefore, leads to a rethinking of how management education and business schools can, or should, be organized, considering the changes in the economic environment.

The following chapters will continue the network perspective and deal with questions like: what does the idea of a network economy mean from a perspective of management knowledge, the managerial job, and the business school curriculum? How can learning be organized from a network perspective? And: should the different parts constituting a business school be organized in network structures and can they be reconfigured to capitalize upon the strengths of network architectures?

CHAPTER 4

THE MANAGER OF THE 21ST CENTURY

*Management knowledge, management skills, and
the management curriculum*

INTRODUCTION

As became clear from the previous chapter, the network economy differs from its predecessors (the industrial and the agricultural era) it fundamental different ways. Consequently, a different economic reality has emerged as well as new organizational logics. Managing in this network economy, therefore, diverges from the characteristics of the managerial job in previous eras. Not only has knowledge moved center stage in the network economy, novel fields of knowledge have also emerged and are developed quickly. Moreover, the art of management has become more complex in this new economic reality, not in the least place by increased market volatility, uncertainty, the scope of corporate activities, and the pace of technological developments. Network economy managers are continuously encountering new challenges, constantly requiring adjusting and adapting the managerial role.

The ever-proliferating set of characteristics and competencies that seem to make the managerial role increasingly illusive is needed to survive in an uncertain future. The managerial job itself resembles the complex structure (and traits) of a network organization on a micro-level. In addition, with a new economic reality and changing views on how business should be organized, management knowledge also changes rapidly. Management knowledge should reflect these transformations and the challenge facing business schools, from this perspective, is to transform management education in such a way that it offers the required skills and knowledge for the network society.

This chapter starts by looking at the new way in which knowledge is produced in the network economy, according to ideas stemming from Gibbons et al. (1994) in which the 'production' and transfer of this knowledge is grounded. In addition, it elaborates on what set of skills, competencies, and what knowledge is relevant for the managerial job in the network economy. Obviously, the managerial role should be geared to the vigorating organizational logics and current developments in organizational behavior, technology, human resources, and other functional fields. But what, exactly, does the managerial job look like in the network economy? Additionally, this chapter will explore the business school curriculum, what it contains, and what functional fields should be represented in the management curriculum.

THE NEW PRODUCTION OF KNOWLEDGE

The newly emerged economic landscape, which has been labeled the network economy in the previous chapter, poses new demands and challenges on business and managerial functions. Managers that are being confronted with these challenges will experience that traditional beliefs, assumptions, and methods of approach will no longer suffice. Knowledge, in particular, becomes the major production factor (or, as some say, the key feature underlying all production factors) in the network economy. However, the nature of knowledge has changed. When focusing on management knowledge in the network economy, this transformationcan be illustrated by looking at the new way in which knowledge is produced.

Gibbons et al. (1994) contend that in this postmodern age one can speak of a new production of knowledge, as opposed to traditional knowledge production and dissemination. Classic knowledge production (Mode 1) takes place independently of context and practical application and refers to knowledge production in the sense of sound scientific practice. In the words of Gibbons et al.:

> *"Mode 1 refers to a form of knowledge production – a complex of ideas, methods, values, norms – that has grown up to control the diffusion of the Newtonian model to more and more fields of inquiry and ensure its compliance with what is considered sound scientific practice. Mode 1 is meant to summarize in a single phrase the cognitive and and social norms which must be followed in the production, legitimation and diffusion of knowledge of this kind. For many, Mode 1 is identical with what is meant by science"* (Gibbons et al., 1994: 2-3).

Hence, knowledge production in the network economy deviates from traditional knowledge production. Compared to the new mode of knowledge production (Mode 2), Mode 1 is based on other premises. Some of the most essential differences are depicted in table 4.1.

Mode 1 Knowledge production	Mode 2 Knowledge production
Problems are set and solved in a context governed by the, largely academic, interests of a specific community	Knowledge is carried out in a context of application
Disciplinary	Transdisciplinary (knowledge resides complexes of heterogeneous networks)
Homogeneity	Heterogeneity
Hierachical, aimed at organizational preservation	More heterarchical and transient

Table 4.1. Mode 1 versus Mode 2.
Source: Gibbons et al. (1994)

The transition of Mode 1 to Mode 2 reflects the transition to a network economy. The new production of knowledge transcends traditional disciplines and epistemologies, and clearly incorporates elements of co-development, negotiation, and balancing 'supply and demand' in this production. The sources of knowledge origination and production become to an increasing extent diverse, just as the demand for differentiated forms of specialist knowledge comes from multiple sources. The localized nature of knowledge production is an essential charactersistic of Mode 2 knowledge production. This organizational dimension is marked by an increase in the number of potential sites where knowledge can be created, the linking of sites together in a variety of ways through functioning networks of communication, and the simultaneous differentiation, at these sites, of fields and areas of study into finer and finer specialities. Next to universities and institutes of higer education, non-university institutes, research centres, government agencies, industrial laboratories, think tanks, and consultancy firms produce knowledge in an interactive process. This interaction is facilitated by the electronic, organizational, social, and informal links that exist in and between networks. The continuous recombination and reconfiguration of specific (sub)fields of expertise forms the bases for new forms of useful knowledge. Over time, knowledge production moves increasingly away from traditional disciplinary activity into new societal contexts (Gibbons et al., 1994).

Within Mode 2, therefore, different contexts are linked together, creating organizational arrangements that are combining the academic venue, the public venue, and the market venue. Examples of such new contexts include the rapid emergence of corporate universities and institutes aimed at start-ups in the sector of advanced technologies (such as BioPartner in the Netherlands, a network and platform for life sciences enterpreneurs) over the last years (see also Chapter 6). As a consequence, working, learning, and researching in Mode 2, bring issues of social accountability, reflexivity, and quality control into play. People from diverse backgrounds cooperate on a temporary (project) basis, working on a specific problem in which they all have a interest. Actors have to consider and appraise each other's needs and inputs and integrate elements of alien contexts into their own contexts. This invokes higher levels of awareness of each other's contexts and requires flexibility in the interpretation, and definition of research problems, while at the same time pointing at to the broader dimensions and implications of (the outcomes of) their research. In addition, quality assessment involves more than mere perr-reviewing individual contributions, placing broader dimensions, like social, economic, and political impact areas, center stage. Hence, Mode 2 knowledge production can be labeled as networking, networked, and network knowledge. Knowledge is differentiated and resides in heterogeneous networks.

From the perspective of management knowledge, a shift towards Mode 2 of knowledge production means a reinforcement of the plea for interdisciplinarity and managing in and between contexts. This indicates the need for skill-building and the ability for a manager to assert him- or herself in complex and a range of different situations (contingency argument). The next sections explore the demands put on and the competencies required for the 21st century manager from the point of view of the network economy, which are fundamentally grounded in the requirements of managing in Mode 2.

ROUNDING OUT THE MANAGER'S JOB FOR THE 21ST CENTURY

The managerial function has undergone considerable changes during the last century. Formerly, a manager was seen as a homo economicus, or a homo rationalis, objectifying and monitoring the individual corporate operations. This epoc was characterized by a rather mechanistic view of management, top-down command structures, and strict hierarchic interpersonal relations. Within this classical view of managers, emphasis was put on the 'controlling' job. Henry Fayol and Frederick Winslow Taylor are seen as two of the most famous representatives of this view, while Luther Gulick and Lydnall Urwick used the acronym POSDCoRB (planning, organizing, staffing, directing, coordinating, reporting and budgeting) to categorize the activities within the managerial job about seventy years ago.

As time has gone by, the business environment has transformed into a different playing field, posing different demands and challenges on the management function. This changed competitive reality urges managers who want their enterprises to be and remain competitive to search globally for opportunities and resources, maximize returns on all the assets dedicated to a business (whether owned by the manager's firm or by other firms), perform only those functions for which the company has, or can develop, expert skill, and outsource those activities that can be performed quicker, more effectively, or at lower cost, by others (Snow, Miles & Coleman, 1992). Within the 21st century playing field, firms are continuously engaged in boundary-busting, adaptation processes, learning processes and creating the required knowledge and skills to achieve a competitive edge in the turbulent environment of the network economy. The fragmenting impact of firms and often paradoxical processes within them, not only makes it difficult to draw a clear line between the firm and its environment, but also causes their employees to view them and their environments as complicated, turbulent, chaotic, antagonistic, complex and ambiguous realities (Baets & Van der Linden, 2000: 41). Due to these fragmentations, as well as the importance and locus of knowledge and skills, the position of the manager can be viewed as being no longer unique. When a firm's most important assets are its knowledge and skills, then the true capabilities and competences of an organization lie in the worker's mind. As Baets & Van der Linden note:

> *"Almost everyone can be considered to be a manager in the tradtional sense, even the secretary/executive assistant, who must possess a sophisticated level of communication as well as professional skills. Strategic leadership, that was typically part of the tradtional management role, for example, is much more widely distributed than ever before"* (Baets & Van der Linden, 2000: 41).

The question then becomes, what knowledge and skills should reside within the managerial role for the new, networked era? To answer this question, the following sections will take a deeper look into the nature of the manager's job, managerial roles, and leadership issues associated with it. First these subjects are elaborated from the perspective of the individual manager – say, the characteristics of the managerial role and the issue of leadership. Secondly, the focus will be on the necessary management knowledge for the 21st century.

TRAITS OF THE 21ST CENTURY MANAGER

Numerous books and articles have been written about the manager and leadership over the past decades. Generally, the hallmarks of leadership are described in two different models: the traits of successful leaders and the behaviors correlating with business success. The former category consists of vision, self-confidence, ambition, intelligence, social skills, while the latter emphasizes that leaders create a vision that others follow; they articulate deeper feelings of their followers and they act in ways that are consistent with the value they represent to others (Frank & Porter, 1997). Empirical studies support the idea of no normative or best style of leadership, and seem to emphasize the contingent character of managerial work and leadership. An effective manager would have to be able to deal with rapid changes, uncertainty and complex and diverse environments both within and outside the firm's boundaries. A vast amount of research on the role and behavior of managers and on defining what leadership actually comprises has been built upon studies by Mintzberg (1973 and 1994), Stewart (1970), and Luthans (1988). In 'The nature of managerial work', Henry Mintzberg concludes that managers have to be 'well-rounded'. Deceivingly simple as this observation may be, it in fact implies that a manager's job is of a very complex nature, commanded by contingency. A manager needs must know at least something about everything, being able to manage in a myriad of situations.

Until recently, however, conventional literature has curiously enough emphasized only single particular traits (Mintzberg, 1994). The *need* for leadership in business renewal, however, is undisputed. Less clear, however, is how to *perform* as a leader. Tom Peters tells us that good managers are doers; Michael Porter suggests they are thinkers; in Abraham Zeleznik's and Warren Bennis's view managers are leaders. Others contend managers are facilitators, coaches, or completers. Recently, an article on contemporary leadership characteristics was published in Fortune magazine, called 'Have you got what it takes?' by Thomas A. Stewart (1999), exploring what qualities should reside within the idealtype manager to succeed in the 21st century's corporate environment. Stewart contends that tomorrow's captain's of industry must be e-commerce adapt and old economy tested; must have powerful analytical skills and superb instincts; must know EPS, TCP-IP, ROE, HTTP, EVA and WAP; must be innovators, visionaries, and change agents; must know the difference between an thin client and a lean supply chain; must be able to say 'no' in a way that doesn't demoralize; must be able to inspire people to exceed their own expectations; must be coaches and team players; must have spent several years working on another continent; must be able to work harder and longer than most people, while keeping their personal lives in balance; must be young at heart, but mature in judgment; and – as he puts it with a wink – must have good teeth and look great in a suit (and in casual on Friday's). This enumeration seems to reflect Mintzberg's idea of 'well-roundedness' in particular.

A recently published study by Andersen Consulting 'The evolving role of executive leadership', aimed at creating a profile of the global leader of the future. The firm interviewed current CEOs and younger people who were labeled as candidates for leadership positions in the future. According to this report, the dreamboat leader is defined as a person who thinks globally, anticipates opportunity, creates a shared vision, develops and empowers people, appreciates cultural diversity, builds teamwork and partnership, embraces change, shows technological savvy, encourages constructive challenge, ensures customer satisfaction, achieves a competitive advantage, demonstrates personal mastery, shares leadership, and lives the values. The result of this study showed that every of these fourteen traits is getting much more important in the respondents' views. These inflated expectations can be explained by the facts that society is increasing its expectations of leaders, business exists by virtue of progress, and the inherent uncertainty of the future. Consequently, Andersen's researchers asked the respondents to additionally rate not less than eighty-two subcharacteristics of leadership. Vision, values and priority setting ranked one, two and three respectively, followed by having a customer perspective, team building, and listening. The image is one of a leader as a partner, a dealmaker, a social director, and a broker. Surprisingly, getting results isn't a top ten issue. Getting the process right, meaning making sure the right people are talking to one another about the right things and have the right tools to do what they decide that needs to be done, is what's important (Stewart, 1999).

Put differently, the leader of the past in this view is a doer, the leader of the present is a planner and the leader of the future is a teacher. Tomorrow's leader, in a sense, resembles tomorrow's business models: it is all about networks and organizing through network logics. Tomorrow's leaders need not know everything about everything, but will be surrounded by people who know a lot more, but trust this leader to balance and judge competing claims.

COMPETENCIES AND SKILLS

According to Baets & Van der Linden (2000: 45) what is becoming prevalent in management is "the need for multi-faceted knowledge, intelligence and competencies to create progress – i.e., having a flexible strategic vision and constantly renewing, preserving the organization's core (…)." Visionary leaders are 'clock-builders', as opposed 'to time-tellers' (Collins & Porras, 1994), creating concepts, facilities, and processes that will carry the organization into new eras and enable organizations to sustain competitiveness over time, while preserving the company's core ideology.

From a competencies-centered view, Baets & Van der Linden (2000) note that discussing competencies enables one to avoid the muddle of traits and motives that are attributed to a manager's role. Unlike 'characteristics', which refer to the whole person, 'competencies' refer to performance: it's role-, context- and person-related. The essence of managerial competencies is in the managerial mindset, which reflects an epistemology, which, in turn, defines knowledge and methods (and their limitations). Managerial competencies support and describe, for example, the behavioral skills needed to communicate, to work in a team, and to understand the dynamics of the context of the work of managers.

Competencies refer to know-how, procedural knowledge, and skills, emphasizing learning as the main source of intelligence to deal with a myriad of situations. A division can be made between generic, organic and changing competencies. Generic (or transferable) competencies can be applied to managers in a range of organizations and roles. Generic competencies refer to more abstract competencies, reflecting the process of thought/inquiry and critical distance and are fundamental to the managerial mindset. Examples of these competencies include critical distance and critical reflection, understanding paradoxes and the ability to listen. Organic competencies are role-specific, or, in a more traditional sense, job-related. In a broader sense they are derived from a firm's strategy, its core competencies, skills, culture, values and mission. Organic competencies refer to processes underlying managerial work and organizational contexts. Examples of such competencies include technical leadership, problem solving and project management. Changing competencies refer to the evolution of changing skills by recombining resources and technologies. These competencies are time-related and connect speed to strategic purposes, information, critical issues, and knowledge management. A distinction can be made between emerging competencies (increasing relevance and importance for the next few years), maturing competencies (gradually decreasing relevance), and transitional competencies (possible decreasing relevance, while remaining present emphasis). The challenge facing business and managers, clearly, is to embed these competencies in both the organization and learning processes.

Though these competencies are present in most managerial jobs in today's industries and business environments, they do not seem to comprise all currently necessary competencies. Especially from the perspective of a network environment and network organization the managerial job demands some specific qualities and competencies reflecting this logic.

Network competencies

Managing within network structures requires some specific competencies. Together with a changed competitive landscape, different organizational principles require adjustments in managerial behavior. Based on interviews with different corporate executives and executive recruiters, Allred, Miles & Snow (1996) conclude from this perspective that future managerial careers will be particularly based on:

- A knowledge-based technical specialty (including computer literacy and turning information into sound advice and practical utility that will provide the competitive edge);
- Cross-functional and international experience;
- Competence on collaborative leadership;
- Self-management skills (managerial careers have become of a do-it-yourself nature);
- Personal traits of flexibility, integrity, and trustworthiness.

These characteristics reflect evolving organizational structures and forms, in particular structures and forms regarding network organization. As organizational structures have evolved, so have the major competencies required by the management function. With smaller structures and flatter hierarchies, today's organizations put different demands upon their executives, guiding them through different careers,but they also provide them with a range of new opportunities. Table 4.2 links different organizational structures to these key competencies. It becomes clear that not only have the required competencies changed, also a more complex, holistic package of managerial demands seems to be today's imperative.

Organizational structure	Key competencies	Career path	Responsibility for career planning
Functional	Technical	Single firm, within function	Functional department
Divisional	Technical, commercial	Single firm, across divisions	Division, firm
Matrix	Technical, commercial	Single firm, across projects	Department, project, firm
Network	Technical, commercial, collaborative, and self-governance	Within and across firms (even an independent professional)	Firm and individual

Table 4.2. Organizations, required competencies, and career path.
Source: based on Allred, Miles & Snow (1996)

As has been illustrated in Chapter 3, network organization requires managing relationships through the entire value chain: collaboration has become the fuel for the firm's engine. Collaboration involves three major types of skills, namely referral skills, partnering skills, and skills related to relationship management (Allred, Miles & Snow, 1996: 21). Referral skills relate to the core competence principle, meaning that problems and opportunities are directed to those nodes in the network that are able to cope best with them and can exploit them to the fullest. Partnering skills are based on the capacity to conceptualize, negotiate, and implement outcomes thath are advantageous to cooperating parties within the network structure. Managers within the network must know-how to quickly, efficiently, and effectively combine other businesses' resources to their own resources in order for all parties to benefit from this collaboration. Relationship management is based on the premise of championing the needs and wants of a firm's cutomers and partners. After all, the glue that binds the nodes in the network together is formed by knowledge and maintaining relationships.

Developing network competencies, therefore, means being able to learn continuously, being able to adapt, and being flexible in the first place. In the network, traditional organizational barriers have disintegrated and managers are being confronted with (behavior, decisions, and interests of) other nodes in the network constantly. It should be noted that the organization's employees, being knowledge workers, have become more independent, responsible, and more powerful network nodes to, whom the manager must reckon with in his daily work. Flatter and less hierarchical organizational structures, democratic organizational processes, power dislocation, power localization and increased organizational interdependency account for the inadequacy and even the demise of traditional competencies. Consequently, there's a pressure on the development of new and specific network competencies by managers, which consist of collaborative skills, negotiating skills, mediating skills, political skills, enterpreneurial skills, social and interpersonal skills and the abilities to combine (developing or facilitating the development of 'neue Kombinationen') and to unleash creativity (invoking lateral thinking). In other words, the network competencies relate to what is necessary to manage (the non-existing) relationships within and between the nodes of the network and the (re)combination of resources, especially knowledge, present in the different nodes of the network.

ROLE CONTINGENCY AND NETWORK ROLES

It has proven to be evident that the managerial job is contextually contingent varying with the needs of a specific job, the approach of the individual person, the type of organization that has to be managed, and the context in which these processes take place. Different managers end up emphasizing different elements in different ways. Mintzberg's concept of managerial work considers the impact on managerial work in three ways, namely the kind of managerial roles that are *favored*, how these roles are *performed*, and the *relationships* that exist between these roles. Managers in different contexts need to emphasize different role, which vary from controlling to facilitating. Regardless of contexts, however, individual managers are often personally predisposed to favor particular roles or aspects of the job. One can distinguish, for example, between a conceptual style of management (focusing on the development of a managerial framework), an administrative style (focusing and controlling), an interpersonal style of management (focusing on leading on the inside or linking on the outside), and an action style (focusing on tangible doing) (Mintzberg, 1994).

Mintzberg made a division into ten different roles concerning managerial work, organized into three categories: interpersonal roles, informational roles and decisional roles. Among the interpersonal roles were figurehead, leader and liaison, whereas informational roles included monitor, disseminator and spokesman. Entrepreneur, disturbance handler, resource allocator and negotiator comprised the decisional roles of the manager (Mintzberg, 1973: 51-94). These roles aren't seen as separate entities into which the activities of the manager can be neatly categorized, but as an integrated construct (Mintzberg, 1989: 21-22). However, the number of managers probably reflects the number of managerial styles. Mintzberg identified eight managerial job types emphasizing different roles. These job types included: the contact man, the political manager, the entrepreneur, the insider, the real-time manager, the team manager, the expert manager, and the new manager (Mintzberg, 1973: 126-129). In all cases, interpersonal, informational and decisional roles remain inseparable (Mintzberg, 1989: 22).

Obviously, there's a infinity of possible contexts within which management can be practiced, as well as the number of 'styles' that can occur. In a recent Dutch study (Van de Velde et al., 1999), managerial activities among top and middle managers were researched. In this study, a questionnaire was designed, including the following thirteen managerial activities, which can be seen as a typical utterance of the variety of the manager's job. These activities are represented in table 4.3.

According to this study, top managers consider traditional management and networking activities more important and devote more time to these activities than middle managers do. Additionally, top managers exhibit some more networking and human resource management than middle managers.

This complex of activities and role contingency are all the more present in the contemporary managerial job, since the new economic landscape requires this 'well-roundedness' of the managing individual. The question now is: when integrating all these activities into the manager's role, what managerial roles can be distinguished for managing in the network economy, taking into account the typical organizational structure and accompanying competencies?

Managerial activities	Tasks
Developing ideas	Taking responsibility for developing new ideas, drawing lines, thinking about and employing new directions and initiatives
Motivating people	Showing approval, providing positive feedback, giving credit, listening to suggestions, asking for participation, offering (formal) rewards, offering challenges, delegating responsibilities
Planning/ co-ordinating	Setting goals, defining tasks in order to reach these goals, dividing people over tasks, giving routine instructions, organizing work, coordinating activities, managing projects
Decision-making/ problem solving	Defining problems, dealing with daily crises, developing new procedures, deciding what action needs to be taken, executing cost-benefit analyses, weighing alternatives, deciding which problems need to be handled, developing visions
Training/ developing	Guiding people, showing them the way, participating in training, clarifying roles, coaching, helping people formulate development plans
Exchanging information	Receiving and giving information, answering procedural questions, spreading outcomes of meetings, giving or receiving telephonic routine information, attending informal staff meetings
Paper work	Handling post, reading and writing reports, doing office work, preparing financial data
Managing conflict	Finding solutions for conflicts between people, or between oneself and others, calling a third party to solve conflicts
Interacting with outsiders	Dealing with suppliers and salesmen, attending external meetings, being actively involved in societal events, employing Public Relations activities
Monitoring/ controlling performances	Inspecting work, walking around to control work, providing feedback on one's own and others' output, carrying out preventive control
Socializing	Chatting about non-work-related topics, informal joking, gossiping, complaining, putting others in their place, lobbying, informal networking
Disciplining/ criticizing	Correcting, calling people to order, applying the rules, giving negative feedback
Staffing	Making job descriptions and profiles, selecting application letters, interviewing, completing procedures

Table 4.3. Typical managerial activities.
Source: Van de Velde et al. (1999)

The network broker

The primary managerial role in a network organization is the broker's role. Network managers operate throughout the network, across hierarchies, combining resources that can be found among network nodes. The brokering function, therefore, lies in the assemblance and the (re)combining of different resources, creating products and services in a way that utilizes the advantages of network production. Snow, Miles & Coleman (1992) distinguish three types of broker roles they deem particularly important to the success of network organizations: the architect, the lead operator, and the caretaker.

The network manager who manages according to the role of the architect facilitates the emergence of specific operating networks rather than having a clear and complete vision of the whole network and the place in the 'whole' that is taken by the emerged network. The architect usually has in mind only a vague concept of the product and of the value chain required to offer it. Consequently, the broker seeks out firms with desirable expertise, takes an equity position in a firm to coax it into the value chain, and helps creating new groups that are needed in specialized support roles (Snow, Miles & Coleman, 1992). Hence, the manager as architect functions as a designer. It depends on the stability and the openness of the network how complex the execution of the architectural role is (see also Chapter 3). In dynamic networks, for instance, the role is of a more complex nature than in internal networks, since the network manager has to identify, select, and manage relationships with suitable business partners.

The second broker role is the role of the lead operator. The lead operator, in effect, builds on the work of the architect, meaning connecting specific firms together in an operating network. A famous example of this kind of network management is displayed by Nike, being only an R&D and marketing firm, brokering the remaining parts of the value chain.

The caretaker sees to it that the network organization continuously develops and operates smoothly. This role implies maintaining and monitoring relationships that exist within and between networks, providing information about the current state of the network to network members, and providing information about individual nodes in order to facilitate the mutual tuning of actions within supply chains in the network. In fact, the caretaker enables the network to learn in order to remain competitive and developing. This managerial role includes having the ability to observe (f)actors of success and failure, or those nodes within the network that function or dysfuntion, and value these from the perspective of their contribution to the network as a whole. Consequently, the caretaker's role is to track down and broach dysfunctional elements within the network and, if necessary, induce disciplinary behavior or corrective action. This disciplinary behavior or corrective action may consist of teaching the network node how to behave and operate in a way that favors the well-being of 'the common good', or even expel the dysfunctioning organization from participating in the network. In essence, the caretaker helps the network to learn.

It should be noted that these network management roles do not exclude each other, but can overlap considerably. In addition, it can be said that, in theory, these roles preceed each other, depending on the development, or life cycle, of the network. Hence, all three roles may be of equal importance to the ultimate success of the network.

LEVELS OF NETWORK MANAGEMENT AND NETWORK MANAGEMENT CAPABILITIES

From the perspective of network management, four different levels can be discerned, based on the managerial complexity of business networks that allows for a number of analytical perspectives (Möller & Halinen, 1992: 416). Each level of network management has its own specific management issues, and therefore requires particular management knowledge, skills, and capabilities.

The first level of network management deals with industries as networks. Network management, then, focuses on different industrial and social networks, in which a range of actors, resources, and activities is present. The industry as a network can be seen as an aggregated system of organizations, whose behavior and acts are highly interrelated with the behavior of the network. This level of network management requires the ability to develop valid and relevant views of networks and the possible future directions of their development (network visioning), and, therefore is closely realted to the issue of organizational learning. Without such a strategic ability, organizations and managers are not able to get a grip on the evolution of the network organization and will not be able to identify business opportunities. Since these networks are by nature highly non-transparent, it is crucial to effectively organize and manage information gathering and knowledge generation.

The second level of network management relates to the management of focal nets and network positions (the firm in a network) and focuses on the relationship between the individual firm and its environment (net management). The focal net consists of those actors that the management deems relevant, or those actors that are located within the firm's network horizon. The focal net mediates the effect of 'macro' forces, such as technological change and economic fluctuations, on individual actors within the network, as well as it translates the behavior of individual to the greater network environment (ibid.). Here, identifying, mobilizing, and coordinating relevant actors, resources, and activities are the critical capabilities within network management. Managing focal nets with different functions (e.g., R&D nets, supplier nets) means managing the firm's network positions, hence being a true tactical matter. Regarding environmental 'macro' forces, the mediating function of focal nets provides the firm with the opportunity to manage and anticipate the effects these 'macro' forces have on the firm itself.

Level three perceives network management as the management of exchange relationships, or relationship portfolios (as contrasted to individual relationships). This type of network management focuses on the interface between the internal management of resources, capabilities, and activities, and the external exchange relationships. Since the exchange relationships include multiple different actors, it is necessary from a managerial point of view to develop relationship capabilities. The relationship portfolio management capability aims for optimizing the firm's resources. It especially relates to managing supplier and customer portfolios, including "analytical aspects, such as competencies in creating and using databases and conducting supplier and customer evaluation, and organizational aspects, such as capabilities to develop organizational solutions for handling exchange relationships" (ibid., p. 418). It should be noted, that different kinds of portfolios require different management approaches. From a strategic point of view, some portfolios and potential business partners, owning special or essential resources and being able to provide access to certain actors and markets, should be given special attention.

Finally, the fourth level of network management concerns the 'micro' level of analysis, which deals with dyadic exchange relationships (i.e., between the firm and another actor in the network). Relationship management capabilities concern coping with individual relationships and largely resembles portfolio management capabilities. One eminent issue from the perspective of this capability is being able to establish the value of important relationships. This, in fact, forms a prerequisite for managing exchange portfolios efficiently.

An overview of the key managerial issues and challenges from the perspective of different levels of network management is given in table 4.4.

MANAGEMENT KNOWLEDGE FOR THE 21ST CENTURY AND THE BUSINESS SCHOOL CURRICULUM

Management as a field of knowledge cannot be seen of as a single and stable concept of looking at or coping with things, nor can it be characterized by a single available paradigm. In management thinking, there are multiple simultaneously competing paradigms, which are used today in many MBA and executive management programmes as the content of a learning method of 'switching frames': re-framing encourages the ability to see things, situations or people in other ways; to put them in different perspectives (Clarke & Clegg, 1998: 10). If one wishes to speak in terms of paradigms of management knowledge, it should be emphasized that such paradigms can be best characterized as paradigms of contingency and structural epistemological renewal (or senescence). Innovations in management knowledge occur at a structural basis, and they are often induced by one or a few highly influential management theorists or gurus like Henry Fayol, Frederick Winslow Taylor, Peter Drucker, Arthur D. Little, Herbert Simon & James March, Henry Mintzberg, Chris Argyris, Edward De Bono, C.K. Prahalad, Gary Hamel & Yves Doz, John Kotter, and Geert Hofstede. Table 4.5 lists the top-25 of the most influential management books of the 20th century, indicating those people and those subjects that have had a prominent place in the development of management knowledge over the past 100 years.

Level of network management	Key issues	Key challenges
Level 1. *Industries as networks (network visioning)*	Networks as configurations of actors carrying out value activities, form the 'environment' the firms are embedded in. They are not transparent but must be learned through enactment. Understanding networks, their structures, processes, and evolution is crucial for network management.	How to develop valid views of relevant networks and the opportunities they contain? How to develop valid views of network evolution for identifying strategic development opportunities? How to analyze strategic groups of firms, forming focal nets, for understanding the network competition?
Level 2. *Firms in a network (net management)*	Firms' strategic behavior in networks can be analyzed through the focal nets they belong to and through the positions and roles they play in these nets. Positions are created through business relationships. Capability to identify, evaluate, construct, and maintain positions and relationships is essential in a network environment.	How to develop and manage strategic nets (supplier nets, development nets, customer nets)? How to enter new networks (market area entry, new product/service field)? How to manage network positions?
Level 3. *Relationship portfolios (portfolio management)*	Firm is a nexus of resources and activities. Which of these activities are carried out internally and which through different types of exchange relationships is a core strategic issue. A capability to manage a portfolio of exchange relationships in an integrated manner is required.	How to develop an optimal customer/supplier portfolio? How to mange customer/supplier portfolios – from organizational and analytical perspectives?
Level 4. *Exchange relationships (relationship management)*	Individual customer/supplier relationships form the basic unit of analysis in a network approach to business marketing. Capability of creating, managing and concluding important relationships is a core resource for a firm.	How to evaluate future value – customer lifetime value of a relationship? How to create, manage and conclude relationships efficiently - from organizational and analytical perspectives? How to manage relational episodes efficiently?

Table 4.4. Key managerial issues and key challenges from the perspective of different levels of network management.
Source: Möller & Halinen (1999: 417)

The continuous development of the corporation in order to remain competitive has been one of the most prominent topics in management. Though many management theorists have tried to demystify the issue of organizational renewal with putting different nametags to (sometimes highly comparable) ideas, organizational renewal can perhaps best be described by the concept of networking and flexibility. Other theorists, on the other side, have focused on managerial and organizational implications within different paradigms. Some of them are merely concerned with business process redesign, some with developing core competences, some with network organizations, some with learning organizations, while some even point to the fact of seeing the corporation as a living or organic being, and even ascribing it a soul.

Rank	Title	Year	Author(s)
1.	The principles of scientific Management	1911	Frederick W. Taylor
2.	The functions of the executive	1938	Chester I. Barnard
3.	The practice of Management	1954	Peter F. Drucker
4.	The human side of the enterprise	1960	Douglas M. McGregor
5.	Administrative behavior	1947	Herbert A. Simon
6.	Organization and environment	1967	Paul R. Lawrence & Jay W. Lorsch
7.	Organizations	1958	James G. March & Herbert A. Simon
8.	Motivation and personality	1954	Abraham H. Maslow
9.	Competitive strategy	1980	Michael E. Porter
10.	Management and the worker	1939	Fritz J. Roethlisberger & William Dickinson
11.	Strategy and structure	1962	Alfred D. Chandler
12.	A behavioral theory of the firm	1963	Richard M. Cyert & James G. March
13.	The theory of social and economic organization	1922	Max Weber
14.	The social psychology of organizations	1966	Daniel Katz & Robert L. Kahn
15.	Personality and organization	1957	Chris Argyris
16.	General and industrial management	1916	Henri Fayol
17.	New patterns of management	1961	Rensis Likert
18.	Industrial organization: theory and practice	1965	Joan Woodward
19.	The human problems of industrial civilization	1933	Elton Mayo
20.	The management of innovation	1961	Tom Burns & George M. Stalker
21.	Quality, productivity and competitive position	1982	W. Edwards Deming
22.	Organizations in action	1967	James D. Thompson
23.	The human group	1950	George C. Homans
24.	The achieving society	1961	David C. McClelland
25.	The motivation to work	1959	Frederick Herzberg, Bernard Mausner & Barbara B. Snyderman

Table 4.5. Top-25 of influential management books of the 20th century. Source: Bedeian & Wren (2001)

Transforming management knowledge: changing paradigms

Thomas Clarke and Stewart Clegg place coping with changing paradigms as one of seven relevant topics in the transformation of management knowledge for the 21st century. The change from classical or neo-classical management orthodoxy to multiple changing management paradigms is the first paradigm shift. Paradigm shifts, they argue, are strategic responses to changing environments, and therefore, one of the key drivers of current paradigm shifts. Next to paradigm shifts, information technology, innovation and learning, a wider conception of stakeholders and the need for new business paradigms based on sustainability, are the key drivers of the current paradigm shift. "At the heart of the paradigms of the 21st century, business will be virtual, intelligent organization networks, competing in a global open economy, in ecologically sustainable ways, appreciative of the many stakeholders with an interest in the company's performance" (Clarke & Clegg, 1998: 57).

Secondly, the conception of business activity as essentially based on local and national markets, with a degree of performance reinforced by local standards and distinctive technologies which will change slowly, is displaced by the paradigm shifts of globalization and glocalization. As Clarke & Clegg contend, it's about separation versus integration, protection versus deregulation, immobility versus mobility, technological leads versus technological diffusion, local standards versus world standards, time lags versus simultaneity and unitarism versus pluralism. Opportunities for business in an age of globalization bring new responsibilities; respect for international social and environmental regulations and for the integrity of different cultures, now becomes a corporate prerequisite for being a true global citizen.

Thirdly, as has been illustrated in Chapter 2, the phenomenon of digitalization represents a series of profound paradigm shifts for business. The rising importance of knowledge and intellectual capital as corporate resources profoundly changes ways in how value is created: knowledge, learning and education are the key sources for competitive advantage. Another outcome of digitalization and the organizational implications of information and communications technologies is the continual acceleration in the rate of obsolescence of organizations' and individuals' knowledge base and skills. To effectively counter this, continual upgrading of skills and life long learning will be needed.

Both globalization and digitalization have been identified as the key drivers of the network economy. Clarke & Clegg also point at the paradigm shifts concerning strategy and organization. Since these subjects have already come to the fore in Chapters 2 and 3, there will not be paid anymore attention to these subjects in this chapter. There are, however, two additional changes severely influencing management thinking, that deserve our attention when focusing on management knowledge for the future. These changes concern the subject of stakeholders and sustainability (or, in a broader view, corporate social responsibility).

In considering the paradigm shift triggered by the subject of stakeholders, the most obvious observation is the transformation from orthodox management beliefs of increasing shareholder value to the modern approach of managing other corporate stakeholders' interests. At the bedrock of the concept of shareholder value, there's the division within companies between ownership and control. This separation, in fact, created the job of 'the manager', who had to represent the interest of those owning the company.

In the theory of classical economists concerned with property rights, agency problems resulting from this separation could only be resolved by the application of objective and demanding financial performance indicators to ensure that managers served the interest of the ultimate owners and not their own (ibid., p. 295). As corporations grew, it has become increasingly untenable to only bear accountability to shareholders. Up until today, the debate of shareholders versus stakeholders is still present in economic and, to an increasing extent, business literature. An important characteristic in this debate is the shift from financial performance indicators (dominated by a shareholder perspective) to a non-financial perspective (dominated by a stakeholder perspective), which is depicted in table 4.6.

From a shareholder perspective	to	a stakeholder perspective
Agency/stewardship theory		Stakeholder theory
Short term		Long term
Shareholder value		Stakeholder values
Tangible assets		Intangible assets
Anglo-Saxon		European/Asian
Property		Knowledge
Transactions		Relationships
Exclusive (Corporate image)		Inclusive (Corporate citizenship)

Table 4.6. From a stakeholder perspective to a shareholder perspective.
Source: Clarke & Clegg (1998: 296)

Both theoretical and practical management implications of this stakeholder approach to organizations have resulted in a 'quest for a business and society paradigm', which has covered corporate social performance as well as stakeholder models, in an as yet unresolved effort to produce an analysis with descriptive accuracy, instrumental power, and normative validity (ibid., p. 351). "Managers may not make explicit reference to stakeholder theory, but the vast majority of them apparently adhere in practice to one of the central tenets of the stakeholder theory, namely, that their role is to satisfy a wider set of relationships, not simply the shareowners" (ibid., p. 107). However, most businesses remain to see stakeholdermanagement to a large extent as a public relations issue, instead of seeing it as a crucial commercial imperative or a modern prerequisite for competitive advantage:

"The importance of developing good stakeholder relationships for successful enterprise (...) is becoming increasingly apparent. This involves not simply acknowledging the significance of these relationships, but making consistent efforts to measure and manage stakeholder relations, in order to achieve continuous improvement in all company operations and, ultimately, increased stakeholder values. In this context many companies are likely to investigate how stakeholder strategies may usefully be applied in business, and how stakeholding is interpreted in other companies and countries. It is harder for companies driven by narrow self-interest to survive public scrutiny; it is still possible for them to make money, but this form of enterprise is invariably short term. Companies that are durable invariably possess a wider and deeper sense of their responsibilities" (Clarke & Clegg, 1998: 367-368).

It is the concept of durability that evokes the last paradigm shift in management knowledge, which is the shift towards sustainability. Though the concept of sustainability can be semantically interpreted as the equivalent of durability (and, therefore, in certain approaches as stakeholdermanagement or even corporate social and environmental responsibility), Anglo-Saxon approaches seem to indicate that balancing the earth's natural resources and preserving essential environmental life support systems is the primary focus. Sustainability, thus, refers to the replacement of the external search for domination over nature by the pursuit of harmony with nature. From a stakeholder perspective this pursuit can be well legitimized by the presence and influence of environment-focused non-governmental organizations, like, Greenpeace.

Functional fields and subtopics

As managers may cynically think, sustainability does not necessary imply the abandonment of industry and consumption, but it – and with it stakeholdermanagement and corporate social responsibility – requires new managerial approaches, a different managerial mindset, an orientation on intangibles, norms and values, ethics, rethinking of strategies, and on non-financial performance indicators. Management knowledge for the 21st century asks for extremely well rounded, inclusive managers who are able to make fundamental new ways of conducting business an integrated part of their business strategy.

That the practice of management and management learning are, by nature, eclectic and multidisciplinary was illustrated (again) by a recent research project, conducted by Contractor (2000). This research was aimed at the internationalization of the business school curriculum by identifying international curricular subtopics, tools, and concepts that faculty respondents deemed crucial to business pedagogy and to the practice of management. As will be illustrated by Chapter 6, calls to internationalize the business school curriculum have come increasingly to the fore. Within the survey held, respondents were initially given 25 international subtopics or concepts (derived from departmental labels) and were then urged to write in their own additional required subtopics that, in their view, were essential to managers. Ultimately, the list presented to the respondents contained 63 international topics, covering a broad range of topics including 'globalization', 'basics of international taxation', 'cultural differences and the practice of management', 'applied economics and related areas', 'technology transfer', and 'social responsiveness and managing the external relations function in a multinational context'. These 63 topics were categorized into (primary and secondary) functional areas, like strategy, organizational behavior, and human resources. The main results of this research are shown in table 4.7, indicating the most frequently selected subtopics and functional areas by top rank. It is clear that topics related to the 'traditional' fields of management and marketing are mentioned most frequently, while a number of topics is included which can be ascribed to 'non-traditional' business school areas. In particular, among the written-in items, some of the topics deemed most important were international law and legal issues, internet resources for global managers, and trade agreements.

A couple of conclusions can be drawn from the results of this research. First of all, the list is very broad-based, including fields like political science, language studies, and geography, indicating a broadening scope of the demands that the managerial job is subjected to. Secondly, the internationalization of management education curricula signifies thinking and developing business school curricula beyond traditional boundaries and cross-functionally. Thirdly, the bulk of the burden of the internationalization of the curriculum will continue to rest on the departments of management and marketing (ibid.).

THE MANAGEMENT CURRICULUM

Business schools have been criticized several times during their development over the past century. They have been labeled as being too theoretical and scientific, therefore not educating students according to the needs of the labor market, as well as being to much labor market driven and not paying enough attention to developing an academic attitude. Already in 1988, in their infamous report 'Management education and development: drift or thrust into the 21st century?', Porter & McKibbin (1988) noted a number of particular curriculum issues deserving discussion, as they put it, among which were international scope, entrepreneurism, and ethics. Within 21st century business school curricula, attention for these issues has indeed risen. In the MACIS project (Management Curriculum for the Information Society, 1999) major flaws of MBA programs have been identified. These flaws include:

–   Very little integration across courses, especially among those offered by different departments, hence resulting in an MBA programme that looks more like 'islands' of functional knowledge with few 'bridges' linking them. This lack of integration is also contrary to corporate recruiters' concerns, aiming to a holistic view of the business;

–   Programmes are more teaching-oriented opposed to learning-oriented, due to the prevailing use of the lecture-based method as opposed to the use of discussion pedagogy (debate, argumentation, tutoring);

- The 'soft' managerial skills are not stressed enough;
- There is limited communication and coordination across the functional departments (or areas of expertise) of the business school, a situation that leads to redundancies in the subject matter covered and/or the pedagogical material used, and to the limited integration mentioned above;
- The pedagogical material used (theories, examples, cases, exercises) often has very little relevance with the business environment of today, with the current management practices and/or with future management trends;
- The delivery mode is rigid and does not exploit the advances of ICT, due to the face-to-face, sit-in class sessions which typically offer no educational flexibility in terms of material used and communication facilities.

Subtopic	Rank	Field
Cultural differences and the practice of management	1.	Management (Strategy, Organizational behavior, Human resources)
The continuing role of governments	2.	Marketing
International aspects of business ethics	3.	Finance
(tied rank) Differences in international markets and distribution; International aspects of strategic alliances; Basic mechanics, opportunities, and challenges of exporting and importing	4.	Economics
HRM in the global economy	5.	Accounting
(tied rank) Globalization: What exactly does it mean in practice?; Social responsiveness and managing the external relations function in a multinational context; Evolution of the firm and foreign direct investment (FDI); International expansion options	6.	MIS/statistics
Basic foreign exchange hedging techniques	7.	Other (Social issues, Political science, Legal issues, Production management, Geography, Language studies)
Information technology in the multinational firm	8.	
(tied rank) Alternative organization designs for the multinational firm; Forwards, futures, and options in foreign exchange; Basics of international taxation	9.	
Pricing and price discrimination in international markets	10.	

Table 4.7. Subtopics and functional fields by top rank.
Source: Contractor (2000: 68)

In addition, the Porter & McKibbin Report (1988) provided research evidence showing that there are considerable discrepancies between what business school curricula offer and the need to change as perceived by business school personnel as opposed to expectations and demands by the corporate sector. The latter would like to see more realistic, practical, and hands-on education with a greater emphasis on the development of leadership and interpersonal skills. This was illustrated by a relatively high percentage of corporate managers believing they were not receiving the proper amount of formal (systematic) management development. Both parties, however, agreed that business schools and their faculties have not been interacting to a sufficient extent with the corporate community, though within business schools little perceived need was displayed to change the ways in which management education was carried out. The report also stated that complacency and self-satisfaction appeared to be the dominant attitudes in many business schools and that major strategic initiatives weren't the focus for concern (Stevens, 2000).

In the development of a management curriculum, educators have to reckon with issues of pedagogy and technology regarding knowledge transfer, but also with skill and competency development and ensuring that courses are based on relevant management knowledge. Views on teaching, learning and the use of ICT both in general and regarding management education have undergone serious changes, which have lead to different approaches to education and learning (see in particular Chapter 5). In addition, the content of management learning, i.e., management knowledge, is subject to numerous paradigm shifts. When society, the nature of competition, and approaches towards business organization change dramatically, management knowledge is altered, not to say reinvented. Characterized by a relatively ill-structured epistemology, the domain of management, therefore, continuously knows different competing beliefs and paradigms.

In the previous chapters the focus has been on the new and network economy and the impact it will have on business strategies, business models and, therefore, management thinking and managerial behavior. Changes in the business environment and its consequences have to be reflected in the ways companies think and managers think. From this point of view, management thinking has developed over the years, of course, necessarily incorporating contemporary challenges society – and business in particular – encounters. Some of the basic and structural challenges included increased technological opportunities and developments and profound socio-economic transformations, resulting from the process of globalization and developments in ICT. The development of the management curriculum has to reflect changes in the business environment and should keep up with the pace of developments within the managerial function, which is the outgrowth of the nature and the dynamics of the general business environment. Business schools have to ensure that future managers have a fundamental and thorough understanding of what the concept of 'management' actually comprises, the contingent and changing nature of the managerial function, and (competing) contemporary managerial paradigms. This means that the curriculum has to stress the relation between the managerial job, corporate behavior, the competitive reality, and macroeconomic trends. The stakeholder paradigm implicitly incorporates these issues, and, hence, forms a good starting point for the composition of the business school curriculum. Furthermore, it is clear that looking at the functional fields and their subtopics concerning management education, experts deem the more traditional managerial areas still important for the business school's curriculum. They add, however, that some specific issues reflecting issues in today's corporate environments, like managing e-businesses, knowledge management, legal issues, corporate social and environmental responsibility, and issues relating to the field of political economy, should also be part of the curriculum of the 21st century business school. Next to these fields of management knowledge, curricula should also pay considerable attention to competence-building, skill-development, and higher order learning.

FINAL THOUGHTS

The development of management knowledge in the network economy is firmly grounded in Mode 2 production of knowledge. Regarding the prominence of network organization it has been noted that a need for the development of specific skills, competencies, and management capabilities has risen, enabling managers to cope with the current competitive reality. Among these were effectively coping with technology, knowledge, information, cross-cultural and cross-functional skills, self-management, collaborative skills, the ability to be flexible and to adapt, relational skills, coping with complexity, creativity, entrepreneurial spirit (finding 'neue Kombinationen), political and negotiating skills, and being able to learn. These issues all related to the broker role, the particular managerial role for the network economy. The network manager, then, can be seen as a mix of a *homo lateralis* (the lateral man), a *homo transversus* (the problem-solving man), a *homo communicans* (the cooperating man), a *homo combinans* (the (re)combining man), and a *homo politicus* (the political man).

The field of management integrates knowledge from a range of disciplines into its 'body of knowledge', which may be one of the reasons that the development of management knowledge is characterized by more or less continuous paradigm shifts. Its eclecticism inevitably engenders the assimilation of paradigm shifts taking place in other domains. The topics that are deemed most important to be present in the management curriculum, however, still reflect some of the traditional managerial fields of knowledge like marketing, accounting, finance, and production. In addition, and mirroring the development of management knowledge, there is a perceived need to integrate managerial topics related to (internet) technology, geo-politics, and political economy.

The management curriculum itself has been a focus for corporate criticism over the years, being accused of being developed on the basis of a view that has been characterized as being too internally oriented. Business schools, many corporate executives will contend, should have a keen eye for what happens outside its walls and try to bridge the discrepancies of what they offer and what the corporate sector really needs. Existing perceived curricular deficiencies have to be overcome, which, perhaps, can be realized best by developing close intellectual partnerships with the business sector. The main challenge business schools are being posed with considering the business school curriculum entails developing curricula and educating managers in order to prepare managers for the network economy, especially relating to the development of the proper competencies and skills. Given the nature of the aforementioned impediments and issues, this promises to be everything but a sinecure for business schools whatsoever.

CHAPTER 5

THE NEW LEARNING

INTRODUCTION

Since knowledge is the key to competitive advantage in the new economic landscape, education and learning become of paramount importance in the network economy. Though education has been a relatively stable institution regarding its presence and its delivery, the rise of the network economy is responsible for creating new dynamics in this field, among which a true paradigm shift.

ICT, particularly, poses questions, challenges and possibilities to the delivery of education and traditional concepts of learning. Applications of educational technology, which have recently been captured by the term e-learning, are enabling learning independent of time, place, and pace. Entire virtual learning environments are being developed and experimented with throughout education.

Underlying these issues, there's a broader transformation to be observed, namely changing relationships between education, learning and work. The distinction is between work and learning is fading and lifelong learning has become a prerequisite in the network economy, not an option. Hence, the context of learning is severely altering. A variety of learning environments is occurring, comprising a broad range of different learners with different learning styles and demands, requiring different pedagogical approaches.

This chapter can be divided in two clearly distinguishable parts. The first part deals with changes in the view of learning. The new learning represents a educational paradigm that is significantly different from the former educational paradigm. The new educational paradigm includes several profound transformations with respect to learning. Subsequently, the focus will be on The new learning and management learning, and some new, active forms of management learning will be explored. The attention then shifts towards the organization of learning through communities of practice and networks, approaches that seem viable future options from the perspective of management learning.

The second part of the chapter elaborates on one specific transformation within the new educational purview, namely the integration of ICT within education. This transformation will have such a prominent impact on learning and is a factor of such importance to business schools that it deserves some special attention. A range of aspects of educational technology will therefore come up in this part of the chapter. Finally, the focus will return to management education by exploring some contemporary issues and examples in educational technology that are relevant from a business school perspective.

FEATURES AND PRINCIPLES OF THE NEW LEARNING ENVIRONMENT

In the network economy, knowledge, education, and learning are key sources of competitive advantage. Knowledge workers need to be educated, or rather have to learn, on a continuous basis since knowledge (especially management knowledge) becomes outdated within a short period of time and since the knowledge worker is working in a rather complex and information- and knowledge-rich environment. The need for education will also increase due to global competitiveness, an increase in demand (due to increasing numbers of non-traditional students, existing students staying on, mature-aged workers needing skills upgrading, and firms keen to develop specific research and training programmes, more career changes, and 'recreational' learning), and the wish for enhancing the quality of life in the future. As a result, educational institutions have been confronted by different demands and have been urged to re-engineer education in a way that fits the new economic realities. Major changes have already occurred within the educational landscape, like lifelong learning requirements, changing student demographics, pedagogical changes, and a more mercantile way of delivering education (seeing students as demanding customers and seeing education as a product schools deliver). This mercantile manner of providing education relates to the challenge of transforming education from a public service concept to a more business-like concept. Such a conception of education is characterized by a need for a market-driven and cost-efficient approach, instead of providing education for education's sake (though education does have a crucial role in forming responsible citizens and in providing basic schooling). The commercial market for education has already attracted sizeable players, like the UK Open University, the University of Phoenix, and a lot of business schools, some of which through partnerships with other players.

Some of the most striking challenges, pressures and responsibilities can be grasped by looking at several additional important transformations that can be observed with respect to the evolution of education (cf. Haug (1999), Pilot (1999), and Van Gastel et al. (1997)). These transformations reflect the most important principles on which the new learning is based.

The most obvious transformation is the development of integrating ICT into all fields of education. Extensive interconnected digital communication networks are giving rise to quick and flexible knowledge transfer and cooperative learning, and are offering possibilities for time-, place-, and pace-independent learning. In other words: learning can benefit greatly from the displaced trade off between richness and reach. ICT applications like the internet, which is an integration of different kinds of technologies, are also offering access to information sources, databases, and digital libraries. As the European Roundtable of Industrialists (ERT) says:

> *"Information and Communication Technology (ICT) is having a profound impact on the way we live our lives – including the way we learn. ICT therefore has an essential role*

to play in European education where it can improve individual performance, enhance quality of opportunity and help combat social exclusion. Whilst ICT is only a tool, its use is nevertheless going to result in fundamental changes throughout the whole Lifelong Learning Chain. It will bring about the emergence of a networked learning community where learning can happen at any place and at any time. It is vital for the future of good health of Europe that this transformation takes place now. This involves a major investment in both human and financial terms but if this investment is not made then Europe and its citizens will suffer a serious economic and social decline as a result of their failure to keep pace with the development of the global knowledge based society" (ERT, 1997: 4).

An equally important transformation is the changing belief that effective education is based on teaching towards the belief that effective education is based on learning. It is the learner that moves center stage, while the emphasis on the instructor and assumptions regarding expert-based knowledge transfer come to mature. Learning cannot be characterized by merely transferring knowledge from teachers to learners anymore, but is increasingly being defined by the (social) construction of knowledge (see later sections in this chapter). Taking the needs and characteristics of learners as starting points for education, the role of the instructor becomes one of a facilitator, or a coach. This transformation represents a whole new, more emancipatory, paradigm concerning the education of people.

Related to this paradigm change, there's a shift from individual learning to learning cooperatively, indicating the need for learning environments in which students work together on projects, develop social skills, in which reflection and discussion are stimulated, and in which students are held mutually accountable. In addition to the learning outcomes, the focus is increasingly on the learning process. This cooperation can also be interpreted as the integration of different learning environments, like the traditional learning environment and practice, or professional environments. Cooperation seen from this context offers possibilities for developing advanced learning environments, especially with regard to management education.

A process of integration can also be observed with respect to courses in the curriculum. Instead of offering courses independently and separately, learning activities should be focused on an integrative approach, aiming at integration of knowledge and skills, reflecting real-life professional environments. From such a perspective, learning can, for example, be organized by means of project-based education, problem-directed education, or action learning. In making education more flexible and customer-oriented, there is an additional trend of modularizing and individualizing curricula. Students are being enabled to co-develop their own learning trajectories.

Next, a change from focusing on subject matter towards developing intellectual skills can be observed, particularly in the field of vocational and professional education. Students have to develop the capabilities to learn autonomously from books, each other, and other resources instead of merely learning from a teacher's lecture. This self-directed learning puts the responsibility of learning with the learner him- or herself. Subject matter, of course, remains important, but is now seen as a tool to be used in productive tasks, while the content, process, and context of those tasks are strongly dependent on the specific fields of knowledge and future professional perspectives (Pilot, 1999).

Learning now means lifelong learning, a transformation induced by rapid changes in the environment. Knowledge and skills become outdated or obsolete within a short period of time and, hence, it's a prerequisite to constantly update knowledge and skills. This transformation is fueled by the rise of the knowledge worker and disappearing boundaries between learning and working. The latter requires a re-examination of the traditional relationships between education, learning, and working. Process-related or procedural knowledge (know-how) and skills (like generic competences for using software packages) instead of mere subject-related knowledge and skills (like learning how to use a specific software package) need to be developed, as well as learning how to learn. Burton-Jones contends:

> *"The shift to a knowledge-based economy demands that traditional relationships between education, learning, and work are fundamentally reappraised. The long-running debate over whether and to what extent education should be a preparation for work, as well as life, is being overtaken by events, with work and learning becoming increasingly interrelated and interdependent. Systems created in the past to provide and support education are clearly ill suited to cater for the forthcoming explosion in demand for access to learning resources"* (Burton-Jones, 1999: 199).

The concept of learning has thus evolved to lifelong learning and just-in-time education, rather than being situated within traditional college years or just-in-case education. Learning now takes place beyond the walls of educational institutions, by different kinds of students, and occurs in fundamental different ways. Since learning will become a lifelong process and one of the major growth markets in the network economy, education has become serious business.

FROM TEACHING TO LEARNING: THE CONSEQUENCES OF A NEW EDUCATIONAL PARADIGM

A focus on teaching provides a different perspective on education than a focus on learning: teaching is expert-based and expert-dominated. Knowledge is, so to speak, handed over by the teacher to the student in a passive way, reflecting the view of students as empty vessels in which knowledge is poured into. Learning in this sense is the mere absorption of knowledge, and this form of education is being practiced in most educational institutions through lectures. Especially from the viewpoint of professional and vocational education like management education, these passive ways of instruction fall short of preferred (or from a customer's perspective: promised) learning outcomes. Business schools have in the course of time integrated alternative ('active') teaching methods into their curriculum, like apprenticeships, simulations, and case studies.

Learning in an active way can be conceptualized by the concept of construction, which is in fact the central concept underlying the new educational paradigm. The construction of knowledge as an educational starting point emphasizes an active role of the student/learner and a coaching role of the teacher. The teacher now becomes a 'guide on the side' instead of a 'sage on the stage'. As opposed to a passive way of learning (which can be labeled as 'instruction') constructive learners take charge of their own learning. Learning in this sense is student-oriented, and the basic idea is that learners interactively construct knowledge in a learning context that is created by both themselves and educators. Papert describes the differences between instruction and construction as follows:

> *"There are two basic ideas of education. One is instructionism; people who subscribe to that idea look for better ways to teach. The other is constructionism; we look for better things (...) to do, and assume that [students] will learn by doing. When we say we educate [students], it sounds like something we do to them. That's not the way it happens. We don't educate them. We create contexts in which they will learn"* (Papert, 1997).

Traditional classroom education, such as lectures, clearly is just one of many possible ways of learning. Educators have emphasized this passive way of classroom learning for obvious and valid reasons, like cost-based arguments and large groups of students. (And who can sustain the argument that one cannot be truly inspired by a lecture given by an overly enthusiastic professor, telling vivid stories from practice based on state-of-the-art knowledge?) Education based on constructionist assumptions turns learning the other way around. Such a constructionist perspective allows self-directed and active learning to takes place. The context in which learning takes place plays an essential role in this perspective.

The question then becomes: what should such a context look like when educators facilitate learning? In order to answer this question, it is necessary to first take notice of different ways of learning. From Kolb's learning cycle, a variety of ways to learn already becomes visible. Additional ways of learning include day-to-day problem solving, experience-based learning, on-the-job learning, action learning, learning through reflection, learning from peer behavior, experimental learning, and learning through conservation, discussion, and debate. Kolb's learning cycle provides some insight into the process of providing adequate (management) education. This 'experiential learning cycle' represents four different kinds of learning processes: reflective observation, concrete experience, active experimentation, and abstract conceptualization. This model combines the need for theoretical knowledge with a need for practical application, hence rejecting the traditional educational belief that knowledge can be rigorously disembedded from practice, transferred to students, and re-embedded into practice. Especially regarding management education and business schools this traditional belief has proven to be an illusive idea.

In a 1996 study, Rajan (1996) identified four types of learning with each type containing four subsets, namely taught learning, mentored learning, distance learning, and experiential learning (shown in figure 5.1). Figure 5.1 shows the percentage of employees that used or were expecting to use the four types of learning over the period 1996 to 2000. Next to the observation that this study shows that 40% of the employees used formal off-the-job classroom-type training routes for their managers at that time, it also suggests that the overall proportion is unlikely to change over the next decade. In contrast, the percentages for mentored, experiential, and distance-based learning routes are likely to grow. Reasons for this include the ascendancy of core skills consistent with the changing market environment and the predominance of self-responsibility for learning in the current culture of employability and ownership of one's own career, as opposed to career-long employment within one organization (ibid., op.cit. Torino Group, p. 33).

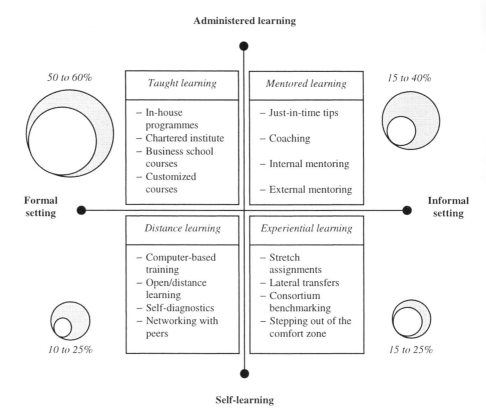

Figure 5.1. Percentage of employees that used or were expecting to use four types of learning over the period 1996 to 2000.
Source: Rajan (1996)

THE NEW LEARNING, MANAGEMENT KNOWLEDGE, AND MANAGEMENT LEARNING

Next to content, other variables in the management learning environment need to be addressed, and, in fact, are increasingly being addressed within management education due to pressures and demands caused by the network economy. Business schools are realizing that traditional educational models have become outdated and that the focus of management learning clearly is undergoing some changes.

Nowadays, especially concerning management knowledge and management education, educators have found traditional teaching methods and the traditional composition of the management curriculum to fall short of effective learning. For effective learning to be realized, several aspects and suppositions traditionally absent in education should be taken account of. As mentioned earlier, creating the right context for learning to take place is a major challenge for educators. Business schools, for instance, are not only confronted with (changing) demands of business regarding graduates, they are also encountering the challenge of managerial epistemology. Management knowledge is, in a sense, a melting pot of the social sciences and a single concept of management learning does not seem to do benefit learning processes. Transferring knowledge will definitely not suffice, nor will merely enabling student to acquire management skills be sufficient to constitute the management curriculum. Developing international, leadership, and network competencies, cross-cultural management, and negotiating skills, as well as fundamental theoretical underpinnings of management science should be part of the modern management curriculum. Figure 5.2 shows the constituting elements of higher education (including business schools) curricula in a triad form (Rajan, 1996), recognizing the development of theoretical knowledge, the development of practical know-how, defined to include core skills (competencies), and the development of appropriate attitudes and behaviors, defined to include personal qualities.

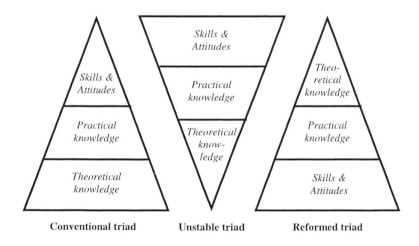

Figure 5.2. The composition and development of curricula.
Source: Rajan (1996)

Traditionally, the triad at the left of figure 5.2 has been the structure of curricula in a descending order of emphasis, while in order to meet today's learning needs, the traditional triangle needs to be inverted, or needs fundamental re-examination at least. Equal emphasis should be put on developing the *art* of management as on the *science* of management (Torino Group, 1998: 45).

Management knowledge, as was illustrated in the previous chapter, is to a very large extent of a situated, distributive, and ill-structured nature, emphasizing the relevance of context and interaction between different relevant communities (e.g., theorists/scientists and practitioners). Management knowledge is not only characterized by the importance of declarative knowledge ('knowing that'), but also by the importance of procedural knowledge ('knowing how'). Therefore, a variety of teaching and learning methods have to be deployed, addressing different kinds of knowledge and allowing them to be transferred to or constructed by learners. Future management educators will have to be experts in the process of education as well as in the content of education, while at the same time allow learning to take place in a proper context. Consequently, the successful business school of the future has a centre or department of management learning. Or, as the Torino Group describes it, this development can be characterized as a transformation from business schools to learning centres. The European context promises the continuation of the current diversity of type, size, and focus of business schools, but underlying this transformation into learning centres, some generic principles can be observed (ibid., pp. 76-78). Such learning centres will start by enabling individuals and organizations to 'unlearn' outdated approaches to management, while also acquiring a deeper understanding of the ways in which new learning can be undertaken. They will incorporate extensive diagnostic and counseling tools and techniques, providing subsequent access to a comprehensive portfolio of learning resources, making wide use of educational technology in addition to faculty and classrooms. Rather than being viewed as a physical entity to which infrequent visits are paid, the centres will act as a focus for continuous learning through networking, benchmarking and identification of best practice. The experience of executives from the public and private sectors will be harnessed through encouraging them to act as coaches and mentors, while a multicultural and global outlook will be inherent in the way such centres think and operate. The development of long-term learning partnerships with clients will demand a relationship marketing approach, which will require the faculty to become client and project managers as well as learning facilitators. A recognition that no single provider can be expected to be 'world class' in every aspect of this wide array of resources and services will lead to collaborative working, not only between business schools but also with some of the newer market entrants. A profile of new learning centres is depicted in table 5.1.

–   Learning to learn and unlearn
–   Partnerships with clients
–   Managers as learning facilitators
–   Comprehensive portfolio of learning resources
–   Professional diagnosis and counseling
–   Focus for networking and benchmarking
–   Multicultural, global outlook to broaden visions
–   Wide use of educational technology/virtual mindset
–   Relationship marketing and client management
–   Collaborative relationships between providers
–   Encouragement of lifelong learning
–   Quality as a core value

Table 5.1. Profile of new learning centres.
Source: Torino Group (1998: 78)

The business school, following Lancaster University's John Burgoyne, would "mount programmes based on clear and thought-through learning principles see(ing) knowledge as diverse in its content and form and dispersed in an uncertain manner. The attitude would be more to facilitate discourse between different forms and owners of knowledge, including practitioners and reflectors (and the approach to management development would be) based as much on expertise in the learning process as on expertise in management problems and disciplines acknowledging the dispersed, multiform, and uncertain nature of management knowledge" (Burgoyne, 1994: 40).

Summarizing, the aforementioned modern educational approaches should be student-oriented and learning-focused, or, using Gibb's terms, management educators will have to augment conventional approaches with enterprising approaches. Such a fundamental shift in educational approaches requires "teachers [to] have action-oriented teaching styles and [to be] capable of using the full range of different process methods" (Gibb, 1991). Consequently, learners (or clients) are being involved in program design, teachers take on non-conventional roles like being coaches and mentors, and insight in how management knowledge can be transferred most effectively and efficiently becomes critical. The characteristics of an enterprising teaching approach are includes a focus on process (as opposed to content) delivery, knowledge generation by participants, sessions that are flexible and responsive to needs, negotiated learning objectives, multidisciplinary, and a problem-orientation.

PEDAGOGICAL IMPLICATIONS: 'ACTIVE' FORMS OF LEARNING

Next, the question raised by the new learning regarding management education evolves into one of pedagogy: how can the new educational paradigm be implemented? The aforementioned quotes of Burgoyne and Gibb already reveal some of the required pedagogical perspectives, namely on-the-job learning, workplace learning, and experiential learning, and an orientation on practice or 'action'. One particular field of interest among management educators from this perspective is the field of action learning. Revans, the intellectual father of action learning has defined action learning as:

> *"[A] means of development, intellectual, emotional or physical that requires its subjects, through responsible involvement in some real, complex and stressful problem, to achieve intended change to improve their observable behavior henceforth in the problem field"* (Revans, 1982: 626-627).

Or consider Pedler's definition:

> *"Action learning is an approach to the development of people in organizations which takes the task as the vehicle for learning. It is based on the premise that there is no learning without action and no sober and deliberate action without learning. (...) The method (...) has three main components – people, who accept the responsibility for taking action on a particular issue; problems, or the tasks that people set themselves; and a set of six or so colleagues who support and challenge each other to make progress on problems"* (Pedler, 1991: xxii-xxiii).

What lies at the basis of action learning, hence, is an active involvement of learners in directing their learning processes and an active, real-world approach towards education. Action learning has also been described as learning from success and failure. Though action learning means different things to different people (Weinstein, 1995: 32) and different schools of thought can be distinguished (scientific, experiential, critical reflection, and tacit) there is agreement on some core features. These features include (Marsick & O'Neil, 1996: 161) the presence of a learning coach, (critical) reflection, team-based learning, involving real work for projects, a focus on team processes, questioning insight, programmed knowledge, just-in-time learning, individual problems, and team problems. Looking at these features, action learning resembles an enterprising approach of education.

As a viable approach to experiential management education and an important element of a training and development strategy, action learning has been adopted in workplace environments (Vince & Martin, 1993). Through action learning, organizational members can be involved in group situations with the goal of helping each group member learn through the process of finding solutions to their own problems. Through this process, learners increase their self-awareness and develop new knowledge, attitudes, behaviors, and skills for making changes and redefining their roles within new contexts (Williams (1992), op.cit. Lankard (1995)).

Within the Management Institute of Lund, Sweden, the emphasis of the learning process is on action *reflection* learning – a synthesis of the best of both classic management development and action learning (Rohlin, et al., 1996). This learning approach has been developed over the years for results-driven and action-oriented managers to take a reflective perspective on their daily activities. The idea of action reflection learning presupposes that learning doesn't automatically result from action; it involves reflection on managers' own and others' real-life experiences and gaining new learning by solving real problems. So, an intermediary step is essential in the learning process, namely an awareness of what happened in the 'action', which enables the learner to think about his or her actions – the moment of reflection (Rimanoczy, 1999). The key elements of action reflection learning reflect the presumptions of action learning to a large extent and include question driven processes, balancing task and learning, discovering learning styles, the presence of a learning coach, just-in-time learning, exchange of learning, a sequential process, a personal journal, a systemic approach, and an appreciative approach.

A learning concept related to the concept of action learning and which is also receiving quite some attention, especially in the field of adult and workplace education, is situated learning. Within this approach, knowledge and skills are being taught in contexts that reflect how the knowledge will be used in real-life situations. Similar to action learning, situated learning emphasizes that behavior is more likely to occur as a result of reflection on experience (Lankard, 1995). Situated learning and action (reflection) learning reflect an active pedagogy.

ORGANIZING FOR LEARNING: NETWORKS AND COMMUNITIES OF PRACTICE

In the early days, management learning only took place in the workplace, and was to the largest extent of a tacit and highly situated nature. Over time, and with the need for more management-wise people, the context of learning was formalized into educational institutions, and management knowledge was disembedded from its original context. 'Management' was now taught in schools, which were expected to deliver 'managers' for the labor market. Consequently, management knowledge, made explicit by means of, for example, theory, had to be re-embedded into practice again. Critics said that these educated managers did not possess the right knowledge, skills, and experience to function properly in real-life environments. Management, they argued, could not be taught in formalized learning contexts, since management learning requires strong interaction with practice. This debate has been alive ever since.

By now, learning in and from practice and real-life contexts has become a major topic again in contemporary management education, and, in fact, reverts to the earliest forms of 'management education'. One of the main reasons of this attention, is the current discontent with traditional educational structures and their effectiveness in providing proper education that prepares students for the labor market and work in practice.

Referring to the distinction between learning about an learning to be, John Seely Brown & Paul Duguid, authors of the most insightful books on the new economy "The social life of information", say that practice shapes and supports learning and traditional training methods tend to isolate people from the sorts of ongoing practice of work itself and that they focus heavily on information (Brown & Duguid, 2000: 129). However, the resources for learning do not simply lie in information, but in the practice that allows people to make sense of and use that information and the practitioners who know how to use that information. "Where in other circumstances knowledge is hard to move, in these circumstances it travels with remarkable ease" (ibid., p. 133) Three characteristics of Brown & Duguid's view of learning are that learning is a demand-driven rather than a supply-driven activity, that is a fundamental social process, and that it is identity-forming (and that learning and identity shape one another). They say:

> "Looking at learning as a demand-driven, identity-forming, social act, it's possible to see how learning binds people together. People with similar practices and similar resources, develop similar identities. (...) These practices in common (for hobbies and illnesses are practices too) allow people to form social networks along which knowledge about practice can both travel rapidly and be assimilated readily" (Brown & Duguid, 2000: 140-141).

Consequently, two types of work-related networks are being distinguished: networks of practice and communities of practice (Brown & Duguid, 2000 and Wenger, 1998). Networks of practice link people to other persons they might never get to know but who are working on similar practices. Between members of networks of practice, the links and relationships are often of a more indirect than a direct nature. Media through which they keep in touch include newsletters, websites, and email.

Coordination and communication take place through third parties and are, therefore, quite explicit (Brown & Duguid, 2000: 142). By the nature of interaction within and between such networks, one could speak of little reciprocity across them. Or, in Evans & Wurster's terms: reach dominates richness.

Communities of practice, on the other hand, are more tight-knit groups by people working together on the same or similar tasks. These communities of practice can be characterized as subsections of larger networks of practice and form small-scale networks on their own. Several striking differences between these networks and communities can be noticed. Following Brown & Duguid, communities of practice are:

> "[R]elatively tight-knit groups of people who know each other and work together directly. They are usually face-to-face communities that continually negotiate with, communicate with, and coordinate with each other directly in the course of work. And this negotiation, communication, and coordination is highly implicit, part of work practice, and (...) work chat. (...) In these groups, the demands of direct negotiation inevitably limit reach. You can only work closely with so many people. On the other hand, reciprocity is strong. People are able to affect one another and the group as a whole directly. (...) These groups allow for highly productive and creative work to develop collaboratively" (Brown & Duguid, 2000: 143).

The basic idea underlying the concept of a community of practice as a model for learning, is that learning is a social activity. In characterizing the process by which newcomers become included in an community of practice, Lave & Wenger (1991) used the concept of legitimate peripheral participation to define learning: required learning takes place not so much through the (reification of a) curriculum as through modified forms of participation structures to open the practice to non-members. Peripherality (an approximation of full participation that gives exposure to actual practice) and legitimacy (needed to be on an inbound trajectory and to be treated as a potential member) are two types of modification that are required to make actual participation possible (Lave & Wenger (1991) and Wenger (1998: 100-101)). The social perspective on learning is summarized by the assumptions regarding learning in table 5.2.

NETWORK LEARNING

Learning viewed from the perspective of communities of practice questions the effectiveness of traditional learning environments, since it presupposes that learning is more than the mere absorption of knowledge made explicit and that knowing involves primarily active participation in communities. The idea of communities seems to provide valuable ingredients to redesign management learning environments into network learning environments.

The concept of communities of practice is strongly related to the concept of network learning. From contemporary views of learning theory, organizations can be regarded as a set of interlocking and shifting relations, a locale internally differentiated where multiple interactions, comprising both social and material elements, take place. Knowing and learning can be viewed of as collective accomplishments residing in heterogeneous networks of relationships between the social and material world, which do not respect formal organizational boundaries (Araujo, 1998: 317). This view of learning resembles principles of network organization. Traditional assumptions of learning and knowledge respectively taking place through and being localized in individuals have proven to be outdated. The situated, transient, and distributive nature of knowledge and consequences for learning have increasingly been emphasized in scientific literature in the past decade (see e.g., Star (1992), Salomon (1997), Hutchins (1995), Lave & Wenger (1991), and Brown & Duguid (2000)).

Learning...

- *is inherent in human nature*: it is an ongoing and integral part of our lives, not a special kind of activity separable from the rest of our lives;
- *is first and foremost the ability to negotiate new meanings*: it involves our whole person in a dynamic interplay of participation and reification. It is not reducible to its mechanics (information, skills, behavior), and focusing on the mechanics at the expense of meaning tends to render learning problematic;
- *is fundamentally experiential and fundamentally social*: it involves our own experience of participation and reification as well as forms of competence defined in our communities. In fact, learning can be defined as a realignment of experience and competence, whichever pulls the other. It is therefore impaired when the two are either too distant or too closely congruent to produce the necessary generative tension;
- *is a matter of social energy and power*: it thrives on identification and depends on negotiability; it shapes and is shaped by evolving forms of membership and ownership of meaning – structural relations that combine participation and non-participation in communities and economies of meaning;
- *is a matter of engagement*: it depends on opportunities to contribute actively to the practices of communities that we value and that value us, to integrate their enterprises into our understanding of the world, and to make creative use of their respective repertoires;
- *is matter of imagination*: it depends on processes of orientation, reflection, and exploration to place our identities and practices in a broader context;
- *is matter of alignment*: it depends on our connection to frameworks of convergence, coordination, and conflict resolution that determine the social effectiveness of our actions.

It...

- *creates emergent structures*: it requires enough structure and continuity to accumulate experience and enough perturbation and discontinuity to continually renegotiate meaning. In this regard, communities of practice constitute elemental social learning structures;
- *transforms our identities*: it transforms out ability to participate in the world by changing all at once who we are, our practices, and our communities;
- *constitutes trajectories of participation*: it builds personal histories in relation to the histories of our communities, thus connecting our past and our future in a process of individual and collective becoming;
- *means dealing with boundaries*: it creates and bridges boundaries; it involves multimembership in the constitution of our identities, thus connecting – through the work of reconciliation – ours multiple forms of participation as well as our various communities;
- *involves an interplay between the local and the global*: it takes place in practice, but it defines a global context for its own locality. The creation of learning communities thus depends on a dynamic combination of engagement, imagination, and alignment to take this interplay between the local and the global an engine of new learning.

Table 5.2. Learning as a social activity: the premises of communities of practice.
Source: Wenger (1998: 226-228)

The idea of network learning builds on principles that resemble principles of network organization. Hence, it has some unique properties compared to traditional learning methods. Network learning distinguishes itself from traditional learning by enabling learning processes that are highly flexible and adaptive, therefore giving rise to the possibility to learn within different fast-changing, dynamic, and relatively ill-structured contexts. Information and knowledge flow from those places in which they currently reside to those places in which they are needed. This knowledge-flow across the network is facilitated by network mediators or knowledge brokers, who know where specific knowledge is located and who facilitate knowledge sharing. Access to knowledge should become easier within this idea of network learning, so the need to memorize, or locally store, information is reduced. The goals of education, in such a network view, shift from knowing a fixed body of knowledge to knowing how to think independently and how to find information when needed (Jacobson & Levin, 1993), therefore emphasizing the development of network competencies. Network-based learning environments can aid students and teachers in jointly constructing both personal and shared knowledge spaces. It is obvious that ICT has a crucial role in developing network learning environments, in the sense of creating quick and easy to create online resources and communication devices, like digital libraries, email, and groupware. Table 5.3 shows some of the features of network learning environments.

- Information flows through networks based on decisions made by mediators (student/teachers or a computer agent) at each node;
- Information and knowledge flow toward where learners need it;
- Information appearing at a network node is stored locally if the mediators expect the information to be of value;
- Over time, mediators at nodes would optimize the organization of locally stored information and knowledge;
- Network-based information and knowledge are not static, fixed 'things', but rather are dynamic, fluid, and changing.

Table 5.3. Features of network learning environments.
Source: based on Jacobson & Levin (1993)

A recent approach to learning-network theory, especially from the view of management learning and management education, has been formulated by Poell et al. (2000), from the perspective of understanding and developing alternative ways of organizing employee learning in relation to work. Within the learning-network theory (LNT) the authors distinguish between the *learning* network and the *labor* network. Each of these networks is characterized by three main components, namely the work/learning processes, the work/learning structures, and the actors. Within the learning network, learning actors, engaged in organized learning play a central role. These actors are stakeholders who act deliberately on the basis of their own theories and interest with respect to work-related learning (ibid, p. 33), and can be labeled as internal (employees, training staff) and external (trade unions, government authorities). These learning actors give rise to three learning processes: the development of learning policies (influencing the general direction of the learning network), the development of learning programmes, and the execution of learning programmes.

The labor network, as a complement to the learning network, is defined accordingly. Next to actors, work processes (constituted by the development of work policies, work programmes, and the execution of work programmes), and work processes. The learning and labor networks of an organization are graphically represented in figure 5.3.

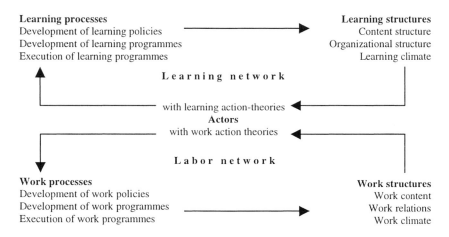

Learning processes   **Learning structures**
Development of learning policies   Content structure
Development of learning programmes   Organizational structure
Execution of learning programmes   Learning climate

Learning network

with learning action-theories
Actors
with work action theories

Labor network

Work processes   **Work structures**
Development of work policies   Work content
Development of work programmes   Work relations
Execution of work programmes   Work climate

Figure 5.3. Learning and labor network.
Source: Poell et al. (2000: 38)

Over time, stable patterns of organizing learning activities tend to develop, which are called learning structures in LNT. These structures develop within content structures, organizational structures, and the learning climates. Four types of learning networks can be distinguished (Poell et al. (2000), based on Van der Krogt (1995 and 1998)): the liberal learning network, the vertical learning network, the horizontal learning network, and the external learning network. Characteristics of these learning networks are depicted in table 5.4.

Concerning the labor network, Poell et al. (2000), following Mintzberg's terminology (1979), distinguish between the entrepreneurial labor network, the machine-bureaucratic labor network, the adhocratic group labor network, and the professional labor network. These types of labor networks are represented in table 5.5.

A liberal learning network is likely to be found in entrepreneurial work, a vertical learning network is expected in machine-bureaucratic work, a horizontal learning network is related to adhocratic group work, and an external learning network is most common for professional work (Poell et al., 2000: 40). It is important to note, that both networks are influencing each other and have their own particular dynamics. First of all, different actors use the networks for different purposes and different objectives through different strategies operating by different principles. Second, as Poell et al. note, power relations between the actors in the labor network are different from those in the learning network. Employees are more powerful in learning networks than they are in labor networks, generally speaking. As the authors say:

> *"The point is that the learning network and the labor network are relatively autonomous, in that they are quite independent as far as their own dynamics are concerned, but very much intertwined because most actors play a role in both networks at the same time. To summarize, the LNT does not prescribe what kind of learning network is best suited for what kind of labor network, it merely describes the relationships between the two networks that are likely to be encountered"* (Poell et al., 2000: 42).

	Learning networks			
	Liberal	**Vertical**	**Horizontal**	**External**
Learning processes				
Co-ordination	Single activities	Linearly planned	Organically integrated	Externally co-ordinated
Development of learning policies	Implicit	Planning	Learning	Inspiring
Development of learning programmes	Collecting	Designing	Developing	Innovative
Execution of learning programmes	Self-directing	Guiding	Counseling	Advisory
Learning structures				
Content structure (profile)	Unstructured (individually oriented)	Structured (task or function oriented)	Open or thematic (organization or problem oriented)	Methodical (profession oriented)
Organizational structure (relations)	Loosely coupled (contractual)	Centralized (formalized)	Horizontal (egalitarian)	Externally directed (professional)
Learning climate	Liberal	Regulative	Integrative	Inspiring

Table 5.4. Four types of learning networks.
Source: Van der Krogt (1995 and 1998)

With respect to management education, this type of learning-network model provides excellent opportunities to educate managers for the workplace and offers possibilities to integrate theory and practice in the learning process of individual learners. The situated and ill-structured nature of management knowledge can be accounted for in such a learning environment, perhaps especially an adhocratic learning network, enabling effective learning processes to take place. The challenge for management educators and business schools, then, is to design a management learning environment that fits the demands of learners (which can, depending on the type of learner, differ remarkably) and the standards and ambitions management learning environments have to comply with and realize according to management educators and business schools. This could mean that, looking at the abovementioned types of learning networks, no particular learning network fits the demands, standards, and ambitions. Consequently, business schools should design a learning network that represents a mix of desirable features.

	Labor networks			
	Entrepreneurial work	**Machine-bureaucratic work**	**Adhocratic group work**	**Professional work**
Dominant actors	Individual employees	Managers/work preparation staff	Multidisciplinary group work	Professional associations
Work content	Broad/simple	Specific/simple	Broad/complex	Specific/complex
Work relations	Contractual	Collective	Team-based	Externally arranged
Work climate	Liberal	Regulated	Organic	Innovative

Table 5.5. Four types of labor networks.
Source: Van der Krogt (1995 and 1998)

With the attention for technology-enabled learning environments (see also the following sections), or as it has recently been called, e-learning, the question of designing learning environments incorporates technological variables, too. The following network model for management learning presented here, accounts for the different requirements put on future managers and business schools. This learning model integrates three interrelated contexts that enable and reinforce each other, namely:

–   The formalized learning environment (e.g., schools, universities, business schools) ('theory');
–   The practical or workplace learning environment ('practice');
–   The technological learning environment ('technology').

The assumption of this network model of learning is that learning takes place in different contexts and that different contexts enhance each other and enable effective learning processes. By such an integration of learning environments, objectives of management educators, such as the development of a profound knowledge base, acquiring managerial skills and competencies, building experience, learning to cooperate, and learning to be adaptive to (culturally) different contexts can be realized. This learning networked learning environment can be visualized as in figure 5.4.

Since the issue of integrating technology in learning environments is one of the major topics of importance in designing contemporary learning environments, the second part of this chapter is devoted to this particular subject. After the following sections, the attention will return to the network model for management education again, and a couple of concrete applications will be discussed.

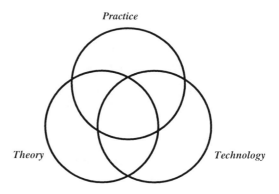

Figure 5.4. The networked management learning environment.

EDUCATION AND ICT: WHY SCHOOLS SHOULD(N'T) INVEST IN EDUCATIONAL TECHNOLOGY

Though ICT is one of the main drivers of the network economy, education does not seem to keep up with the rate of investments in ICT by, for example, business, and seems unable to follow the pace of rapid technological change. Though this situation in higher education institutions is less dramatic than in basic levels and secondary education, this is a problematic observation made by numerous authors; the actual reality of the role of ICT in education does not reflect the potential of ICT by far, nor does it do justice to a new educational paradigm were the responsibility for learning lies primarily with the learners themselves.

Different reasons can be brought up for this backlog. First of all, there is a resistance to change engendered by seemingly unfaltering traditional educational and academic values. Among educators and learners there is an ingrained culture of face-to-face communications and paper-based systems (Burton-Jones, 1999: 201), while the mere lack of a perceived need to improve education and learning processes is another reason for the slow innovation and diffusion of learning technologies. The latter reason can be explained by "public perceptions of education, which have been conditioned by traditional ways of thinking about its role, including its relationship to employment and jobs, and socially ingrained acceptance of the traditional roles of educators and learners" (ibid., p. 202). Concerning issues of knowledge creation, organization, and dissemination, ICT imposes significant changes upon teachers and learners, their personal learning and teaching styles and pedagogical assumptions. According to Dillemans et al. (1998: 108) the structure of schools is not one to properly respond to the demands of the new society for more participation, less strict lessons, and more creativity, but it is designed to satisfy the needs of a mass society and mass production. The curriculum is mainly focused on routine and repetitive working, punctuality, and obedience, whereas ICT calls for a reorientation of the position and flexibility of administrative structures (Van Bolhuis & Colom, 1995).

Secondly, education in particular has to deal with the lack of funding potential because of budget constraints. Integration of ICT requires large investments in hardware, software, training, support and retrofitting (modifications to the schools to accommodate the telecommunication infrastructure) (Rothstein & McKnight, 1994). Some authors therefore argue that, considering limited budgets, schools should invest in older, and thus cheaper, technology, while others insist on keeping up with ICT advancements. As we will be shown in later, large-scale investments in ICT are not necessarily certain to yield enhanced educational quality or more positive learning outcomes, nor can it be said ICT will undoubtedly make education more cost-effective in the long run.

As both Van Bolhuis & Colom (1995) and Burton-Jones (1999) note, another explanation for the fact that education does not invest extensively in new technologies is to be found in the lack of specific, pedagogical, and scientifically correct software: the technologies themselves have been a limiting factor themselves. Strommen (1992) points at the fact that implementation of ICT is being hampered by the systematic lack of awareness of the appropriate uses of technology in the educational setting. Education has traditionally been one of the latest adopters of technological applications.

Whereas the abovementioned reasons are hindering educational investments in ICT, there are several compelling reasons why educational institutions are making and should make continuing and significant investments in ICT. These reasons generally fall into three categories (Green & Gilbert, 1995: 7). First of all, there are reasons with respect to competitive positions. Growing numbers of students come to schools with computer skills and expectations regarding technology, and colleges and universities will have to invest in ICT in order to attract and retain students.

Second, these investments have to do with teaching, learning and curriculum enhancement: ICT can improve the quality of instruction and productivity. New technologies offer almost limitless possibilities for virtual learning and cooperation between students in different locations. Massy & Zemsky (1996) see two general potential benefits of ICT based on the contribution to increasing learning productivity. First, they state that ICT offers economies of scale. After a front-end investment, the cost of usage per incremental student is apt to be low. Moreover, access to very large amounts of information can be obtained at low incremental cost. Secondly, ICT offers mass customization: technology allows faculties to accommodate individual differences in student goals, learning styles and abilities, while providing improved convenience for both students and faculty on an 'any time, any place' basis. These benefits cover several characteristics of ICT-supported education like time-, place-, and pace-independent learning. ICT will empower students to have greater control over the learning process, with all the benefits associated with active learning and personal responsibility. With these technological applications information-rich environments can be created. Additionally, budgetary pressures confronting education have also directed the attention towards the promise of technology to improve productivity. ICT has been expected to yield new levels of institutional and instructional productivity, though ICT has often failed to live up to the expectations. Green & Gilbert (1995) see substantial benefits in widespread academic use of information technologies in the areas of content, curriculum and pedagogy. As for curriculum and pedagogy, they state that ICT applications function as additional resources that enhance the instructional tools used by faculty and the learning experience of students. Next to enhancing productivity by consulting remote libraries, databases, and using sophisticated statistical tools, these technologies offer possibilities for developing distance education. Both will enrich students' learning experiences and can reduce the cost of instruction. Concerning content, the use of ICT has already changed some disciplines in how scholars think of their work and the focus of their activities.

Third, there is the argument of student preparation for the labor market. Employers increasingly demand computer skills as ICT continues to permeate business and society. Enhanced productivity by ICT-based (organizational) processes also plays a major role from this perspective.

The advancing development of ICT has led to the collapse of space and time. Moreover, the traditional trade off between richness and reach has been displaced by ICT: by now, a greater reach not necessarily inhibits lower richness anymore (and vice versa). Multimedia applications are increasingly being seen as substitutes for face-to-face communications and allow establishing virtual teams of which the members work together intensively from very remote places. With respect to education, ICT can contribute in making education more cost-effective (though there has been a lot of discussion on this as will be shown by following sections). Multimedia offers possibilities to address diverse learning styles and to enhance the quality of education. As Brickell notes:

> *"As one of the most recent developments in Information Technology, interactive multimedia technology stands to offer a particularly significant contribution to the improvement of education and training. Sound, direct manipulation of interface objects (such as menus, tools, or instructional screens), visualization of processes and dynamic video images are all features of today's interactive multimedia systems. The technology can not only be used to improve the quality of instruction, but more significantly it can also be used by learners to achieve a variety of learning objectives"* (Brickell, 1993).

LIMITATIONS OF ICT

Though new learning technologies have a huge potential, several determining features of ICT should be considered, which could lead to possible drawbacks in implementing ICT in educational settings. As a consequence, neglecting these inherent features could lead to decreased efficiency and effectiveness in using ICT applications.

First, it should be noted that the amplifying function of ICT could lead to a diminishing attention given to other factors concerning education. For example, the amount of time and effort students and teachers are putting into adopting and learning to use ICT could get so large that there's less time left for other activities. This is obviously the case in a strongly technology-driven environment. Moreover, the nature of technology selects the aspects of experience that will be amplified and reduced (Bowers, 1988: 32). The second pitfall to be aware of is the selective function of ICT, which encompasses the fact that experienced users will have advantages over less experienced users. Third, the non-neutrality characteristic of ICT is to be taken into consideration. Consistent with the amplifying function of technology it influences the conception of data and information by users and can therefore be classified as a non-neutral medium. The next feature to take critically account of is the media-richness of ICT that varies with the medium. Different technological applications have inherent different levels of richness of data. Using a less appropriate medium in a certain educational setting will lead to a loss of information, biased transmission and interpretations, and, therefore, to a loss of quality of education. In the fifth place, the issue of information overload should be taken into account. Since capacities and interactive features exponentially rise in ICT applications, it has become nearly impossible to process and use all available information (sources). These developments can make people hesitant or even resistant in using new learning technologies. Consequently, learners and teachers have to develop learning skills, like learning how to isolate, process, and analyze the right information (coping with the information overload) instead of trying to understand the content of all available information. Seventh, and last, the efficient and effective use ICT can be decelerated by the absence of new forms of assessment with which the efficiency and effectiveness of new learning technologies can be measured (Strommen, 1992).

Both Strommen (1992) and Angehrn & Nabeth (1996: 1) point at the fact that education has traditionally been a sector in which the implementation ICT applications lagged other sectors. Angehrn & Nabeth (ibid., p. 3) note that from a *technical* viewpoint, the low utilization rate of computers in education can be attributed three main limitations of the current generation of technologies: (1) poor quality of human-computer interaction, (2) the limited integration of different media (documents, pictures, video), and (3) limited networking capabilities. Increasing technological standards and quality will probably reduce these drawbacks. Another barrier facing the implementation of learning technologies is the fact that teachers and instructional designers come to distance education from traditional backgrounds, bringing with them assumptions about teaching and learning that are not theory-based and do not translate well to technologically mediated instruction (Schieman, Taire & McLaren, 1992).

EFFECTIVENESS OF EDUCATIONAL TECHNOLOGY

So the key question underlying most of the aforementioned issues is: should education invest in ICT? Or, put differently: how effective is technology in education? Does ICT generate clear and positive learning results? Do the cost associated with the implementation offset the potential of ICT? To properly analyze the effectiveness of ICT, three dimensions have to be taken account of, namely the effectiveness of ICT-mediated instruction compared to face-to-face instruction, what ICT enables that would otherwise not be possible, and the cost effectiveness of ICT (Blurton, 1999).

The effectiveness of ICT-mediated instruction

An extensive amount of research has been conducted for more than 70 years on the first question, that eventually leads to conclude that there is no significant difference to be observed in performance measures between learning with and without technology. This no significant difference phenomenon is the outcome of most research findings (over 350 research projects) related to the effective use of technology, mainly distance learning, compared to alternative methods or techniques of teaching (Russell, 1999). In contrast to radio, the emergence of television in classrooms got a lot of interest from researchers, which functioned as the main application of educational technology until the 1980s. By then, interest rose again, since video and computer technology emerged, and it still continues to rise with rapid the advancements in interactive and multimedia technologies. Table 5.6 lists an overview of research findings per decade since the 1940s.

Decade	Number of studies	Technology reviewed	Outcome measures	Summary/trend
1940s	5	– Radio – Correspondence courses	Exam scores, Standardized tests	3 out of 5 studies found students did 'as well as' or 'better'
1950s	40	– TV in classroom	Achievement tests, EPPS Profile, Final exams/course grades, Aptitude scores, Dropout rate	Most studies reported 'no significant difference'. Students report 'preferred' face-to-face instruction
1960s	73	– Correspondence courses – TV in classroom – Telecourses	Achievement tests, Final exams/course grades, Retention tests, Achievement tests, Behavioral measures, Spacial relations, I.Q. tests, Reasoning tests	Most studies reported 'no significant difference'. Preference for 'face-to-face' continues
1970s	19	– Radio – TV in classroom – Telecourses	Aptitude tests, Final exam scores, Achievement tests, Retention tests	All studies reported 'no significant difference' or 'equally effective'
1980s	61	– TV in classroom – Telecourses – Videotaped instruction	Completion/dropout rate, Final exams/ course grades, G.P.A., Achievement scores	While most studies report 'equal to' or 'no significant difference', a few teletraining studies report improved performance at post-high school level
1990s	49	– Interactive video – Television – Computer simulations – Distance education	Final exams/course grades, Retention scores, Cost-effectiveness measures, Assignment completion rate, Individual assignment scores	Nearly 30% of studies report favorable outcomes based on student preference, better grades, cost-effectiveness, greater homework completion. Most report 'no significant difference.'

Table 5.6. Research on the no significant difference phenomenon.
Source: Nettles, Dziuban, Cioffi, Moskal, and Moskal (1999)

Looking at the results of these studies, several trends seem to emerge. In the 1950s and 1960s, students reported preferring direct, face-to-face instruction, perhaps because the technologies were new and the learning environment was unfamiliar to them. More recently, perhaps as a result of students having become more technologically adept, results indicate a developing preference for distance learning, particularly among those enrolled in post-high school programs. Next, many early studies were designed to prove that technology in the classroom would not 'harm' student performance, while later studies seem more interested in discovering whether students might actually benefit from technology driven instruction. While most studies report no significant difference in the statistical analysis of the outcomes measured, still many studies report scores equal to or better than traditional classroom scores. Several studies conducted in the last decade, however, identified populations of graduate students who performed better with distance learning. Kulik (1994) (as cited in Glennan & Melmed, 1995), for example, in a meta-analysis of over 500 individual studies, found that:

–   students usually learn more in classes in which they receive computer-based instruction;
–   students learn their lessons in less time with computer-based instruction;
–   students also like their classes more when they receive computer help in them;
–   students develop more positive attitudes toward computers when they receive help from them in school;
–   computers do not, however, have positive effects in every area in which they were studied. The average effect of computer-based instruction in 34 studies of attitude toward subject matter was near zero.

It has to be noted, however, that Kulik's research involves studies prior to the 1990s, when the use of ICT was often restricted to drill and practice and tutorial software programs. Nowadays, the use of ICT in schools has moved toward engaging students in authentic learning tasks in which students use computers, software, and network access to simulate events, communicate, collaborate, analyze data and access information sources. Research on these ICT application has not been extensively conducted yet, though a number of studies indicate positive learning and affective outcomes (cf. Means & Olson (1995), Software Publishers Association (1996), Special Issue on Educational Technologies (1994), op.cit. Blurton, 1999: 8), of which the results of two recent studies are worth mentioning. First, a study by the Bertelsmann Foundation of students in a German and a US school concluded that "the use of media and technology improves learning outcomes, instills key qualifications for the information age, and increases motivation (Bertelsmann Foundation, 1998). Second, a 10-year longitudinal research project Apple Computer (1995) stated that "[d]ispelling widespread myths, the researchers found that instead of isolating students, access to technology actually encouraged them to collaborate more than in traditional classrooms. And instead of becoming boring with use, technology was even more interesting to students as they began using it for creating and communicating."

ICT-enabled opportunities

The second dimension in establishing the effectiveness of ICT in education considers what possibilities learners, teachers, and education in general are being offered what otherwise wouldn't have been possible. From this perspective, Blurton (1999: 9) distinguishes between the support of new pedagogical methods, the access of remote resources, the opportunity to collaborate, the extension of educational programs, and the development of skills for the workplace. ICT has the potential to enable students to learn in new ways: self-paced, self-directed, situational, and instant learning experiences have become reality. New pedagogical models in which knowledge can be constructed by social negotiation and students engage in collaborative learning are induced by advanced ICT applications (see for a further elaboration following sections). It should not be forgotten, however, that though powerful learning experiences become possible, ICT remains pedagogically neutral. This means that next to the possibility of creating complete virtual learning environments, ICT can also be used to support traditional forms of education, such as lectures. The way of using ICT remains a human decision, and is not inherent in the technologies themselves (ibid., p. 10).

Concerning the access of remote resources, the issue of connectivity plays a vital role. Internet, the pinnacle of connectedness of networks, provides a seemingly limitless access to information resources, such as databases and libraries. While traditional physical sources are complemented with digital applications, increasingly more resources become available only in a digitally accessible form. Connectedness also is of major important from the perspective of collaborative learning. Albeit local or globally dispersed, ICT enables students to cooperate with each other, their tutors, and their mentors (for example, from the business community). With the characteristics of connectedness, time-, place-, and pace-independence, ICT can additionally contribute to the extension of educational programs by enabling worldwide delivery of education (distance or distributed education) and lifelong learning.

Lastly, using ICT enhances the development of skills for the future workplace of students. As has been illustrated in the previous chapters, in the network economy value is increasingly being created through services and knowledge instead of goods and handicraft. Personal, organizational, and national wealth creation is to be strongly related to the production and dissemination of knowledge and depends on research, education and training, adaptability or flexibility, and on the capacity to innovate. Having advanced ICT skills and knowing how to use discipline-specific applications may help students to secure suitable employment and enhance their productivity once employed (ibid., p. 18). The constant updating of knowledge and skills is another factor in the personal and professional development of students and employees.

The cost-effectiveness of ICT

The cost-effectiveness of ICT in education is the third, and perhaps most difficult to establish, or ambiguous, dimension. Not only does Moonen (1994) from a review of literature conclude that there is confusion about the concepts of effectiveness, efficiency, utilization, and feasibility in cost analysis in education, there are also different analytic frameworks in which social programs, for example educational policies, can be evaluated (Dillemans et al., 1998: 99). Moreover, integrating technology within educational environments poses difficulties upon the performance or cost-effectiveness measures, since additional transformations, such as adapting organizational arrangements to ICT, have to be made (see also Chapter 2). It has been shown that disappointing results of technology-based innovations are due to the shortcomings in the way evaluators have used the methodologies to assess the effects (Herman (1994), op.cit. Dillemans et al. (1998: 99)).

Blurton (1999: 20) states that assessing the cost-effectiveness of ICT in education is difficult – if not impossible – for at least four reasons: (1) meaningful data is lacking (since there are too many variables to be measured in different studies); (2) variability in the implementation of ICT (similar objectives can be reached by different applications); (3) difficulty of generalizing from specific programs (since within a specific course an array of applications can be deployed); and (4) difficulty of assessing the value of qualitative educational differences (what metrics can be used in measuring effectiveness?). In determining the effectiveness, one could also add the costs of not investing in ICT – i.e., the costs of not preparing citizens to participate in an information-based global society (ibid., p. 23). Nevertheless, a number of studies can be reported that try to establish the relative costs of ICT in education. Potashnik & Capper concluded:

> *"Print, audiocassettes, and prerecorded instructional television (lectures) are the lowest-cost technologies for small numbers of students (fewer than 250), while radio requires 1000 students or more to achieve comparable per student costs. Computer conferencing is a low-cost approach to providing interactivity between teachers and students, but live interactive broadcasts and video conferencing are still very high-cost technologies, regardless of the number of students enrolled"* (Potashnik & Capper, 1998).

Davis's study on the cost-effectiveness of ISDN in education, concludes that ISDN can be cost-effective for secondary schools and universities, providing that the institutions have an ethos which welcomes innovation with flexible learning and new technology (Davis, 1996). On the other hand, some scholars have argued that that ICT will not necessarily lower the cost of education (Bates, 1995), is not cost-efficient (Pournelle, 1994) and will be subject to continuously rising costs in the coming years (Cambre, 1991). Not only does the continuing reduction of prices of ICT applications make investments a costly matter, also faculty training and technological maintenance will contribute to rising costs.

TECHNOLOGY-ENABLED LEARNING ENVIRONMENTS

In the network learning model, the technological learning environment existed next to the formalized and the workplace learning environment. Different kinds of learning environments can be realized through a range of technologies. Dillemans et al. (1998: 45) distinguish three main streams with respect to instructional technology-enabled environments (or technological learning environments, TLEs), namely tutorial environments, explorative environments, and interaction environments.

Tutorial environments, embedded in behaviorist and objectivist theories, help learners in realizing predefined learning goals. In these kinds of environments, learning outcomes are produced by the instructional environment, instead of by the learner and differences between instructional environments that affect educational quality in a negative manner are avoided by replacing teachers with computers. Tutorial environments can be deployed especially for rather simple tasks, that require ample drill and practice, routine, and programmed instruction, increasing learning efficiency. Tutorial environments, hence, do not reflect current perspectives on instructions and learning, which stress the importance of constructive, meaning-oriented, and self-regulation activities by the learner (Shuell (1992), Simons (1993)). Human-machine interaction is the common form of interaction within these environments (Dillemans et al., 1998: 46-48).

Contrary to tutorial environments, the location of learning support within explorative environments is not embedded in the technological environment. Unless learners have all the necessary capacities and skills, the open, explorative instructional environment either explicitly or implicitly needs to provide support that helps with their use of such information environments. Two types of explorative environments can be distinguished, namely information tools and multimedia and simulation and modeling tools. While the former may assist learners in acquiring declarative knowledge, the latter aims at supporting the acquisition of procedural knowledge and skills. With respect to multimedia, the main advantage lies in the potential to bring together the characteristics and effects of single instructional environments, hence integrating instructional styles and a variety of information sources. Multimedia technologies will keep changing rapidly in the future, which will expand the capabilities of existing tools even further. Learning environments will be influenced by a variety of advanced technological applications, providing information anytime, anywhere, and in different forms. Distance education, virtual universities, and online campuses have already become a reality. Examples of information tools and multimedia applications are interactive video, CD-ROM and hypermedia. Simulation and modeling tools enable students to conduct experiments in situations where real-life experiments would be too costly or to dangerous. Within such environments, learners can practice their skills in safe settings, but they can also investigate (simulated) aspects of the world. Modeling tools go even further, enabling students to shape (simulated) worlds themselves (ibid., p. 52). Though with these technologies, complex learning environments with a lot of different variables to be influenced can be constructed, and learning effects can be enhanced, the main disadvantage of mainly human-machine interaction remains.

Interaction environments, however, facilitate human-human interaction by means of telecommunication technologies. Though these environments offer the promise of learning through advanced technologies, the actual deployment of these technological possibilities remains the responsibility of the learner. Examples of interaction environments are audio- and videoconferencing.

As Dillemans et al. note, generally speaking, any system that provides an integration of these three instructional environments is to be preferred above a set of more isolated elements. The internet has provided the potential for integrating of these separate environments.

TLEs can be positioned along 6 different dimensions on which they can differ from one another (see Dillemans et al., 1998). With this categorization, the functional use of educational technology can be valued. Here, these dimensions are briefly examined.

1. *Information modality*
    A distinction can be made between verbal, para-verbal and non-verbal information. For example, when using audio-conferencing applications, both verbal and para-verbal information can be transmitted, whereas non-verbal information is excluded. Limitations to the information modality can have serious impacts on communication and interaction;

2. *Linearity*
    Transportation of messages can be conducted in linear or alinear ways. In linear environments, information and the diffusion of it is controlled by the instructional designer, whereas in alinear environments learners are confronted with a rich amount of information which they can explore according to their own needs and in their own style (Conklin, 1987);

3. *Type of interaction*
    On this issue one can distinguish human-human and human-machine interaction. The authors note that if the quality of interaction is more the product of the way students cope with instruction, rather than of the technology itself (Hoogeveen, 1995), designers must re-examine the assumptions, models and strategies embedded in instructional design;

4. *Number of participants*
    The number of participants interacting by mediation of ICT applications is subdivided by one-alone, one-to-one, one-to-many and many to many. Speaking in pedagogical terms, this dimension can determine the efficiency and effectiveness of learning materials;

5. *Time/Place (in)dependency*
    ICT applications enable educational programs to be offered independent of time and place. Learners do not have to attend classes at the same time nor do teachers have to give real-time lectures. This time (in)dependency is

specified as the (a)synchronous aspect of communication of which e-mail is an example. Considering this dimension, Lauzon & Moore (1992) introduce the term 'twenty-four-hour classroom'. The same goes for place (in)dependency: for example, online courses can be attended at home by the students and people all around the world can join a project team;

6.   *Immediacy*

Immediacy deals with the amount of time from sending a message to the response to this message. Teleconferencing, for example, allows for immediate feedback, whereas e-mail is a medium which is characterized by less immediate responses.

Considering these dimensions, learning technologies can be functionally classified. A classification of some of the aforementioned tools is to be found in Table 5.7.

		Information modality	Linearity	Number of participants	Time (in)dependency	Immediacy
Explorative environments	**Interactive video**	Dynamic visual displays, computer text	Linear or alinear	Not applicable	Not applicable	Immediate or non-immediate
	CD-ROM	Text, dynamic visual displays	Linear	Not applicable	Not applicable	Immediate or non-immediate
	Hyper-media	Text, dynamic visual displays	Alinear	Not applicable	Not applicable	Immediate or non-immediate
Interaction environments	**Audio-conferen-cing**	Audio	Linear or alinear	One-one One-many Many-many	Synchronous	Immediate
	Audio-graphic conferen-cing	Audio, still graphics	Linear or alinear	One-one One-few Few-few	Synchronous	Immediate
	Computer conferen-cing	Dynamic visual displays, mainly written word	Linear or alinear	Many-many	Asynchronous	Non-immediate
	Video-conferen-cing	Audio, still graphics, nonverbal information	Linear or alinear	One-one One-many Many-many	Synchronous	Immediate
	Internet	Dynamic visual displays, mainly written word	Alinear	Many-many	Asynchronous	Non-immediate

Table 5.7. Classification of tools.
Source: based on Dillemans et al. (1998)

PEDAGOGICAL MODELS AND APPLICATIONS OF ICT

It should be noted that the role of the instructor changes dramatically by the implementation of (a combination of tutorial, explorative and) interaction environments in the educational system: (1) instructors will be replying to questions from students rather than asking questions; (2) teachers act more as guides and tutors (they should give as much individualized feedback as possible, and become real-life facilitators of learning); (3) to design a course for a telecommunication environment requires considerable attention and time; and (4) teachers will inevitably also have to deal with technical problems related to specific technology used (Dillemans et al., 1998: 53).

Additionally, according to recent theories, technology can be used to engage learners in a meaningful dialogue, rather than the traditional model of being a tutor. Technology can be used as a tool to extend human minds, to provide an environment for learners and teachers to 'construct' their knowledge. Technology also makes it possible for learners to work collaboratively and to promote active learning. In fact, ICT has created a new educational paradigm in which the learner moves center stage and the role of both the instructor and technology will change dramatically. First, the instructor will spend less time in the lecture theater and more time interacting with individuals and with small groups. The instructor can focus on the structuring of information, demonstrate processes, and attempt to spark insights in the student. Secondly, the instructor will spend less time preparing traditional lectures and more time structuring material in a format where it can be presented in an interactive manner through the use of information technology. Thirdly, the roles of information technology systems will include implementing active agents with which students can interact to pursue the acquisition of information, reinforcing and practising the processes of structuring of information, and participating in interactions with simulation systems which give students experience in process formulation (for example, virtual reality). And fourthly, information technology will provide a basis whereby the interactions among instructors and need not be confined to a single geographical location, but can be conducted through visual and verbal interactions from physically disjoint locations. This paradigm shift is represented in table 5.8.

Old paradigm	New paradigm	Technology implications
Classroom lectures	Individual exploration	Networked PCs with access to information
Passive absorption	Apprenticeship	Requires skill and simulations
Individual work	Team learning	Benefits from tools and e-mail
Omniscient teacher	Teacher as guide	Relies on access to experts over network
Stable content	Fast-changing content	Requires networks and publishing tools
Homogeneity	Diversity	Requires a variety of access tools and methods

Table 5.8. Old paradigm versus new paradigm.
Source: Multimedia Instruction Committee Report (1995)

The difference between traditional models of education and new models of education mentioned before parallel the pedagogical distinction between objectivist and constructivist models of education. Of course, it is not only technological advancements and possibilities have given rise to constructivist pedagogical models. Great societal demands concerning continuous innovation, development, and adaptation require an approach towards learning that puts the learner at the center of lifelong learning processes and enables the learner to become an independent, self-regulated learner. The constructivist approach towards learning highlights the importance of promoting learners' activity from the start on. The interplay between learning goals, selected tasks and outcomes (external parameters) and specific characteristics of learners (internal parameters), refers to active, constructive, self-regulated and goal-oriented learning (Dillemans et al., 1998: 24).

But one should not make the mistake seeing the pedagogical models as substitutes, or contradictions. In fact, tailoring learning environments to specific learners' needs requires taking into account additional variables like epistemology (nature of a specific field of knowledge) and the stage in the learning trajectory (beginner or advanced, pre- or post-experience). No size fits everyone, figuratively speaking, and not all technological applications, learning models and instructional techniques are equally compatible. The different pedagogical models will be briefly elaborated on in the next sections, as well as related technological applications and implications.

The objectivist perspective

The basic assumption of the objectivist perspective is that the external world is a given and can be represented in an objective way (e.g., by the expert). It is also conceived to be mind-independent, which means that the world can, known be by everyone in an objective and absolute way (Bednar et al., 1992: 20). Only the boundaries of our ratio ('bounded rationality') may place limits to the intellectual capacity to get to know the world. Reality can be mirrored by the mind and be described and mapped in terms of entities, properties, and relations completely. The objectivist perspective, therefore, has a strong focus on declarative knowledge instead of procedural knowledge or conditional knowledge (knowing when).

Prior experience does not play a dominant role in the way people interpret reality (Duffy & Jonassen, 1992: 2). Logical reasoning and (positivist) science can help to give the 'correct' and general account of reality. Theoretically it is possible that during the learning process people acquire a common agreed and complete picture of a part of the world. Knowledge than is perceived as a 'package', an entity, that can be transferred into people's mind. Learning in this objectivist perspective refers to the responses given by people to the stimuli from the external environment. Hence, learning highly depends on these external stimuli and is therefore always adaptive (in contrast to e.g. explorative of generative learning). By focussing on these external stimuli there is a total lack of attention to the importance of internal stimuli, like motivation. Differences in the understanding of these stimuli are the result of efficiency or imperfect knowledge transfer from the expert to the learner (Leidner & Jarvenpaa, 1995: 267). The instructor, viewed as the source of objective knowledge, controls the material and pace of learning process (programme control).

The constructivist perspective

The constructivist perspective originates from a very different strand in educational psychology and philosophy, called humanism. Humanism is associated with basic ideas about freedom, autonomy and the notion that human beings are capable of making important choices within constraints imposed by heredity, personal history, and environment (Hiemstra & Brockett, 1996: 3). From an epistemological point of view, this perspective holds that there is real world beyond our experience, but meaning is imposed on the world by ourselves instead of the existence of a world independent of our meaning. In contrast to the objectivist learning model, students are not assumed to absorb knowledge passively from external resources (e.g., experts, books, and databases) but are active constructors of knowledge by integrating and combining new information with their own experiences and prior knowledge. Learning is conceived as an active construction process during which learners give meaning (based on their prior knowledge, experience, and attitude) to their environment. From a constructivist point of view, learning is a situated and social activity. This means that knowledge is constructed within different realistic contexts depending on variables of the environment, which is the educational setting. On the level of the individual learner and instructor, variables are also defined in accordance with and influenced by their personal, cognitive and cultural characteristics. Different types of interaction which occur between (variables of) learners and instructors, define learning as a social activity. As Blurton (1999: 9) states:

> "Modern constructivist educational theory emphasizes critical thinking, problem, solving, authentic learning experiences, social negotiation of knowledge, and collaboration – pedagogical methods that change the role of the teacher from disseminator of information to learning facilitator, helping students as they actively engage with information and materials to construct their own understandings. That is, students learn how to learn, not just what to learn" (Blurton, 1999: 9).

By focussing on the declarative (and in some cases procedural) knowledge, the objectivist perspective, as contrasted to the constructivist perspective, ignores some of the most crucial drivers behind the individual learning process, which are also important elements within technology-supported learning environments: prior knowledge, motivation and self-efficacy, metacognition.

Within the constructivist model of learning, two other relevant approaches, or offsprings can be distinguished: the cooperative or collaborative model of learning (learning emerges through interaction of individuals with other individuals; knowledge is being created through the sharing of it) and the sociocultural model of learning (knowledge cannot be divorced from the historical and cultural background of the learner). An important implication of the cooperative model for instructional methods is that the instructor's role is to facilitate maximal information and knowledge sharing among learners rather than controlling the content and delivery of learning (Leidner & Jarvenpaa, 1995). The major implication of socioculturalism is that students should participate on their own terms with their different backgrounds. Instruction should not deliver a single interpretation of reality nor should it present a culturally biased interpretation of reality.

Pedagogical models and educational technology: ICT strategies

When considering the issue of the use technology in education, the discussion of how classrooms should be organized becomes apparent, varying from instructor consoles and the use of simple key response pad in classes to complete virtual learning environments. In an article by Leidner & Jarvenpaa (1995), four different strategies for integrating technology in classrooms are presented, based on organizational change theories, to which (functional) ICT applications are attributed These visions partly reflect the instructional environments as defined by Dillemans et al. (1998), which have been discussed previously. The following four visions are particularly interesting since Leidner & Jarvenpaa relate them to pedagogical models. The visions are:

1.   The vision to *automate*;
2.   The vision to *informate up*;
3.   The vision to *informate down*;
4.   The vision to *transform*.

Within the vision to automate the role of ICT is to provide operational savings and improve quality by performing structured, routine, operational tasks reliably and efficiently. Teaching nor learning is fully prone to being automated, since, at best, these activities are of a semi-structured nature. It is the objectivist model of learning that best fits the vision to automate. Characteristic ICT applications within this vision are instructor consoles equipped with presentation software and display controls, instructor consoles and stand-alone student computers, computer-assisted instruction, and distance learning.

The vision to informate up sees the ICT as a management control tool to keep managers informed of detailed aspects of their organization's performance (Schein, 1992). Translated to educational settings, the instructor is being enabled to provide feedback to students concerning their understanding of class material in a timely fashion. The instructor can now clarify misunderstandings and misinterpretations. Both the objectivist and the cognitive information processing model of learning are promoted by this vision. Applications within this vision are key response pads and email between instructor and students.

Using technology to provide students (or, in general, lower levels within an organization) with information to allow them to critically analyze information or discuss issues among a set of peers, is the aim within the vision to informate down. The constructivist model of learning applies to this vision, as well as collaborativism, and cognitive information processing. ICT applications can be divided in information classroom technologies (providing information to learners – e.g., learning networks, hypermedia, simulation technologies and virtual reality) and communication classroom technologies (providing communication facilities to learners).

The vision to transform holds the most radical perspective by allowing ICT to completely change organizations into virtual structures. Within the context of education, this vision contends ICT to redraw the physical boundaries of the classroom, to enable more teamwork, to allow learning to be a continuous time-independent process, and enable multi-level, multi-speed knowledge creation. Virtual classrooms can be organized by and exist with pedagogical principles from all the aforementioned models. Both asynchronous communication across distances and groupware-supported asynchronous communication across distances are applications that can be distinguished within this vision.

Table 5.9 depicts the integration of the aforementioned visions of technologies in classrooms, the pedagogical assumptions of these educational technologies and the preferred model(s) of learning for the particular vision and technologies.

Vision and ICT applications	Pedagogical assumptions	Model of learning (primary and, if applicable, secondary fit)
The vision to automate		
Instructor console	Instructor is the center of classroom activity; Presentation technologies can make the delivery of information more memorable and interesting	Objectivism
Instructor console and stand-alone student computers	Students learn better if they can emulate what the instructor is doing on the computer; Learning is more effective when it is interactive	Objectivism Constructivism
Computer-assisted learning	Students benefit when they control the pace of learning; Feedback should be frequent	Objectivism Cognitive information processing
Distance learning	Weakness in education is the lack of availability of good courses and faculty; Accessibility in remote locations or smaller schools can be efficiently provided via telecommunications	Objectivist Socioculturalism
The vision to informate up		
Key response pads	The instructor needs feedback; The ability to elicit responses via technology is superior to hand-raiding	Objectivism Cognitive information processing
Instructor-student email	Feedback, even delayed, is better than no feedback; Limited access to instructors limits communication	Cognitive information processing
The vision to informate down		
Learning networks	Delivery of information is not a pressing problem, but rather the lack of current information from realistic contexts; Students create knowledge through information exploration	Constructivism Cognitive information processing
Hypermedia/internet	Students need to create their own knowledge structures	Constructivism and Cognitive information processing are both the primary model of learning
Simulation/virtual reality	The more real the context, the more effective the learning; Students should be provided the means to experience the phenomenon during class	Constructivism
Synchronous communication classrooms	Participation is critical to the learning process; Anonymity encourages participation	Collaborativism Socioculturalism
Groupware-supported synchronous communication classrooms	Structure imposed on communication is effective in helping students learn; Communication is more efficient when structured	Collaborativism and Cognitive information processing are both the primary model of learning Socioculturalism
The vision to transform/virtual continuous learning spaces		
Asynchronous communication across distances	Learning is an ongoing process; Time should be flexible; learning need not be geographically dependent	Collaborativism
Groupware-supported asynchronous communication across distances	Ad hoc communication is more effective wen supported with a structure	Collaborativism and Cognitive information processing are both the primary model of learning Socioculturalism

Table 5.9. Integrating technology and pedagogy.
Source: Leidner and Jarvenpaa (1995)

Until recently, the vision to automate was the strategy that could be found within education in particular. Relatively basic technological applications contributed to the learning process in way that primarily had to do with cost-savings and replacing educational routines. Though only a few schools have been able to effectively integrate educational technology into the learning processes in a way that reflects the vision to transform, some progress has been made in integrating ICT according the visions to informate up and down. Especially the latter vision is compatible with principles of the new educational paradigm. Looking from the perspective of realizing a networked learning environment, however, the vision to transform seems to offer the best starting point. It should be noted the mentioned virtual structures do not only relate to the mere digitalization of the learning environment and the relevant contexts. It does also point at the virtual links or relationships between different learning contexts, which was the basis for the network learning environment. In the next section some concrete applications of advanced management learning environment using educational technology are being dealt with.

MANAGEMENT EDUCATION AND ICT

A lot of effort put in the integration of ICT into educational settings has resulted in what Leidner & Jarvenpaa have called the automation of classrooms. This process of automation does not lead to an advanced and enriched learning environment, but resulted in substituting or complementing blackboards with digital aids. As Alavi et al. (1997) note, these efforts to automate have often led to improved efficiency of effectiveness, but have not led to fundamental changes in learning and teaching. They say:

> "The integration of information technology into management education is by no means trivial, and it is not simply a matter of providing computer access and training to faculty and students. Effective use and integration of computers into classrooms requires a departure from traditional interaction modes, so that a technology-mediated learning environment becomes pedagogically effective and even superior to alternative modes of learning and instruction" (Alavi et al., 1997: 1312).

ICT provides management educators and management learners with great opportunities, like just-in-time and just-in-place learning, and collaboration between students on remote locations, but how to transfer procedural management knowledge and tacit dimensions of knowledge? A recent approach to management development is the Business Navigator Method, which combines the case method of learning and business simulation games. The Business Navigator Method defines a framework for the integration of computer and telecommunication technologies underlying the next generation of management development tools (Angehrn & Nabeth, 1997: 277). The objective of this method is to develop a virtual interactive business environment (VIBE), a simulated 'real-life' business environment, to which students can be visits. Such a VIBE is divided into three network levels, namely the physical network (the actual/physical business environment), the organizational network (the 'information owners', agents, or gatekeepers within the organization), and the information network (the sources of information, like interviews, documents, databases). One of the true benefits of the Business Navigator Method is that an extended set of pedagogical objectives can be realized, which, according to Angehrn & Nabeth (1997), include dimensions that are difficult, if not impossible, to reach through traditional educational methods. These objectives include:

–   Learning how to manage complexity (e.g., information overload, complex social interactions);
–   Learning how to deal with constraints (time, skills, perspective);
–   Learning how to develop efficient information gathering and interpretation strategies ('sense making');
–   Understanding the role of information (and information ownership related to different organizational structures) in companies;
–   Richer discussion material given the difference of individual strategies;
–   Richer experience ('case writer perspective' rather than 'case reader perspective') involving both action and analysis.

In short, learning through the Business Navigator method comprises two phases. The first phase is concerned with gaining navigation experience in a VIBE, on an individual basis or in networked teams. The second phase consists of group discussion and the comparison of experiences (co-located or in distributed teams) enhancing both the quality and diversity of the ensuing discussions and reflection (p. 279). One of the tools based on the Business Navigator Method is the EIS simulation (Executive Information System), in which learners are being challenged to intervene in a division of a large enterprise during a simulated six-month's period. The learners' mission is to progressively convince the twenty-four managers of the division to adopt a major innovation. The department managers populating the VIBE have different roles and display different patterns of resistance to change, which can be influenced by the learner through the application of an extensive set of organizational development tactics ranging from information gathering techniques to individual meetings, the organization of pilot projects or executive development programmes (ibid., p. 281). In sum, Angehrn & Nabeth observe the following strengths of learning tools based on the Business Navigator Method (ibid., p. 280):

–   The creation of a powerful, safe experiential (learning by doing) experience;
–   Capturing and mirroring the complexity of today's business environment;
–   The expansion of personal, organizational, and industry knowledge;
–   Emphasizing the importance of managing time and information;
–   Interactively stimulating continuous reflection on quality and speed of decision-making processes;
–   Complementing opportunity and problem-finding with interpretation, sense-making, problem-solving, and communication skill development;
–   Developing team-building sensitivities and skills;
–   Stimulating reflection on personal experiences and being able to appreciate the variety and diversity of management thinking and action.

Virtual learning communities

Earlier this chapter, the idea of communities was presented and explicated from a learning perspective. Communities are a promising venue for learning and, for instance, knowledge management. The organization of communities has recently received considerable attention in literature related to new models of learning, organizational science, and the field of management. The concept of communities integrates different contexts enabling the development of rich learning environments and provides a 'social', instead of a mere cognitive, way of learning. Communities transcend traditional boundaries between relevant, and traditionally separated, contexts for learning and, hence, offers fertile soil for the organization of professional and vocational education, like management education. One particular challenge is how to manage, or rather facilitate, the emergence and development of these community-based arrangements. As a supporting medium, ICT has an essential role in this process of development.

Here, the idea of virtual communities comes into play. Establishing virtual communities is one of the most promising venues from the perspective of lifelong learning and for developing network learning environments. Rheingold (1993: 5) has defined virtual communities as "social aggregations that emerge from the [internet] when enough people carry those public discussions long enough, with sufficient human feeling, to form webs of personal relationship in cyberspace." This definition gives an idea of how virtual communities can be seen, but it clearly has its limitations. Social aggregations do not only emerge through personal and emotional relationships, nor does it merely imply discussion. Of course, though an important element in reflective learning, functions of virtual communities are not restricted to providing a technological platform for discussion. What is really important, is the fact that these social aggregations do emerge through the use of technology, creating opportunities to use them for functional purposes (like learning or knowledge management) and that they resemble aforementioned aspects of the community concept. An example of a functional purpose of virtual communities is learning. From this perspective, virtual communities can best be defined as a group of people with similar learning interests who collaborate in an electronic learning environment in order to share knowledge, experiences, resources, and best practices with a view to accrediting the learning undertaken through assessment and feedback (Fraser, 1999).

A virtual community, therefore, can be used as a prominent tool for supporting lifelong learning by integrating instructional content with collaborative work environments and online reflective dialogue. Through content-delivery technology as well as communication technology, virtual communities help to support the building of deeper understanding through participation and engagement of learners. They can open the doors to institutions of learning as well as, for example, institutions of business and allow the community inside, thereby enabling actors other than teachers, to become participants in and witnesses to learning processes. It's possible to bring together different kinds of learners, teachers, experts from practice, and businessmen, amongst others, to scaffold (Vygotsky, 1976) each other, and to work with and alongside each other, engaging them in thought-provoking discourse on their own terms, enhancing each others' learning processes (Ramondt & Chapman, 1998).

Focusing on technology, it is important to note that virtual communities have aspects of philosophical, political, ideological, and experiential significance. Fernback & Thompson contend:

> *"Ideologically, community within cyberspace appears to emphasize a shared belief in the principles of free speech, individualism, equality, and open access the same symbolic interests that define the character of American democracy. Experientially, community within cyberspace emphasizes a community of interests, usually bounded by the topic under discussion, that can lead to a communal spirit and apparent social bonding"* (Fernback & Thompson, 1995).

Entrepreneurially, it is added here, virtual communities challenge existing traditional forms of organization, especially regarding the organization of learning, by providing a mode of organization that integrates ICT with organizational purpose, building on both the (pedagogical) strengths of the community concept and the delivery and communication possibilities of ICT applications. In addition, virtual communities allow learners to take charge of their learning process in an easy and flexible way and learning to take place according to the new educational paradigm in which knowledge is interactively constructed. Virtual communities, therefore, must be affordable, intellectually accessible, available to use it (ibid.), and provide the possibility to be constructed in both a bottom-up as well as a top-down (interactive) manner, which should be seen as some of the main challenges for management educators and business schools.

Returning to the network learning model, virtual communities of management education are located at the centre of the model, i.e., at the intersection of the formalized, practical or workplace, and technological learning environment. It should be noted that within this network learning model the focus of community regarding the learning environments varies depending on different variables. Conceptually, this means that varying with the value of the particular variable, the learning environment can be designed according to the conceptions of educators and schools regarding the fit between the nature of the learning environment and the variable. An example of a relevant variable is the type of knowledge that should be acquired by the learner: some knowledge cannot be efficiently or effectively acquired or transferred by means of attending lectures (e.g., procedural or tacit knowledge), while other types of knowledge can (e.g., declarative knowledge). Consequently, educators can prefer organizing a lecture instead of workshops in which case studies are analyzed. The same goes for knowledge transfer through the use of technology: some applications of educational technology only allow for specific kinds of knowledge to be transferred. A second example of a variable in this model is the stage in the learning process. This variable refers to intra-curricular differences in the desired educational approaches (first year students versus graduating students), but also to inter-curricular differences (pre- versus post-experience management education). A meta-variable in this model can be the general objectives of (business) schools concerning the learning outcomes, such as the desired level of graduates, labor market, the composition of the curriculum (e.g., research orientation), and the objectives related to image and reputation considerations.

FINAL THOUGHTS

Without any doubts, the use of ICT applications in constructing learning environments has – for good reasons, it appeared – exploded over the past years. ICT provides numerous opportunities for developing learning environments that fit personal demands of learners, that fit the demand of flexibility, that fit the challenges posed by the need for lifelong learning and the integration of learning and working, and that fit educational strategies of offering effective and real-life learning experiences in cost-efficient ways. In addition, ICT fits the new educational paradigm which is characterized by its learner-centered nature, explorative and collaborative learning environments in which knowledge is created interactively, a coaching role for teachers, and time-, place-, and pace-independence of learning, among other things. The internet, in particular, integrates different elements of technological learning environments, enabling the development of advanced learning environments. Educational technology, however, still has to cope with its drawbacks and its skeptics.

As has been illustrated in this chapter, ICT plays an essential role in developing a networked learning environment for management education by, for instance, enabling time- and place-independent communication and collaboration between relevant communities. Establishing virtual communities and technology-enabled real-life simulations are some of the applications that are most probable to become prominent tools in both management education and business research. By means of new educational approaches, management education is being redesigned for the 21st century.

However, the 'new learning landscape' is revolutionizing the purview of education in general and management education in particular. Advancements in ICT and the nature and consequences of the network economy will drive major changes in management education. Davis & Botkin argue:

> *"Business, more than government, is instituting the changes in education that are required for the emerging knowledge-based economy. School systems, public and private, are lagging behind the transformation in learning that is evolving outside them, in the private sector at both work and play, with people of all ages. Over the next few decades, the private sector will eclipse the public sector as our predominant educational institution"* (Davis & Botkin, 1994: 170).

Though these authors paint a bleak, a speculative, and perhaps a too radical picture, this passage contains some truths. The penetration of private sector organizations, like publishing companies, software houses, and corporate universities, into the market for management education is a risk for business schools and centres for innovation in management education are to be found outside universities and business schools (Ives & Jarvenpaa, 1996: 33).

Hence, some new and powerful players have already entered the market and they will be not the last ones; new dynamics will emerge, not in the least place concerning a diversified demand for management education and the nature and structure of competition; new opportunities will arise in this transforming market and business schools will encounter severe threats. One of the most important questions from this angle is if business schools are able and equipped to adapt to the circumstances in this rapidly changing environment.

CHAPTER 6

THE INSTITUTIONAL PERSPECTIVE

Business schools' markets, organization, and strategy

INTRODUCTION: NEW INSTITUTIONAL REALITIES

It has been only four years ago that Peter Drucker was quoted in Forbes Magazine saying: "Thirty years from now the big university campuses will be relics. Universities won't survive. It's as large a change as when we first got the printed book" (Forbes Magazine, 1997). Since 1997, a lot has changed: technologically, economically, as well as socially. Higher education has moved center stage in discussions on economic development and growth since knowledge and learning are of paramount importance in the network economy: the nature of work has changed, and the distinction between working and learning is rapidly disappearing. The fact that expressions like the intelligent enterprise, the knowledge worker, and smart products have become established indicates their relevance and illustrates new organizational realities.

Almost half a decade after Drucker's assertion, it appears that universities are still able to survive. However, the environment in which higher education is developing, is undergoing severe changes (see also Chapter 5). Since knowledge and learning have gained so much importance, the function of providing education has partly been shifting to the business sector. Traditional educational institutions are encountering a global competitive playing field in which non-traditional players, like new media enterprises and publishers, are competing for students. Increasingly, partnerships between various players are emerging in order to capitalize on each other's particular strengths and reap the benefits the market for learning is promising. The organizational form of higher education is changing consequently.

Over time, management education has changed, not only in the way it is delivered or relating to the content of the management curriculum, but also the types of management education that have been offered. By now, undergraduate education, graduate education, post-graduate education, pre-experience education, post-experience education, part-time education, and executive education are all part of business school offerings. Some business schools have been specializing themselves in some of these offerings, for instance executive education, while others offer a package in which all of these offerings are represented. The way in which management education is being delivered has also changed. In addition to traditional business schools, a number of ambitious partnerships between business schools, technology providers, and other corporate partners has emerged. These partnerships aim at seizing market opportunities by providing different kinds of management education in innovative and customized ways.

This chapter focuses on the following question: what do the institutional dimensions of universities in general and business schools in particular change in the network economy look like? The term 'institutional', here, encompasses two distinct meanings, which will be dealt with in this chapter respectively. First, it refers to the social-economic environment of higher education, which increasingly becomes internationalized. Second, it refers to the institution, i.e., the university and the business school itself, and its organization, management and strategy. What is apparent from both these perspectives, is that universities, business schools, and other institutions of higher education are central actors in de further development of the network society. These institutions are the developers and purveyors of the resource that is of paramount importance in the network economy: knowledge. Restrained financial resources due to decreased government funding and the interest of other parties outside the academic venue in knowledge produced by higher education have directed the activities of universities and business school towards the marketplace (cf. Gibbons et al., 1994), making the institution and faculty more or less free entrepreneurial agents (cf. Slaughter & Leslie, 1997).

THE INSTITUTIONAL ENVIRONMENT

As was indicated by the previous chapters, thinking about and the provision of education has revolutionized. Education is increasingly being delivered in a way that capitalizes on the possibilities and the strengths of new technologies. Since knowledge has turned out to be one of the essential resources in the network economy, continuous learning and training have become a prerequisite for individual and corporate survival: lifelong learning is today's and tomorrow's educational groundwork. The shelf life of knowledge is short in the network economy and knowledge and skills need to be updated on a regular basis, so that the knowledge worker is able to keep adding value to the network he or she belongs to. According to a variety of sources, ranging from scientists to multinational company's CEOs, education – in particular the e-learning component – is the single booming market of the 21st century. Cisco's John Chambers claimed education over the internet is going to be so big it's going to make email look like a rounding error. Knowledge and learning are at the center of a company's competitive advantage, due to which knowledge management and developing learning programmes have to a certain extent become a meta core competence of organizations. In fact, business can now be seen as a sector which will be at the forefront of transferring knowledge and providing education taking the place of government, which once took over the prominent role of the church in education (cf. Davis & Botkin, 1994). As a result, the nature of the educational playing field is changing, incorporating non-traditional and commercial suppliers of education, and structures through which education is being organized is transforming. Both education and industry initiate cooperative network efforts. In addition, the educational playing field is globalizing and growing in scale. Universities and business schools are aiming for market expansion and have been developing overseas sites to serve their clients better and reap the benefits of their market positions.

The commercialization of higher education

The commercialization, or 'marketization', of higher education, has been subject to blazing discussion and has recently been called academic capitalism (Slaughter & Leslie, 1997: 208). The idea of academic capitalism holds that universities perform institutional and professional market or marketlike efforts to secure external funds, and is a response to developments with the environment of higher education. Not only are budget cuts at the heart of the development of this concept, the fact that universities still are knowledge-based institutions and have a central societal role, and, therefore, are amidst the development of the knowledge-based society are crucial in this regard. This unique and important position has also driven university activities (education, research, and consultancy) towards the commercial playing field. Businesses from a wide range of industries are very eager to establish some kind of relationship with academia. Market and quasi-market funding mechanisms and profit motives are increasingly an integral part of higher education. According to Slaughter & Leslie, this new reality can be characterized as

> *"[a]n environment full of contradictions, an environment in which faculty and professional staff expend their human capital stocks increasingly in competitive situations. In this environment university employees are simultaneously employed by the public sector and increasingly autonomous from the public, corporate body. They are academics who act as capitalists from within the public sector; they are state-subsidized entrepreneurs"* (Slaughter & Leslie, 1997: 210).

Especially technosciences, like biotechnology, ICT, and new materials technology, and academic professional fields that are close to the market, like management and applied sciences, are engaging and will increasingly engage in academic capitalism. Additionally, other kinds of management of entrepreneurial endeavors will increasingly be part of the core of higher education. Examples of such endeavors include the development and management of offices for patenting and licensing, technology transfer, arm's length foundations, spin-offs, incubators, research parks, consultancy and (in-company) education offices, and training centers.

These developments make that the educational playing field, in particular the field of management education, has become much more dynamic than ever before. The next sections will elaborate on these subjects and comprise both developments relating to higher education in general as well as developments concerning business schools in particular.

The internationalization of higher education

Within the network economy, global competitive structures are emerging, seemingly disregarding international social and economic borders. Paradoxically, in order for these structures to function properly, an awareness of these borders is pivotal. From an American perspective, Joseph S. Johnston, Jr., former Vice President for Programs of the Association of American Colleges writes:

> *"A massive challenge now confronts American higher education: the challenge of internationalization. Our colleges and universities must become environments of teaching and learning – as well as research and service – that reflect and address the increasingly interdependent nature of our world. Their success with internationalization (...) will depend on their ability to get beyond borders – both the literal, geopolitical ones that demarcate nation-states and the figuration (and often less permeable) ones that define the academic disciplines"* (in Johnston & Edelstein, 1993: 1).

Though this passage refers to the American situation and universities in particular – which is characterized by a relative isolation – it also applies to European higher education and business schools. All the more, perhaps. In fact, the market for management education can be viewed of as being big global business by now, attracting new (commercial) competitors eager to yield a profit. European competitors, which in general do not quite have the reputation of the top US business schools, will have to expand their horizons and increase their international focus. When US business schools are entering the European market for management education, they will constitute a great competitive challenge to European business schools. Therefore, European higher education in general and European business schools in particular will be forced to internationalize, exploit overseas markets like the US market, the Latin American market, and the Asian market, and live up to the high quality and competitive standards this fierce competition will bring. In the global network economy the notion of (national and regional economic) competitiveness not only provides a strong argument for the development of higher education as such, but also for the internationalization of higher education. Institutions, thus, are faced with intensifying competition and are looking for opportunities to expand their markets.

A second argument for the internationalization of business schools lies in the fact that business very much values the understanding of other cultures, since business itself to an increasing extent operates in global networks. This relates to the fundamental rationale for international education, which, according to Johnston (ibid.: 6), should not arise from forces external to the university, but from a profound conception of the goals of education itself: being educated means to acquire general knowledge of the larger world, understanding of the different constituting national cultures, and the position of one's own culture in it. Consequently, curricula in higher education in general and particularly in business schools should internationalize.

Internationalization, accreditation, and brand value

A difficulty in the internationalization process arises from the (in)comparability of certificates administered by institutions of higher education. Sofar, it has been difficult to make a comparison between nations' different diplomas regarding undergraduate and graduate studies, hampering international employability. Following the certification system of distinguishing between undergraduate (bachelor level) and graduate (master level) education, the European Ministers of Education have signed a joint declaration (the Bologna Declaration), thereby adopting a system of easily readable and comparable degrees. The main aims underlying this adoption are to promote the international employability and mobility of European citizens and the international competitiveness of the European higher education system. The Sorbonne Declaration of 1998, which forms the foundation of the Bologna Declaration, has stressed the importance of universities' role in building a so-called Europe of Knowledge, which is able and ready to equip its citizens with the proper knowledge and competencies to encounter the technological, economic, and social challenges of the network society. Within this two-tier system, a student has to successfully complete the bachelor phase (with a minimum of three years), after which the student can choose to pursue a masters degree or a doctorate degree.

The internationalization of higher education, the intensified competition to get the best students, scholars, research funds and matching funds (Spoun, 1998: 45), and the development towards a uniform and globally comparable education system pose different challenges upon business schools within the market. One key future issue will be the issue of branding and a global 'brand war' in the field of management education seems no exaggerated forecast. Exploiting the brand value means that schools will compete on the basis of reputation, quality of faculty and infrastructural facilities, and the value potential clients attribute to the culture or 'myth' of the school in question. Within such brand war, smaller institutions are likely to be overwhelmed by the larger well-known schools, since students will perceive graduating from a highly valued brand as advantageous outside their locality or country (Burton-Jones, 1999: 205).

Business school rankings, ROI-indicators, quality evaluation reports, accreditation agencies and alumni associations emerge to aid students and governments in picking the winners (Byrkjeflot, 2001: 13). Accreditation agencies, following the trend in higher education, are internationalizing too. The American Association of Collegiate Schools of Business (AACSB) has already approved European and Asian business schools, while Equis, the accreditation system initiated by the European Foundation for Management Development (efmd) approved its first US school in 2000.

Within the global and uniform playing field, it seems obvious that the strong brands of the highest ranked and well-known business schools will dominate the market for management education. In fact, there have been initiatives by renowned business schools to establish learning sites overseas to capitalize on their quality image, worldwide reputation, and their well-known staff. However, these expansions do not seem to really pay of as yet: Harvard formerly had an annex in Verviers, which has been terminated; the University of Chicago's Graduate School of Business has campuses in both Barcelona and Singapore, that, as has been reported, do not yield a profit yet; INSEAD has a site in Singapore, but students seem to want to go to France. Though this global market for management education has not reached its final dimensions sofar, these steps indicate the dominance of the world's largest, renowned business schools exploiting their brand names through the opening of global campuses.

From a European higher education perspective, the fear of potential global competitive dominance of a small number of world-class universities has resulted in the Granada Declaration. The polarization between these world-class universities as opposed to a large number of universities having difficulties to keep their current prestige and attractiveness has been deemed not desirable. Such a competitive imbalance should not result in a loss of the richness of universities' vast plurality of traditions, national and local cultures, and different perspectives. The strategic option that the Granada Declaration proposes, is a strategy of pursuing partnerships, in order to build collaborative knowledge, facilitated by the use of ICT networks.

A STRATEGY OF PARTNERSHIPS

The Granada Declaration, in fact, relates to destabilizing patterns of university professional work that have been the result of the rise of the network society and the impacts its drivers, globalization of the (political) economy and virtualization/digitalization processes, have on society. Dramatic changes in academic work and institutional and system management have occurred consequently, and many authors have pointed at the changes in higher education, often focusing on how the center of the academy has shifted from a liberal arts core to an entrepreneurial periphery, describing the increasing 'marketization' of the academy and detailing the rise of research and development with commercial purposes (Slaughter & Leslie, 1997: 208). The idea of this marketization, which has been labeled 'academic capitalism', holds that universities perform institutional and professional market or marketlike efforts to secure external funds, and is a response to developments with the environment of higher education. Not only are budget cuts and performance measurement based on financial indicators at the heart of this advancing idea, the fact that universities still are knowledge-based institutions and have a central societal role, and, therefore, are amidst the development of the network society, cannot but have the consequence of other parties' increased interest in (commercializing) academic knowledge. This unique and important position has also driven university activities (education, research, and consultancy) towards the commercial playing field. Businesses from a wide range of industries are very eager to establish some kind of relationship with academia. Market and quasi-market funding mechanisms and profit motives are increasingly an integral part of higher education.

Globalization and the trend towards the forming of partnerships between industry and academia are particularly influencing management education and business schools. These "new partnerships among education and media organizations and also among consulting forms, corporate universities and other knowledge-based firms represent a formidable challenge to our ways of conceptualizing business education and to the traditional system for creation and governance of management knowledge" (Byrkjeflot, 2001). Some of the most prominent business sectors eager to engage in relationships with educational institutions are the media conglomerates (see Intermezzo 1). These transnational media conglomerates, rather than public education, are predicted to play a central role in the more culture-centered capitalism of the future. The digital revolution gave these media companies the leverage to realize global connectedness and to expand and simultaneously commercialize the cultural sphere (Rifkin, 2000).

INTERMEZZO 1

Rupert Murdoch joins with 18 universities in distance education venture

The media baron Rupert Murdoch has linked his giant News International company with the 18-member university network Universitas 21 in a move designed to capture the major share of the rapidly growing global market for online higher education.

Mr. Murdoch announced Tuesday that News International would set up a joint-venture company with Universitas 21 through News International's London-based subsidiary, TSL Education Ltd. and said the venture company would begin offering custom-designed higher-education programs over the Internet next year. These would be aimed at college graduates who are already working, and would lead directly or indirectly to the awarding of degrees and diplomas by Universitas 21.

"News has taken a strategic decision to enter the distance-learning market using our global distribution platforms, our advanced technologies, and our marketing reach", he said. "A mutually profitable partnership between leading providers in higher education and one of the world's leading media companies is a very strong proposition."

The Universitas 21 network was incorporated as a company in London last year. Its 18 members are spread across 10 countries in Asia, Australia, Europe, and North America. Under the new arrangement, Universitas 21 member institutions will provide the quality-assurance structure, assessment, and degrees for all courses offered. Later this year, the joint venture is expected to call for proposals from groups or individual scholars anywhere around the globe who are interested in designing and developing new e-education programs.

Alan Gilbert, chairman of Universitas 21, said Tuesday that he hoped the new company would be operational by September and would offer its first courses by mid-2001. He said the revenue stream would begin flowing back to member universities as soon as the first student signed up for a course. "We don't think the individual campus brands or the old-fashioned forms of pedagogy and their adaptation to distance education from face-to-face teaching is the way e-education will go", said Mr. Gilbert. "Nor do we think the individual university brand is any longer the most potent in the global market. A U.S. university brand, for example, would look somewhat imperialistic if offered in China."

Mr. Gilbert said graduating students would receive a diploma issued by Universitas 21 and bearing the names and logos of the 18 member universities. "Properly branded, advertised, and promoted, it will be hugely powerful, much more so than any individual university trying to franchise its brand around the world."

Mr. Gilbert said that for the universities involved, the aim was to generate income that they will be able to spend on their campus-based operations. "What we want to do is to preserve our universities as the best campus-based institutions in the world where we can continue to offer philosophy and classics and things like that which are hard to pay for in commercial terms, but which you can do if you are well-resourced."

In addition to the need for branding learning, Byrkjeflot (2001) distinguishes three reasons why media, education, and firms increasingly develop alliances and partnerships with each other. Each of these reasons relates to characteristics of network organization. The first reason is the convergence in learning markets as a result of the development of new learning and publishing technologies. While the market for traditional student learning has historically been the main market for education, the promising markets for the future are employee learning and info- and edutainment. As Martin Kenny, President of Simon and Schuster's Education Technology Group, explains:

> *"Partnership will evolve to include the delivery (...). The technology is allowing us to do things with content that we have never done before (...). The use of the technology will drive the pace and the course of change. We have a lot of businesses coming to us directly with opportunities to do training at the workplace which sound a lot like what used to happen at the university venue. So this is something where people are coming to us, and our development is skewing this way, too. Our role in the development of planning as we see it is not one-to-one, not one-to-many, but many-to-many. And that's a model we see really proliferating"* (in Byrkjeflot, 2001: 8).

The second reason is that the huge new media firms command dense and overlapping networks that are linked to networks that, in turn, are not connected to each other. It can be simply seen as a business opportunity to take on the role of a broker to bridge gaps in social structures (cf. Ronald Burt's theory of structural holes). Applying network theory to education and e-learning, this means that content makers and technology or network providers complement each other. These brokers can also be entrepreneurs, instead of the media companies, brokering the relationship between new media providers, business schools, and customers. The third reason lies in the trend towards globalization, which is intensifying competition and is making existing supply structures more transparent. The need for quality, certification, accreditation, and differentiation, then, has become greater. This also relates to the withdrawal of national governmental interference, meaning that education has to look for substituting funds. As a result, it has become more important for educational institutions to engage in commercial research and consultancy and organize themselves in networks.

Business schools, specifically, have been increasingly active in developing partnerships and networks, in order to seize a share of the lifelong learning market and to benefit from knowledge transfers made possible by these networks. The next section explores four types of cooperative structures between different parties.

PROSPERING THROUGH PARTNERING: EXAMPLES FROM NETWORKS IN PRACTICE

By now, more and more business schools seem to be practising what they have preached. They have partnered up with fellow and erstwhile competing business schools and additional (corporate) partners, in order to develop industry-relevant, global programmes, sometimes provided through the use of advanced learning technologies. True networks of management education have emerged, incorporating those actors who command specific competencies and resources to organize management education for the 21st century. Classified by means of looking at different partners involved, four types of partnerships relating to the organization of management education and educational resources can be distinguished, namely partnerships between (cf. Byrkjeflot, 2001):

-       Type 1: Media companies;
-       Type 2: Business schools;
-       Type 3: Corporations and business schools;
-       Type 4: Media companies, business schools consultancy firms, research think-tanks, technology providers, and corporations.

Each type of partnership will be dealt with individually in the following sections. The partnership typologies will be illustrated by a number of recent examples.

Type 1 partnerships

The media industry has witnesses a considerable industry concentration, characterized by huge mergers and acquisitions and anti-trust lawsuits. In 1983, the media industry was controlled by 50 corporations, while only 14 years later, this number had dropped to about 19 (Bagdikian, 1997). Regarding the distribution of academic management knowledge, the trend towards concentration in the journal publishing industry seems to indicate that this distribution is being monopolized. Small companies and non-profit organizations owned most journals until the 1960s. By now, a corporation like Reed Elsevier – by far the world's biggest journal publisher – has acquired the bulk of them, which has resulted in an aggressive raise of subscription fees (Byrkjeflot, 2001: 19). The recent merger between Reed

Elsevier and Harcourt, another huge media company, has been investigated by antitrust authorities (Kirkpatrick, 2000). The trend of digitization has resulted in new market opportunities within the publishing industry for old-media-new media partnerships. Within these partnerships, the content provider is able to build extensive digital libraries and to develop new distribution channels through technology providers. The recently announced alliance between Simon & Schuster and Lightning Source is an example of such a partnership, in which Simon & Schuster's digital content is enabled to reach a vast group of retailers by providing end-to-end digital capabilities from file conversion to delivery and other fulfillment services for both eBook and print-on-demand orders (Byrkjeflot, 2001: 19).

Type 2 partnerships

As was noted before, business schools have since long been active in establishing and participating in alliances and networks. Not only does the need for cooperation with industry (e.g., in order to guarantee curriculum relevance) play a role, the development of new learning technologies, the need for internationalization, student and faculty exchange, and the need for seizing market opportunities induced by the trend towards lifelong learning and executive education are increasingly becoming important.

PIM and CEMS

Two well-known business school alliances are PIM (Program in International Management) and CEMS (Community of European Management Schools). PIM, established in 1973 by HEC, New York University and London Business School (LBS), is organized as a consortium of top business schools from throughout the world and aims for the exchange of graduate students and counts as the first international student exchange network. It allows for the mutual recognition of both the quality and reputation of partner universities and networking on best practices in exchange coordination, new program development, academic equality issues, and global trends in business education (see PIM website).

Many of the European PIM-members are participating in the CEMS-network, which was founded by Esade, HEC, University of Cologne, and Bocconi with the support of a number of international companies in 1988. Being a non-profit organization, it was originally thought of as a pooling of resources in a strategic alliance and as a defense against the spread of the American format in business education (Spoun, 1998). One of the aims of CEMS is to strive for the development of a European standard in management knowledge and management education and to become a pan-European management university. By now, CEMS has borne over 2000 management graduates, while it continues to have about 250 graduates a year. The CEMS graduates receive the CEMS Master's degree in Management, which is claimed to be a degree that is grounded in academic excellence and cultural diversity. CEMS includes international corporate partners, whose association with CEMS is presented as strategic alliances. It has established its own organizational apparatus which has a legal autonomous status, its own budget, a European head-office based in Paris with 6 employees, a board, its own magazine (the European Business Forum, together with PriceWaterhouseCoopers) and its own diploma. The organizational model of CEMS can be characterized as a simple network model and is depicted in figure 6.1. By now, CEMS is a community of 17 leading universities and about 57 international corporate partners. CEMS has always defined itself as an alliance, with its degree being "not combined, but common". The student is the most important criteria of legitimation and it is for this reason that CEMS has put such an emphasis on producing graduates having the right profile as defined by the corporate affiliates (Spoun, 1998: 99).

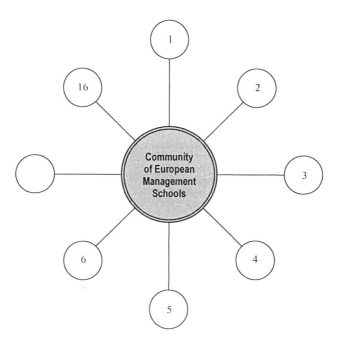

Figure 6.1. CEMS organizational model.

PRIME

Founded in 1997, the Programme for International Managers in Europe (PRIME) aims at providing a global approach to international management in Europe, blended with an in-depth understanding of cross-cultural national realities, both in the form of open programmes and in-company programmes. PRIME involves the following institutions: Copenhagen Business School, Erasmus University Rotterdam, HEC, SDA Bocconi, WU Wien (Vienna Economics and Business University), and (in a contributing role) Esade.

Its primary objectives are to prepare managers for an international career by providing them with the skills and abilities needed to successfully manage in an open global market economy from higher managerial positions within companies. The programme also gives the participants the opportunity to benchmark themselves, their positions, responsibilities, and companies to the other participants and helps them in developing and maintaining international networks. Some of the pedagogical objectives include interactivity through the use of small groups, learning to work in cross-cultural teams and learning from diverse European experiences. Its main target group consists of relatively young though experienced international managers and executives.

PRIME is organized through five modules (technology and business environment, strategic decision-making, leadership, key business skills, and organization and performance) that are organized by the partner business schools in five different European countries, thereby especially emphasizing European diversity. Its organizational form can be characterized as a carrousel model, as is depicted in figure 6.2.

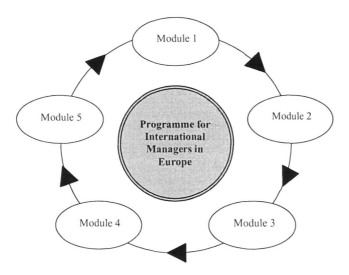

Figure 6.2. PRIME organizational model.

More recent examples of business school networks for management education include Trium Emba, Universitas 21, and the Global eManagement programme (GeM).

Trium Emba
Trium Emba, offering an executive MBA, can be seen as a response to the consequences new online learning technologies bring for the competitive structure in management education. In contrast to the CEMS-network, it has no centralized

physical organizational structure, but it is organized as a loose alliance. However, while CEMS aims to be European, the Trium Emba organization, consisting of New York University Stern School of Business, the London School of Economics and Political Science (LSE), and HEC, claims to offer an authentic global executive MBA programme. Trium has partnered up with two guest institutions, the Chinese University of Hong Kong and Fundação Getúlio Vargas in São Paulo, Brazil, whose campuses will be used to educate students. One additional salient characteristic is the presence of LSE, which was incorporated in the partnership for its knowledge on international economic, political, and social policy – elements that usually are not part of the MBA curriculum.

A comparable example of such a business school partnership is the agreement between the University of Virginia's Darden Graduate School of Business Administration, the University of Michigan Business School, and the University of California at Berkeley's Haas School of Business. The agreement implies that these schools will offer common e-business courses through online instruction to each other's MBA students (The Chronicle of Higher Education, 2000b). Students will receive class preparation materials over the internet and will communicate with each other and their teachers by means of videoconferencing and through internet chat rooms. Though there have been other business school partnerships, this cooperation is unique in the sense that it involves three top business schools from three geographic corners of the US. Moreover, this partnership links two business schools that are located at the centre of the US's high-technology corridors – Silicon Valley and Northern Virginia – with a school that can be seen as a pioneer in using technology around the globe.

Universitas 21

Universitas 21 is a UK incorporated company with a network of 18 universities in 10 countries, which was established on the initiative of three Australian universities in 1997. This incorporated entity is able to leverage the reputation, resources, and experiences of its members. Through the network structure, a framework is created that enables members to pursue agendas that would be beyond their individual capabilities, hence aiming for synergy. This operational synergy is supported by a strategy of branding: the company's core business is provision of a pre-eminent brand for educational services supported by a strong quality assurance framework. It offers experience and expertise across a range of vital educational functions, a proven quality assurance capability and high brand value (see Universitas 21 website).

This quality assurance and international brand value contribute to the organization's purpose of developing international curricula for graduate students with credentials that are internationally portable and accredited. In total, the associated universities enroll about 500,000 students a year, employ some 44,000 academics and researchers, and have a combined operating budget of 9 billion US dollar.

London Business School and Columbia Business School
"Both Columbia and London have extraordinarily successful and sizable executive education operations. This is the new frontier for executive education, and it's very exciting. This alliance builds upon our individual offerings. It provides the unique opportunity for us to offer clients an additional pool of talented faculty and experiences, as well as geographic reach", says Columbia Business School dean Meyer Feldberg about the recent alliance between LBS and Columbia in New York. It is the first formal alliance between two of the world's most prestigious business schools, formalizing a two-year partnership for executive programmes (both in-company programmes and short open enrolment courses) (FT.com, 2001a).

According to LBS and Columbia representatives, the benefits of this cooperative effort are an upgrading of the quality of executive programmes, complementing each faculty's strength with expertise in different areas, developing and providing truly global (going beyond US- and Euro-centric attitudes) and customized programmes, overseas branding opportunities. Becoming increasingly attractive in recruiting new faculty and retaining existing faculty, and joint research possibilities. Both schools will continue to individually serve current and new clients.

The partnering business schools are also engaging in cooperation with corporate partners in the development and offering of its courses and programmes. LBS and Columbia will link up with the Sumitomo Corporation of Japan. The aim of this cooperation is entering a new market by running an open enrolment programme in general management in Japan. Ian Hardie, associate dean for executive education at LBS, says "neither school would have had the capacity or the courage to embark on such a programme alone." In addition, both schools will be able to use the online programmes developed by the two schools under the agreement with technology partners Quisic (LBS) and UNext (Columbia) (ibid.).

INSEAD and Wharton
The demand from the world's largest companies for international management raining has led to the emergence of an alliance with a possibly even bigger global reach and scale, which was recently forged by INSEAD and Wharton School, two of the world's leading business schools (rated seventh and first worldwide respectively). Through this cooperation, INSEAD and Wharton will be enabled to provide custom executive education programmes and open courses by using the schools' campuses in Philadelphia, San Francisco (both Wharton), Fontainebleau, and Singapore (both INSEAD). Next to their existing courses, INSEAD and Wharton will develop a number of new courses combining faculty strengths, of which some of the first will be a course in global management and an MBA update for those who already have management degrees. Additionally, the schools will co-brand some of the existing courses. Course credits will be linked to both schools, though each school will continue to hire its own faculty and grant its own degrees. Both schools expect to offer a joint global executive MBA someday, and maybe the alliance will eventually offer degrees as a single institution (Business Week, 2001).

The partnership will include the development of a Centre for Global Research and Development to, among others, raise global awareness of emerging business and societal issues, collaboration in the delivery of Ph.D. courses, the exchange of faculty in both person and via technology, and offering students the opportunity to use each school's career management services. Part of the alliance, which is claimed to be more broad-based than other business school alliances, will be the joint development of new markets such as Latin America, India, and Japan. Together, these business schools account for 333 full-time faculty, 149 visiting and adjunct-faculty, nearly 5,500 undergraduate, MBA, and doctoral students, about 14,000 annual participants in executive education, and close to a 100,000 global alumni network. Of the near 140 faculty members of INSEAD, up to 30 of them already had established links with Wharton. Many of these management scholars completed their doctoral degrees at Wharton, while others have been or still are visiting professors at Wharton (FT.com, 2001b).

GeM

The GeM-programme (Global eManagement programme) is offered by the GeM-consortium, an international network of business schools which share a common curriculum in e-management at a Masters level. It specifically focuses on the role of ICT in helping organizations rethink and redefine their operations, value chain, competitive advantage, markets, and market opportunities. The founding members of the GeM-consortium include Athens University of Economics and Business, Copenhagen Business School, Erasmus University Rotterdam Rotterdam School of Management/Faculteit Bedrijfskunde, Georgia State University, Norwegian School of Economics and Business Administration, and the University of Cologne. Later, Esade, Monterrey Tech, and the University of Denver have become participants in the GEM-consortium. Reykjavik University students will also be offered the GeM-curriculum. Each member contributes to the development and improvement of the programme, which has been organized through different 'rings' ('ring model', see figure 6.3), which resembles a network architecture. This ring model entails that each GeM-school is linked with a maximum of four universities into subgroups, which are called rings. A ring is composed on the basis of the preferences of the schools involved and has its own curricular calendar and its own set of international seminars.

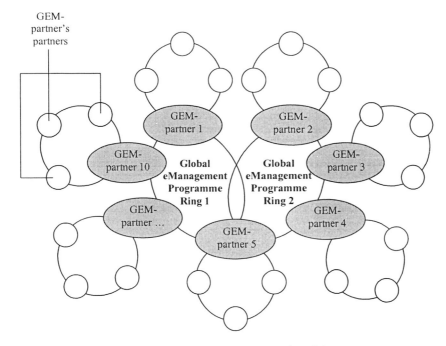

Figure 6.3. GeM organizational model.

Type 3 partnerships

The challenge of continuous learning, the blurring boundary between working and learning, the need to develop workplace competencies, and the need to develop competitive advantage in the network economy, have been some of the most important drivers of the emergence of corporate universities (CUs). The general basic tenet that defines a CU is that it functions as the strategic umbrella for developing and educating employees, customers, and suppliers in order to meet an organization's business strategies (Meister, 1998: 29). Though CUs differ in scale and scope, they are usually organized around a set of similar objectives. These objectives include (see, amongst others, Meister, 1998: 30):

–   Providing tailor-made learning opportunities that support the organization's critical business issues;
–   Training the value chain, including customers, distributors, product suppliers, and the universities that provide tomorrow's workers;
–   Encouraging leaders to be involved with and facilitate learning;
–   Utilizing CUs for competitive advantage and entry into new markets;
–   Cost reduction in travelling and housing expenses by keeping learning within the borders of the company.

The benefits associated with CUs have caused a true explosion in the number of CUs. Compared to one-and-a-half decade ago, the number of organizations with a CU or corporate college has risen from 400 to about 2,000; by 2010, it is expected that CUs will outnumber traditional universities. It is projected that 30% of all learning will be delivered over corporate intranets by 2003 (FT.com, 2000a). One of the world's most famous CUs, McDonald's Hamburger University, has trained mote than 50,000 of its restaurant managers over the past 37 years.

Though there is a myriad of collaborative patterns and partners in developing corporate learning programs, an increasing number of companies is choosing to set up a CU in cooperation with business schools. A clear and important motivation for this is that a CU is able to provide learners with accredited certificates, diplomas, and degrees, and educating them through the use of a renowned faculty. Though from the employees' point of view there is the demand of getting qualifications that are portable from a career point of view, employers are using this as an argument for recruiting and retaining their workforce.

Both Henley Management College and Ashridge are examples of British business schools that are active in assisting companies in setting up CUs and training programmes. Henley helps consultancy firms and other multinational companies in setting up their own CUs, while Ashridge uses a tailored development approach in which a careful diagnosis and design of learning programmes is applied to individual companies. In collaboration with Electrolux, Ashridge has developed the International Business Leadership programme. The programme was designed to provide an in-depth understanding – in as real a context as possible – of what it actually means to network and operate on a true international level. It brings together around 25 international managers for two one-week modules, which take place at Ashridge and a place near the Stockholm-based Electrolux centre respectively.

Another recent example of close collaboration between business schools and industry is the Centre for the Network Economy, a cooperative effort by the London Business School, Andersen, and Lucent Technologies. The genesis of the Centre for the Network Economy is a response to the surge in the practice of e-business and the fact that the idea of the emerging network economy has caught the interest of LBS faculty across a range of disciplines. The centre will be sponsored by its two founding corporate affiliates, complemented by an international consortium of businesses and expects to work together with a range of other business schools, like the Massachusetts Institute of Technology Sloan School of Management, INSEAD, via its Singapore campus, and Boston University.

Together with Henley, Cap Gemini Ernst & Young has developed its Virtual Business School (VBS), which is recognized by the firm as a key strategic tool for generating business synergies and innovation. The VBS includes Centres for Leadership Development, Research and Innovation, Connected Learning, and Post-Graduate Learning. Each centre develops learning programmes, events, and activities that provide Cap Gemini Ernst & Young employees the opportunity to engage in distance education for a variety of qualifications, including an MBA and doctorate qualifications. Part of the cooperation is the firm's consultants work with Henley faculty on joint research, publications, and conference opportunities (Byrkjeflot, 2001: 23). Last year, the VBS won the Corporate University Xchange European Excellence Award, demonstrating it has been able to align corporate learning to the organization's business strategies and being successful in developing learning alliances with leading universities. In addition, it has proved that it used technology to create a continuous learning environment, and developed and implemented innovative marketing and branding techniques (Cap Gemini Ernst & Young website).

A second example including Henley as an academic partner is the ABB Academy. The ABB Academy, launched in December 1999, will address ABB's middle to top management from different segments, businesses, countries, cultures, and generations. It will focus exclusively on the group's key global strategic business issues. Henley Management College supports the three initial educational programmes, which are the Top Management Programme, the Profit Centre Management Programme (for business unit managers with worldwide responsibility and for company, divisional or local business unit managers at country level), and the International Management Programme (for managers who currently have a functional responsibility). Henley will help ABB Academy develop itself into a independent full-fledged, state-of-the-art school (Summit, 2001). Arne Olsson, ABB Senior Vice President, Corporate Staff Management Resources, explains why ABB has chosen not to send its managers to business school, but instead to develop learning programmes and set up a corporate university with the assistance of Henley:

> *"Business Schools can deliver first class products, but they cannot deliver from the really top managers information on where we are going, what are the issues, problems and challenges. You can never do that externally. (...) People told us they want to get strategic messages directly from the top, to build networks with peers, to get a better understanding of ABB's culture and values, and to get specific tools, ideas, and project management techniques to help them manage better"* (FT.com, 2000b).

Type 4 partnerships

Recently, a considerable number of initiatives involving business schools, media companies, new technology firms, and a legion of other firms has emerged. These complex partnerships and networks operate as for-profit providers of education and are a contemporary response to the opportunities of the learning market, capitalizing on the parties' particular complementing strengths and competences. The division of activities between the parties involved is usually indicated as the division between content, technology, and services.

UNext

A first example is UNext, a privately held company which calls itself 'the internet education company'. UNext is part of Knowledge Universe, a group of more than 40 business firms focussing on e-learning, and was founded in 1996 with initial investments from Larry Ellison (CEO of Oracle) and the investor/philanthropist Michael Milken. The company cooperates with eminent scholars through its online university Cardean University. One of the goals of Cardean University is to engage students in authentic, real-world business scenarios with defined learning outcomes. UNext claims it proprietary technology to provide a unique level of active collaboration among students, and between students and instructors. The pedagogical approach is one of coaching students to realize their own abilities, rather than instructor-centered lectures.

The associated schools with Cardean University are Stanford University, Columbia Business School, University of Chicago Graduate School of Business, Carnegie Mellon University, and London School of Economics and Political Science. The agreement with such renowned schools is an indication of the perceived market potential, though the calibre of these schools did surprise universities:

> *"The implications of the deal have sent a shudder through the business school world at a time when the industry is changing more rapidly than ever before. As with the businesses they educate, business schools are now faced with the need to internationalize, develop strategic alliances and use technology effectively while protecting their intellectual property, the one thing that differentiates them from other business schools"* (FT.com, 1999).

Pensare

Similarly, Pensare – meaning 'to think' in Italian – has partnered up with top-tier universities, professors, business leaders, and recognized industry experts. Pensare also has strategic alliances with a number of academic partners, including Duke University's Fuqua School of Business, University of Pennsylvania's Wharton School, The University of Southern California Annenberg Centre, and Harvard Business School Publishing. In addition, it cooperates with INSEAD Online, the Edvantage Group, a Scandinavian- and UK-based e-learning company, and several management gurus.

At the heart of Pensare's offerings is the concept of learning through the use of communities. Its mission statement says that Pensare's mission is to create corporate knowledge communities using the internet, where content from renowned business and academic thought leaders and internal best practices can be shared to solve critical business problems (Pensare website). In terms of technology, Pensare's Knowledge Community and Pensare's Learning Platform serve to facilitate this knowledge creation and knowledge sharing. It has been Pensare's aim to bring the best courses from the associated schools to one online location, from which companies can pick and choose in order to create their own, customized MBA programme. Business Week reports that it is Pensare's aim to grant 20% to 30% of US MBAs within a period of five years. Students in the 20-month Duke MBA Cross

Continent programme learn through a combination of education via a physical location of a classroom, and via internet. Since Duke has a European campus next to its US campus, Pensare acquired the exclusive distribution rights to the jointly developed curriculum for resale among its corporate customers and other business schools seeking to develop their own degree-granting programmes. As part of this agreement, Pensare will set up the internet-based technology platform, produce the courses in an online format, and provide ongoing support for the programme (op.cit. Byrkjeflot, 2001: 25).

FT Knowledge, Thomson Learning, Docent

FT Knowledge, part of Pearson plc., owner of the Financial Times Group, is one of the world's leading education companies. It has partnered with Cambridge, Wharton, and the University of Michigan Business School, and has reached an agreement with Blackboard, which provides platforms for online courses. FT Knowledge will also provide the content for the new MBA courses for Regent College, that expects to enroll as many as 5,000 new MBA students within five years as a consequence of the deal with FT Knowledge (Byrkjeflot, 2001: 24).

In November 2000, Thomson Learning, a global provider of lifelong learning information with over 5.8 billion US dollar revenues, announced a plan to cooperate with Universitas 21 to develop and deliver online learning materials. Within this partnership, Universitas 21 will award students the qualifications after successful completion of courses. The unique structure of Universitas 21 enables it to take a powerful international brand, credible quality assurance, and multi-jurisdictional certification and add Thomson Learning's expansive content and course development experience. The result is an e-university built in a fraction of the time and cost it would take without a partnership of this magnitude. Bub Cullen, President and CEO of Thomson Learning's international division, says:

> *"The brand recognition, credibility, staff and student body that Universitas brings to the formation of e-university is phenomenal. Together, we can create a high-quality e-learning experience for customers around the world"* (see Universitas 21 website).

Docent, a provider of e-learning infrastructures and services, maintains alliances with over 90 international organizations in a wide range of educational, consulting, and technology specialties. It is the developing company of Docent Enterprise, an internet-based software platform for knowledge sharing and provides full-fledged infrastructures for the development, delivery, management, and measurement of e-learning for employees, customers, partners, and professional communities. To achieve this, it partners, among others, with Accenture, Elsevier Training, FT Knowledge, Harvard Business School Publishing, Microsoft, McGraw-Hill Lifetime Learning, and INSEAD.

PERSPECTIVES ON KNOWLEDGE INSTITUTIONS: CONCEPTS OF UNIVERSITIES AND BUSINESS SCHOOLS

The aforementioned partnership typology is derived from current developments in the field of management education. As the playing field for business schools is evolving, business schools are exploring new models of organization that fit the changing environment by engaging in partnerships and networks. These new models of organization are not only limited to cooperation with other business schools or other content providers, such as media companies, but also stretch out to non-traditional partners. These partnerships and networks including a myriad of partners are evoking a new marketplace, with different dynamics. Actors that were previously operating autonomously with their own specific interest have now become interdependent. Such organizational models are catching on rapidly and clearly present a particular perspective on the organization of business school.

In more general terms, an extensive amount of literature has been developed by now regarding the future of education, ranging from elementary schools to universities and from the changing nature of pedagogy to e-learning applications. Many stereotypes of future educational institutions have been described, of which lately 'electronic versions' of schools have received paramount attention. Particularly cyber-prophets have been hallowing ideas of 'e-schools', 'e-universities', 'cyber-learning', and 'virtual education'. With respect to higher education, this electronic version has been labeled among others as the virtual or digital university, and, as has been indicated by the previous chapter, e-learning. Some predictions read that brick-and-mortar universities will have to make way for their online or virtual equivalents, which are sometimes referred to as clicks-and-mortar institutions. However, a preoccupation with and overemphasis on technological developments and their influence on education enshrouds other important developments within the sector of higher education, such as the extension of higher education's activities into commercial or contract research and consultancy activities, the composition of the marketplace for learning, and partnerships between education and industry.

In the following sections, some of the contemporary issues within higher education (in particular universities and business schools) are being discussed, following some prominent and some of the most eye-catching contributions that can be found in current literature. Consecutively, the concepts of the distributed university/business school, the virtual (distributed) university/business school, The synolic business school, the business school as a learning centre, the hybrid business school, and the networked business school.

The distributed university/business school

The first idea of universities/business school in the network economy presented here, is, in fact, a direct reaction to the glorification of the role of ICT and encompasses a distributed perspective on universities. According to Brown & Duguid (1995) the true value of the university lies in the complex relationship it creates between knowledge, communities, and credentials. Technology, especially ICT, alone cannot meet the demands the future puts upon universities; what is needed, are structural transformations within institutional arrangements. They say:

> *"Of course, communications technology will undoubtedly support and transform many of the interactions of researchers and students, teachers and learners. Moreover, its marginal cost is also much cheaper than the conventional classroom. Undoubtedly, its contribution to the university of the future will be immense. Yet the feasibility and financial viability of technological intervention are, we believe, as much issues for concern as celebration. Implemented without due understanding of the institutional character of educational forms, intervention might only further polarize an already divided system. For instance, rather than disappearing, the conventional campus with all its rich and respected resources could easily become the reserve of those who can afford it. Those who cannot, would be offered the Net as their alternative. And though catalogs might claim that such an education and the degrees granted would be virtually the same, we suspect they would be materially different. The Net degree (...) would almost certainly not command the same respect as its distant campus cousin. In consequence, despite all the claims that the Net is a means to overcome inequality, the already steeply tiered system of higher education would probably become only further divided by the unequal financial resources of its students"* (Brown & Duguid, 1995).

The university's core activities

At the core of the activities that the university as an institution deploys lies the provision of degrees, which, next to traditional status, is the main reason universities have the role and position within society as they do. Though for some education is an end in itself and some have higher aims and goals, a vast majority of students (especially the traditional group of younger students) engages in higher education because that's the only way a degree or diploma is earned. In fact, completing an MBA not seldom means a salary increase from 75 to 150% (see table 6.1).

Return on investment is an important reason to participate in a recognized and highly valued MBA programme. Such learners can be labeled as 'certificate learners'. With such a degree, people can get the jobs, status and salary they are looking for. The different ways these degrees are valued by actors inside and outside the educational system (mis)represent what a university really does. Though as long as the degree represents certain things about the degree holder with reasonable accuracy, it can certainly obscure other (more important) things. Or put differently, next to being a receipt indicating the 'delivery of knowledge' (which in fact is a misrepresentation of how people learn – see Chapter 5) a degree also indicates social experience gained during college years. A mere knowledge-delivery view radically devalues learning and knowledge creation that occurs outside the classroom and beyond the campus. Especially in this knowledge-based society, it is a fallacy that learning ends after a university career. Moreover, from an outsider's point of view, degrees contain a certain amount of intangibility, expressed in, for instance, reputation of the particular educational institution it is received from. Brown & Duguid express this as follows:

> *"Where [employees and clients, for whom most degrees are ultimately earned and with whom they are exchanged for status and income] would scrutinize a delivery rigorously, they rarely look beyond the central letters (B.A., M.Sc., etcetera), the name of a school,*

*and a mumbled 'major'. No inventory is taken of all those classroom hours the degree
(mis)represents. No one outside academia really wants to examine a transcript"*
(Brown & Duguid, 1995).

Business school	Country	Rank	Last year	Salary today ($)	Salary increase (%)	Value for money[a] (rank)	Career progress[b]
Wharton	US	1	2	162,610	225	2.8 (5)	62
Harvard	US	2	1	173,120	216	2.7 (6)	78
Stanford	US	3	3	168,318	206	2.5 (8)	59
Chicago	US	4	6	157,872	245	3 (3)	38
Columbia	US	5	5	157,775	251	2.9 (4)	47
Sloan	US	6	4	149,934	200	2.6 (7)	58
INSEAD	France	7	9	129,272	143	4.1 (1)	55
LBS	UK	8	8	115,577	160	2.4 (9)	50
Kellogg	US	9	7	134,341	192	2.6 (7)	50
Stern	US	10	13	127,255	204	2.5 (8)	44
IMD	Switzerland	11	11	130,367	120	4 (2)	72
Anderson	US	12	14	131,494	184	2.8 (5)	51
Tuck	US	13	15	152,799	209	2.7 (6)	49
Haas	US	14	12	126,780	171	3 (3)	56
Johnson	US	15	10	117,507	197	2.5 (8)	49
Michigan	US	16	16	113,106	171	2.2 (10)	45

[a] The amount earned for every dollar spent on the course.
[b] Reflects the changes in company size in which alumni are employed and the level of seniority achieved three years after graduation.

*Table 6.1. Salary increase with an MBA and other benefits.
Source: FT.com (2001)*

Though of high importance, there is of course more to a university's activities than granting degrees. As indicated in the previous chapter, learning occurs through the (legitimate peripheral) participation and enculturation in different communities. Re-engineering the university system, then, should involve widening the access to communities next to credentials. Universities provide students access to different communities, such as the academic community, the professional community (practice), and the student community. Different kinds of learning take place and a range of experiences is gained. Education socializes students, makes students unreflectively familiar with diverse communities and helps them learn how to learn (ibid.). Especially in case of academic disciplines, which are traditionally separated from each other and not seldom from practice (as opposed to theory), the challenge is to integrate these and offer students holistic and integrated learning processes (cf. Elfring & Van Raaij, 1995). An additional task for universities should be to find ways to address people beyond the conventional degree courses and to open campus communities to participation of 'outsiders', such as alumni, business and local communities. The use of live links, videotapes, email, ftp sites, world wide web documents, and advancing ICT applications should help universities to capture the otherwise transient practices on campus to make them useful in other circumstances. Such learning technologies – though not all designed for educational uses – succeed because they implicitly honor community and conversational paradigms (Brown & Duguid, 1995).

One of the ways to establish an enduring relationship with students is to establish learning contracts to the incoming students. With such a contract, relationships after graduation can be maintained, offering possibilities to offer alumni tailored courses while at the same time the university can expand their financial base and maintain links with expertise from practice. Brown & Duguid see the technological possibilities and the traditional resources of the universities as complements of each other: the challenge is to take advantage of the technologies of the future without losing sight of the resources of the past. The university in the digital age, then should aim for:

1.   Enabling students to engage in open learning, exploration, and knowledge creation;
2.   Simultaneously providing the resources to help them work in both distal and local communities;
3.   Offer them the means to earn exchangeable, equivalent credentials for work done in class, online, or through hands-on experience.

However, in order to achieve this, the university needs to become considerably more flexible than it is today. The authors see a role for a distributed educational system constituted by the separate elements of a degree-granting body, the academic staff/faculty, campus facilities, and students.

The role of degree-granting bodies and faculty
The function of granting degrees can be picked up by degree-granting bodies (DGBs). These bodies would function primarily as administrative bodies. They would receive their own degree-granting credentials from exactly those bodies that assess universities now and would compete for students and faculty, just as universities do now. DGBs would vary in size and set degree requirements and core courses as they see fit. Depending on the outcome of these options, their degrees would gain recognition, reputation, status, and exchange value.

Faculty can develop into becoming independent contractors, having to find (one or several) DGBs to sanction their teaching. Scholars could, in this system, contract individually or in teams, but wouldn't have to assemble in one place. Fees could vary, depending on the type of teaching offered and the reputation of the instructor. DGBs might pay a per capita fee to reward a teacher's ability to attract high-quality students to the DGB. Research, additionally, might be administered by a DGB, or staffed and funded separately.

For both teaching and research, faculty could find their own facilities. Such facilities could look very much like today's campus, but yet be quite independent of either the

DGB or the faculty. The quality of the facilities would be an element on which competition for faculty and students would be based. Both faculty and students using a particular facility might come from several DGBs and the constitution of the faculty would become a regional magnet for both staff and students. DGBs, faculty, and students might not use campus facilities at all, though, given the need for socialization, most DGBs and many faculty might insist that as part if their degree, candidates spend a set amount of time on campus in groups rather than online individually.

Students are confronted with a dramatic increase in choices if the university is broken up into different parts. Choices could depend on the reputation of the faculty, or the relative amount of time required to be on campus instead of learning through online facilities. Learners might choose a DGB whose degree in an area of interest is known to have a particularly high exchange value., or, for instance, one that was prepared to validate certain kinds of in-work experience. A distributed university system might allow much greater flexibility for local sites of professional excellence, like research centres, law firms, or hospitals. "Essentially", Brown & Duguid say, "a student's university career would not be through a particular place, time, or preselected body of academics, but, rather like the their current explorations of the Net, through a network of their own making, yet endorsed by the DGB and its faculty. A student could stay home or travel, mix online and off-line education, work in classes or with mentors, and take their own time" (Brown & Duguid, 1995).

The virtual university/business school

One of the hallmarks of techno-enthusiasts with regard to higher education has been the development of a true virtual university or business school. The concept of a virtual university is seen as the ultimate techno-organizational form of higher education, based on technological networks. This virtuality means that the university doesn't exist in the physical reality, but that it exists only in cyberspace. With both proponents and adversaries, the virtual university has given rise to a fierce debate. Cunningham et al. say in this respect:

> *"Picture a future in which students never meet a lecturer face-to-face in a classroom, never physically visit the on-campus library; in fact, never set foot on the campus or into an institutional lecture-room or learning centre. Such is the future proposed by the virtual university"* (Cunningham et al., 1998: 179).

Such a description opens the discussion of the (societal and social) roles universities fulfill and the value universities add to the development of individuals (see the previous section). According to Newman & Johnson (1999), the vision of the virtualization of universities is based on a naïve sociology, which ignores the role of apprenticeship and implicit craft knowledge in the generation of technical progress and scientific discovery (ibid., p. 80) and the role face-to-face interaction, group dynamics and socialization processes play in the development process of students.

Bricks or clicks
Though the idea of a virtual university has already tempted several authors to predict the death of the regular, i.e., physical or campus-based, university, it still seems more of a illusion for now than it has proven to be a reality. In addition, many authors doubt if such a virtual university is desirable, or even achievable. There are, indeed, some institutions of higher education that appeal to the concept of a 'clicks-and-mortar' – as opposed to a 'bricks-and-mortar' – university, although they aren't in fact fully virtual. The Open University in the United Kingdom, for example, provides a good deal of education through ICT, but complements this with regionally-based classroom instruction. The University of Phoenix also combines online and on-campus education, respectively attracting 9,500 and 65,000 students. Some traditional universities, among which are some of the world's most prestigious, like Duke University (business), the University of California at Berkeley, the University of California at Los Angeles (through UCLA's Extension), and the University of Washington (Uwired programme) have followed a similar path (Dumort, 2000: 548-549). Additionally, several new commercial enterprises have spawned, cooperating with world-class universities. The UNext company and its for-profit subsidiary Cardean University bring together the University of Chicago, Columbia University, Stanford University, Carnegie Mellon, and the London School of Economics and Political Sciences. Looking at the homepages of UNext (http://www.unext.com) and Cardean University (http://www.cardean.edu), it becomes clear that UNext wants to become the premier knowledge studio dedicated to creating and delivering educational products over the internet, while Cardean University offers advanced business courses to companies around the globe. Curriculum and course content are developed through the mobilization of senior faculty members of the affiliated schools, who are selected and compensated by their schools. The universities receive substantial up-front payments, plus a percentage of profits made, in return. Recent articles report that Columbia, which was the first university to sign with UNext/Cardean, receives 5% of profits, in cash or in UNext stock, with a minimum payback of 20 million US dollar in the next five years (McGeehan (2000), op.cit. Baer (2000: 465)).

As Baer notes, the instructional model used by Cardean University is of a different nature compared to those used in academic distance learning in its use of faculty, its cost, and projected scale. In order to develop a wholly new business curriculum that is fine-tuned for delivery via internet to an audience of experienced executives and managers, Cardean expects to invest 1 million US dollar per course. Next to the course development by senior staff from the affiliated universities, Cardean staff, among which instructional designers, support development of courses. Then, instruction will be performed by separate teaching faculty who are Cardean employees and adjuncts. Meanwhile, IBM is under contract to develop a highly interactive internet-based platform for course delivery. Courses will be marketed under the name of Cardean and not in the names of affiliated universities. For now, Cardean will provide individual courses and non-degree 'course clusters' to its corporate customers, but UNext and Cardean clearly intend to offer an accredited Cardean MBA and perhaps other degrees in the future (taken from Baer, 2000: 466).

Cardean University, just as the Pensare initiative, which includes Columbia Business School, Stanford, University of Chicago Graduate School of Business, Carnegie Mellon, and the London School of Economics and Political Science, is one of the contemporary exhibits of 21st century management education. However, not all virtual endeavors have been successful, as is shown by the California Virtual University, which in fact offers little more than being a website (see California Virtual University website).

Models of virtualization
Harris (2000) distinguishes four models of virtualization, namely the learning utility, the networked bureaucracy, the insular model, and the interstitial model. A university that operates as a learning utility can be characterized as a provider of low-cost and mass-customized vocational training material. In its goal to maximizing student numbers it relies heavily on the remote delivery and assessment of teaching material. Within the model of a networked bureaucracy a broader spectrum of teaching modes is adopted; the commitment to reaching large numbers of students is balanced with the need to maintain tutorial support. The Open University, for instance, is committed to using ICT to enhance 'learning' productivity, says Daniel (1996), but it combines this with a strong academic ethos and commitment to research embodied in its faculty. The Open University continues to operate according to many norms and structures of a conventional university, but combines this with advanced learning technologies and strategic alliances. The insular model of virtualization can operate in ways that circumvent questions of productivity and new learning technologies. Following such an insular path would presumably require a highly differentiated, high-cost position in the market. This model usually applies to institutions that teach very small numbers of students. The interstitial model combines selective investment in new media and/or information networks with traditional methods and is likely to be adopted by many more conventional institutions. These universities will typically seek to combine the economies of scale and flexibility offered by ICT with a low-risk approach to investments and online learning. "This strategic 'hedging' (which has also been observed by Sabel (1991)), produces a very diverse mix of options in combining traditional methods with remote access" (op. cit. Harris, 2000: 587-588).

Sir John S. Daniel, vice-chancellor of the Open University in the United Kingdom, speaks of mass distance education in terms of mega-universities. A mega-university is defined as a distance-teaching institution with over 100,000 active students in degree-level courses (Daniel, 1996: 29). The one common feature of mega-universities is that they promote distance and open learning. The term 'open', then, refers to the aim of opening access to higher education, rather than just one of the means it would use (broadcasting) (ibid., p. 31). Mega-universities have, in the course of time, managed to realize a cost-effective way of providing education. For instance, a government review of the UK's Open University in 1991 compared its costs per graduate with those of three other institutions. It appeared that the Open University's costs were significantly lower: between 39% and 47% of the other universities' costs for ordinary degrees, and between 55% and 80% for honors degrees (see Daniel, 1996).

The distributed virtual university

Recently, the concept of a distributed virtual university has been coined by Van der Perre, Roosendaal & Van den Branden (2000). Within the idea of the distributed virtual university, the use of ICT is of central importance to its functioning not only in the sense of providing education through ICT, but also to establish networking between participating universities that initiate activities together. Hence, the distributed virtual university integrates the functions of a technological network and an academic network (cf. Universitas 21). The distributed virtual university has some particular advantages over other virtual forms of education, related to costs, educational richness, access, critical mass, lifelong learning, interoperability, accreditation, research, and quality:

–   *Costs*
    In the creation of a global campus, some of the costs can be shared (e.g., the development of the virtual campus platform, the development of joint programmes and courses, the provision of teacher training in the effective use of information and communication technologies). Other costs can be reduced (e.g., by bundling the request of various partners into one block while negotiating with providers about cheaper and to the educational needs tailored services). The creation of a database for reusable learning and teaching materials will get a far greater number of entries, and its maintenance may become more cost-effectiveness by sharing costs and income;

–   *Educational richness*
    The development of joint courses provides an international dimension and richness that supports the globalization of education and life. Students within each partner university can be provided with a more attractive offer, by extending the own programmes and courses with elements that are only available in partner universities;

–   *Access*
    Certainly at post-graduate level, it is a competitive advantage to offer students the possibility to get direct access – be it virtually – to top experts in other European universities, knowing that they can be considered and approached within the partnership as own professors;

–   *Critical mass*
    For highly-specialized courses, such as Ph.D. courses, the distributed environment can provide the critical mass both at the level of availability of

expertise for development and at the level of availability of participating students, to create a cost-effective production;

–   *Lifelong learning*
    The partnership can act as a broker to the outside world, through the provision of a common online directory, thus providing each participating university with a continuing education and lifelong learning offer that is more extended and shortens the time to market;

–   *Interoperability*
    A partnership can act as a more effective pressure group to realize interoperability of equipment and platforms and the creation of standards;

–   *Joint research*
    Where pedagogy of ICT-based education and training is still largely missing, well-balanced joint research may lead to faster and better results;

–   *Cross-accreditation*
    A firm partnership is also an effective instrument to realize cross-accreditation of programmes and courses, and may thus support a real and realistic European credit transfer system;

–   *Quality*
    Although complementarity between partners is the first focus, a sound competition that unavoidably accompanies it can boost quality within each partner institution.

The distributed virtual university has several limitations, however. First, it can suffer from the disadvantage from a loss of control, due to the existing independence of the individual institutions. Secondly, a distributed environment is synonymous with a decreased visibility of the individual partners. This may prevent prominent and internationally recognized institutions from participating in a distributed virtual university.

INTERMEZZO 2

The critics: Noble's crusade

There have been numerous critics on the concept of the virtual university regarding the prominent role and place techno-enthusiasts see for technology while seemingly ignoring the social element involved in educational change, and the role of commercial providers and interference of industry with education. One of the most prominent critics – who, in turn, has encountered a lot of criticism himself – is

David Noble, who agitates against the high-tech commercialization of higher education.

For Noble, the increasing integration of technology in the classroom equals a veiled integration of commercial stakes into educational institutions. "[U]niversities", he says, "are not simply undergoing a technological transformation. Beneath that change, and camouflaged by it, lies another: the commercialization of higher education. For here as elsewhere technology is but a vehicle and a disarming disguise" (Noble, 1998). Higher education has over time evolved from an institution in which knowledge was accumulated for general societal purposes (or be viewed of as an end in itself) to centres of knowledge capital. Those who think they can benefit from this knowledge have capitalized upon higher education and exploited it for commercial purposes – universities, confronted with budget cuts, not in the last place.

According to Noble, two phases of this change can be distinguished, namely the commoditization of the university's research function at the expense of its educational function, and, secondly, mainly as a response to the first transformation, the commoditization of instruction. The point raised by Noble, then, is that this second transformation of higher education is not the work of students or teachers, but is induced by market forces. Education, after all, is the single booming market of the 21st century. Commercial content, technology, and service providers are eager to capture a part of this market, while higher education, in turn, is also engaging in software and content development to reap the benefits of their current knowledge potential.

This commoditization of higher education has two important implications. First, there is the role for the university as a market for these commodities. The first implication raises traditional labor issues about the introduction of new technologies of production for the faculty, while the second raises major questions about costs, coercion, privacy, equity, and the quality of education for students (Noble, 1998). Concerning the first implication, teachers as labor are drawn into a production process that is designed for the efficient creation of instructional commodities. Not only will their activities be restructured in their nature, but their autonomy, their independence, and their control over their work will be reduced and be conversed into the hands of the administration, Noble argues. At the same time, working times and intensification of work will be extended with the use of technology. Additionally, the university's administration will claim the ownership of online course material allowing to hire less skilled and cheaper workers to deliver the technologically prepackaged course (ibid.). In the long run, Noble warns, faculty will become redundant:

"Some skeptical faculty insist that what they do cannot possible be automated, and they are right. But it will be automated anyway, whatever the loss in educational quality. Because education (...) is not what all this is about; it's about making money. In short, the new technology of education, like the automation of other industries, robs faculty of their knowledge and skills, their control over their working lives, the product of their labor, and, ultimately, their means of livelihood" (Noble, 1998).

Regarding implications for students, the market-like and product-like characteristics of education brings up new issues. First of all, there's the issue of affordability of education, which may become more capital-intensive through investments in ICT and underlying for-profit motives. Secondly, there's the issue of product and market development. While students are studying through technology, technology is studying them., collecting data regarding their learning process and experiences, in order to enhance product quality. Such an issue places question marks with privacy issues and tuition fees: who should pay whom?

There are major stakes at play concerning the future of higher education, since it has become and is increasingly becoming big business. A critic like the historian David Noble paints a bleak picture of current and future developments, but he raises some interesting and intriguing points. But are these points realistic? Will higher education – in particular face-to-face instruction – become for the elite again? To a certain extent his point are indeed realistic, we would say. Education *is* big business, and commercial interests, both from the perspective of business and higher education, *are* present. Moreover, Nobles points aren't just pure speculations; most of his argument is underpinned with real-life practices within the sector of higher education. In Canada, for instance, universities have been given royalty free licenses to Virtual U software, an educational software platform directed by an industrial consortium, in return for providing data on its use to the vendors. UCLA's WEB-CT software also allows for tracking, storage, and retrieval of online student activities.

But Noble, too, has received a lot of criticism on his 'cry for reflection' on the automation and commercialization of higher education. Brad DeLong (1998), professor of economics at U.C. Berkeley, for example, sees Nobles argument as being a contemporary equivalent for earlier critics' arguments against the printing press. He argues that books are sold by (online) multinational conglomerates for a fraction of the price that a student would have to pay for personal lessons from the author or professors. Moreover, books are complements to instead of substitutes for personal engagement, lecture-discussion-and-office-hours part of higher education.

White (1999) accuses Noble of being very ill-informed on ICT applications and says his manifest is saturated with an anti-technology attitude. He says:

"Noble is right to oppose university administrators and their profit-motivated corporate partners in their plots to use technology to control higher education. This top-down process to change is deservedly doomed to failure (...). Unfortunately, rather than focusing his attack on the process, [Noble] is unable to control his strong anti-technology bias and risks losing the support of those he needs most – faculty and students – with indefensible attacks on the technologies of distributed learning and instruction" (White, 1999).

The Synolic Business School (the challenge of double integration)

As was indicated by Chapter 4, management education has undergone some rigorous critiques and subsequent changes over the years. Van Baalen & Leijnse (1995) use the term 'the synolic business school' to characterize the revised school for business and management education. This revision has been induced by the introduction and development of interdisciplinary action-oriented pedagogical approaches and new methodologies which forces to rethink the institutional structures of business schools and universities in general (ibid., p. 21). The term synolic, derived from the Greek word 'synolos' and meaning complete or all together, refers to a comprehensive design of business schools. Van Baalen & Leijnse put it as follows:

> *"The synolic business school has a clearly stated mission and a faculty committed to interdisciplinarity and is combining different, interdependent pedagogical and research objectives: interdisciplinarity, life-long learning, and learning alliances. Achieving these goals stresses the importance of institutional integration in two directions, vertical and horizontal (Knapper & Cropley, 1985). The former refers to the organization and co-ordination of the different business programs at different levels. The latter refers to linking the school to other learning settings, especially to work"* (Van Baalen & Leijnse, 1995: 21).

They continue:

> *"The educational goal of the synolic business school is to create an interdisciplinary attitude and to equip the students with an adequate methodology and skills for their future action-oriented research. (...) The function of interdisciplinary, pre-experience business education within this comprehensive system is to provide the students with a sound educational basis for a life-long learning process in business"* (Van Baalen & Leijnse, 1995: 22-23).

The issue of interdisciplinarity can be viewed of in different ways. First of all, it refers to interdisciplinarity within the management curriculum, meaning developing courses leaning on the integration of knowledge from different scientific areas or disciplines. Secondly, interdisciplinarity with respect to management education refers to the integration of academia (theory) and business/industry (practice) (cf. network learning in Chapter 5). Elfring & Van Raaij call the pursuit of combining both modes of interdisciplinarity the challenge of double integration. "In order for management research to remain relevant", they say, "a more dynamic approach to research is needed. The business environment is changing and boundaries become more fuzzy between formerly separate entities such as disciplines, nations, private/public, between and within organizations. Management science should mirror these fuzzy boundaries, not with fuzzy approaches but with an integrated problem-oriented approach related to (...) both monodisciplines and the practice of management" (1995: 32).

The business school as a learning centre

The concept of business schools as learning centres has already been mentioned in the previous chapter. In this paragraph, it will be elaborated as a vision on the future of business schools.

The idea of the business school as a learning centre capitalizes on a range of contemporary environmental developments facing management education and management development. These developments include changing needs and wants of learners, new providers entering the marketplace for education, changing learning methods and increasing cooperation between industry and academia.

A 1993 market survey conducted by Ashridge Management College on trends in learning preferences in executive education clearly shows a shift from structured expert courses delivered by experts or gurus in management to the need for courses that are tailored to specific individual and organizational learning needs. This shift can be derived from the results from this survey, which are depicted in table 6.2.

From the percentages corresponding with these three types of course delivery, it seems that all types bargain on future demand, though a clear development towards a Type 3 mode of delivery can be distinguished. As a starting point, there will be an assessment of individual performance and behavior, combined with an analysis of the culture of the organization in question. The preferred outcome is usually continuous development underpinned by action planning and follow-up activities (Torino Group, 1998: 74).

Percentage of respondents saying	Type 1 Structured expert courses	Type 2 Interactive courses	Type 3 Courses tailored to individual learning needs
More use	13	29	51
Same use	40	52	25
Less use	30	15	6
No use	16	5	18
	Fits current policy *Leading edge thinking* *Best experts*	*Participation/projects* *Balance of learning* *methods* *Interactive*	*Individual assessment* *Small groups* *Follow-ups*
	Academically driven *business school*	*Development centres* *Consultants*	*Centres of learning*

Table 6.2. Trends in learning preferences.
Source: Torino Group (1998: 75)

In general, business schools are organized by the underlying principles of a type 1 mode of delivery, i.e., driven by an academic culture. Realizing a transformation to becoming centres of learning will, then, be the primary challenge for business schools.[1]

---

[1] As the Torino Group notes: "The danger that confronts both schools and their clients which embark upon this path is that they can become-side-tracked by the latest management fads promoted by gurus and consultants. In 'Management redeemed: debunking the fads that undermine our corporations', Hilmer & Donaldson (1996) argue that such fads lead managers to 'false trails', where their usefulness is taken on

The profile of such learning centres depends on the impact of the aforementioned developments in general and on rethinking the role management education and management development play in the business sector in particular. This changing role can be characterized by a shift (1) from imparting functional knowledge to supporting integrative learning, (2) from explaining generalized concepts and theories to designing individually and organizationally tailored approaches, and (3) from a focus on initial career education delivered by remote and controlling providers to a continuous involvement in lifelong learning through the development of partnerships. Underpinning themes and an indication of the range of services would include the following (ibid., pp. 77-78):

–   Such centres will start by enabling individuals and organizations to 'unlearn' outdated approaches to management, while also acquiring a deeper understanding of the ways in which new learning can be undertaken;

–   They will incorporate extensive diagnostic and counseling tools and techniques, providing subsequent access to a comprehensive portfolio of learning resources, making wide use of educational technology in addition to faculty and classrooms;

–   Rather than being viewed as a physical entity to which infrequent visits are paid, the centres will act as a focus for continuous learning through networking, benchmarking, and identification of best practice. The experience of executives from the public and private sectors will be harnessed through encouraging them to act as coaches and mentors, while a multicultural and global outlook will be inherent in the way such centres think and operate;

–   The development of long-term learning partnerships with clients will demand a relationship marketing approach, which will require the faculty to become client and project managers as well as learning facilitators. A recognition that no single provider can be expected to be 'world class' in every aspect of this wide array of resources and services will lead to collaborative working, not only between business schools but also with some of the newer market entrants.

The future facing business schools, thus, poses challenges on the dimension of the interface with the client (the business school as a distance supplier or as an integrated partner) and on the dimension of the types of services offered (the

---

trust, their implementation assumed to be easy and effective, and their attractiveness undermines rational thinking. They refer to this as 'instant coffee' management, and plead for the replacement of such faddism with the 'thinking organization' which understands that competitive advantage stems from the development of critical thinking skills in all managers. Most recently, the wide-spread adoption of business process re-engineering to restructure and de-layer organizations is an example of the way in which a management technique can be pursued with almost religious zeal" (Torino Group, 1998: 76).

business school as a supplier of a structured, packaged product or as a development-based change facilitator of management education and management development). This is depicted in figure 6.4.

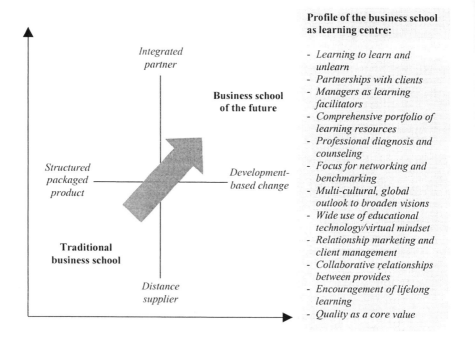

Figure 6.4. Transformation of business schools and a profile of new learning centres. Source: Torino Group (1998: 78 and 80)

The Hybrid Business School

The idea of the Hybrid Business School, as developed by Baets & Van der Linden (2000), capitalizes on the different demands the business and educational environment put on organizations and the social, economic, and technological developments that are taking place in the network economy. It can be seen as a corporate learning strategy using elements from business school organization. As such, the Hybrid Business School is characterized by a constructivist, learner-centered approach, a continuous or lifelong learning premise, new managerial paradigms, competencies and skills, learning communities, an integrated view on working and learning, and advanced technological learning arrangements. Considering the integration of technology in learning, the Hybrid Business School goes beyond the mere delivery of information through a technological infrastructure and modes of distance and online education that are displayed by a considerable number of educational institutions nowadays. In fact, the Hybrid Business School aims to integrate virtual education and knowledge management within organization in order to bring learning closer to corporate practice. It therefore combines the value and opportunity of sharing tacit knowledge, while at the same time using the potential of explicit knowledge, and the offering of personalized, practice-oriented, and continuous education. Examples of the usage of advanced technological learning applications within the Hybrid Business School include knowledge management technologies, like case-based reasoning systems, group decision support systems, and artificial neural networks. Learning through these technologies complements face-to-face communication, which ideally should take place by means of creating dialogue instead of lectures.

The mode of organization of the Hybrid Business School strongly resembles a network approach. Within this network business and business schools cooperate through the development of management knowledge (albeit it 'general' management knowledge or company-specific management knowledge), the development and implementation of integrated knowledge networks, and the development and implementation of learning platforms. As Baets & Van der Linden argue:

> *"Ideally, business schools and companies should cooperate in the implementation of the overall concept of virtual education and knowledge management. The more closely the basis of management education and the knowledge base of a company are linked, the more added value it will have for a company. Business schools must therefore organize their courses differently by feeding into knowledge networks"* (Baets & Van der Linden, 2000: 68).

The Hybrid Business School should be balanced on two dimensions, namely the delivery dimension and the content-driven dimension. The delivery dimension relates to the ICT infrastructure upon which courses are built as well as to the pedagogical strategies that underpin the learning processes of the individual learners. Concerning the technological applications, there's a range of technologies to be deployed, ranging from distance learning delivery systems to technologies that facilitate interactive communication and cooperation between learners. The pedagogical principles are based on a constructivist learning design, putting responsibility for learning with the learner himself and stimulating collaborative efforts and interactive knowledge creation and diffusion. The pedagogical material is organized in order to accommodate virtual or hypertext learning platforms and can be divided into three categories consisting of:

1. A concept/principle library;
2. A case/illustration library;
3. An activity learning set.

The concept/principle library accounts for the absorption of subject matter and, hence, functions as a learning base for content. This absorption is the minimal requirement for the learner's knowledge level. The function of the case/illustration library is to offer more than anecdotal information, and to provide a more profound conceptual understanding by showing how concepts were applied (know-how) as well as the underlying logic (know-why). Each case, then, illustrates an in-depth description to capture the underlying aspects of a certain strategy, decision, policy.

or process. Through the use of a case-based reasoning system, learners/workers can consult a database to search for comparable cases, which not only account for a practical reference set, but also stimulating analytical skills. The activity learning set consists of tools, applications, and exercises to involve learners actively in the learning process. Within this learning process the learner is enabled to translate a managerial phenomenon to a conceptual level, come to an understanding by continuous questioning, and to translate this understanding again to the current practical corporate situation (ibid., p. 145). Action learning, critical reflection, conversation, and the participation in communities of practice are crucial elements in this learning context. A typical learning environment within the concept of the Hybrid Business School should include (ibid., p. 146):

–   Schedules (guidelines, monitoring);
–   A media centre or resources with hypertext links to managerial concepts, case/illustrations, and managerial skills or competencies;
–   A course room for discussions, debating, and the formation of a knowledge-web;
–   Video-conferencing facilities;
–   Participant profiles (in order to facilitate the formation of dynamic networks or communities).

THE NETWORKED BUSINESS SCHOOL

In Chapter 3 the concept of the network organization has been expounded and it became clear that network organization has a lot to offer to organizations trying to survive in the 21st century's competitive landscape. Perhaps it can be seen of as *the* mode of organizing viable today, capitalizing on some of the most prominent features of today's economy and reflecting the fundamental structure of the network economy. Among these prominent features were the importance of information and knowledge, and the economic drift towards the globalization of economic activity. The decomposing of value chains, primarily invoked by the possibilities of technological network architectures, has led to the disintegration of traditional firm structures, such as divisional, multifunctional, matrix, or network organization.

Within the network, that is composed of different complementing and sometimes competing nodes, it is the knowledge and the maintenance of relationships that functions as the glue holding the network together. Therefore, it is the management of the network, characterized by the management of knowledge, relationships, and trust, that is of paramount importance to effectively exploit the advantages the network structure offers. Above all, it offers organizational flexibility by enabling organizations to deploy different resources, residing in different locations (nodes) in the network, when and where necessary. The prerequisite organizational arrangements for realizing a network structure in the organization of business schools require a shift in the thinking of the organization of education: it should be realized that educational institutions consist of different, clearly distinguishable, elements that serve different (societal) functions. The networked business school, therefore, partly reflects the idea of a distributed university/business school. However, the networked business school takes this distributed view considerably further.

Essentially, what lies at the core of the networked business school, is a combination or constellation of nodes that perform different roles in the network. The network, here, can be defined as the network that includes the relevant actors or nodes that should be included for delivering management education. In this sense, the networked business school, like the distributed university/business school, is of a virtual nature: virtual not in technological sense, but in a way that the different functions or elements constituting the business school have no single location in which the different functions or elements are brought together physically. Instead of a physical presence, it exists in one's mind or in concept. Its outcome, of course, can be physically observed; hence, it's the specific organizational arrangements behind its functions that differentiate the networked business school from other business schools. This, however, is exactly what a network is actually all about and is precisely what gives the network organization its competitive advantage.

Tasks and objectives

One particular task of the networked business school is that it participates actively in various networks, creating a myriad of communities that are of interest to the business school's stakeholders. It engages in a Mode 2 production of knowledge, thereby transcending the traditional presumptions and boundaries of Mode 1 knowledge production (see Chapter 4). As important as this is to higher education in general, it's even more important for educators in the field of management education. One thing that has become clear throughout the history of management education is that it is crucial from the perspective of developing or educating managers to achieve a combination of decontextualized (theory) and contextualized learning environments (practice, skills, experience). Business schools have been criticized in the past for providing management education that can be characterized as being too much influenced by a focus on just one of these extremes (too scientifically, too practice-oriented) instead of integrating these perspectives. Through a strategy of making the business school more permeable, or opening it up to the external environment, by engaging in partnerships and networks of business schools, industry and other parties, and by continuously facilitating the creation of communities, the networked business school aims at achieving the right balance and opportunities for a range of different learners.

Networking, hence, means contacting and contracting with different parties that have been identified as relevant from the objectives the business school aims to achieve. These objectives include the provision of management education

1.   through open, interactive, explorative, and mainly constructivist learning environments;

2.   in which management knowledge, skills, and experiences are continuously generated and reflected on by engaging in and coupling different contexts;
3.   in which learners primarily have the responsibility of their own learning process and progress while at the same time guided by a coach on the sideline;
4.   in which learning through the participation in different communities is stimulated and underpinned by the assumption that participation of different actors and networks (Mode 2 production of knowledge) is an essential condition for management learning;
5.   and which is facilitated by a broad resource base consisting of both traditional business school resources, primarily regarding physical off-line facilities, and new learning technologies.

In addition, and following Brown & Duguid's vision of the distributed university (1995) and Van der Perre, Roosendaal & Van den Branden's concept of the distributed virtual university (2000), the networked business school should offer learners the means to earn exchangeable degrees for work done in class, online, and through hands-on experiences (work). Degree-granting can be picked up by one or more independent supra-network organizations, who individually value different aspects in management education and business school curricula. For instance, some specific degree-granting bodies will emphasize the amount of practice-oriented and experiential modules in the curriculum, while others will grant degrees using criteria like the academic or scientific quality of the curriculum. A distinction between degree-granting organizations can also emerge on the basis of the difference between pre- and post-experience training, while they can also differentiate themselves on the basis of image and reputation. Another possibility, which in fact resembles current practice, is that individual business schools, conglomerates of business schools (e.g., CEMS), and conglomerates of business schools, media companies, consulting firms and other parties (e.g., UNext and Pensare) will grant degrees. However, contemporary examples of such cooperative practices, the internationalization of education, and the convergence in education expressed by the bachelor/master structure all indicate that the issue of branding will become an eminent feature of certification. Hence, degree-granting will become increasingly a function of degree-branding. The value of the degree, then, will be established by the reputation of the business schools and industrial partners involved in the network, as well as the quality of the curriculum and the management of the network. Within the idea of the networked business school, value-added is defined according to network economy standards.

Organizational structure

The question now is: how will the networked business school be organized? As is the case with a true network, the different functions within a business school (e.g., different types of education, research activities, consultancy activities, alumni policy, and business contacts), individually, are organized by means of a network logic, while at the same time the different functions, mutually, are organized through network logic. The business school as a whole is managed as a part of different networks itself.

This network organization enables the business school to engage in Mode 2 knowledge production. As has been illustrated in Chapter 4, Mode 2 knowledge production entails knowledge production in the context of application, transdisciplinarity, heterogeneity, organizational diversity, social accountability, reflexivity, and quality control organized on a fundamental different basis than was the case in Mode 1. It takes a strategy of partnerships and co-development to realize a true Mode 2 type of knowledge production. The networked business school offers its students a flexible curriculum, which can be organized by the preferences and standards of students themselves, relating to both subject matter and institution. The nature and academic level of the curriculum, in the end, determine the specific value of the diploma, which can be underpinned by an orientation on theory, practice, or both.

Looking at the different tasks and objectives of the networked business school, it becomes clear that organizing the networked business school is not a clear-cut and a rather complex task. For example, it depends on the number and the nature of the stakeholders (those who are affected by or have an interest in the activities and existence) of the business school. The identification process of stakeholders can differ from school to school, and different ranks can be assigned to different stakeholders by different schools (even by different parts within the same business school). Organizing the business school in a way that enables adequate management of different sets of stakeholders, then, becomes a complex task. Taking into account contemporary business school strategies directing towards quite extensive cooperative ventures with different parties, illustrates this all the more. When transcending traditional borders and operating within different interfaces and varying contexts, organizing for coping with resource dependency and managing relationships of interdependency become one of the most challenging tasks for business schools. In more general terms, this means that business schools should have a conception of what is important from a strategic point of view and develop a clear vision on the role of the institution within society as a whole, within its relevant networks, and the role it plays for its students in particular.

The networked business school should also organize for learning or, rather, organize for ensuring an appropriate learning process for students. Again, looking at the networked business school's tasks and objectives, this means organizing and managing across old-fashioned boundaries of discipline, both within the business school itself, as well as relating to its external boundaries. From the perspective of learning, the business school should strongly stimulate autonomous learning (i.e., a sideline or coaching role for the teacher), peer-to-peer learning, team-based learning, experiential learning, and learning through the use of technology. One important way to do this is to accommodate the management learning environment with an advanced ICT infrastructure, on which different technological applications can be operated. Examples of these applications are content resources, exploration- and experience-based learning (like simulations and games), community-based learning technologies, and applications that allow for contact between students and faculty as well as interaction among students. Such a technology-enabled management learning environment based on educational principles of constructivism requires a different mindset of business schools, its management, and its faculty. Regarding models of virtualization of learning, the networked business school deploys a hybrid form of virtualization, allowing for different objectives to be met. This means that this hybrid model integrates elements of the different virtualization models (the learning utility, the networked bureaucracy, the insular model, and the interstitial model as defined by Harris (2000), see earlier this chapter) into one flexible model of virtualization. Consequently, the networked business school is able to deliver low-cost, mass-customized courses for large numbers of students, while at the same time it commits to principles of personalization, differentiation, and blended learning in its offerings, enabling low-scale and high-cost provision of education for particular markets, too.

In addition, the networked business school should be equipped for the demands and challenges of today's learning society. The networked business school, therefore should tool up itself for different kinds of learners (like pre-experience learners, post-experience learners, executive learners, and recreational learners) and an attitude of continuous learning, meaning different kinds of learners (including alumni) returning to the business school for advanced or different management courses.

Speaking in terms of managerial roles regarding the organization of the networked business school, all three network brokering roles (architect, lead operator, caretaker) are applicable, individually or integrally. These business school network managers operate throughout the network, identifying, selecting, assembling, and combining resources from varied sources that are located within the network for the purpose of the benefit of the network as a whole. Network managers 'wander' through the business school network, allocating the needed resources, originating from different relevant actors as identified by the business school, wherever and wherever needed.

It should be noted that, though there is a prototypical or idealtypical concept of the (full-fledged) networked business school, different kinds of networked business schools can emerge. Alternative organizational structures can exist varying with the scale, scope, focus, and objectives of business school activities. For example, a networked business school can be characterized as being primarily an academic network, engaging in networks with fellow (academically grounded) business schools and universities. Other examples concern the networked business school engaging mainly in facilitative partnerships with corporations in order to develop corporate universities or partnering with technology and content providers in order to create (partly) online MBA courses.

CASE STUDY OF THE NETWORKED BUSINESS SCHOOL: IMD LAUSANNE

About IMD

In January 1990, the International Institute for Management Development (IMD) was formed as the result of a merger of two renowned international management education centers, which were once created by Alcan (IMI Geneva) and Nestlé (IMEDE Lausanne). Its core business is developing the leadership capabilities of international business executives at every stage of their careers. For 95%, IMD's market consists of executive development, while MBA programmes constitute only as much as 5%.

Today, it is one of the world's leading business schools. Both in 2000 and 2001, IMD ranked 11th in the Financial Times MBA ranking, as the third best overall European business school following INSEAD (7th) and London Business School (8th). The next European Business School, IESE, ranked 24th. Within the Financial Times ranking, IMD appeared to be the highest ranked 'small' MBA programme (IMD does not have a Ph.D. programme) worldwide. The Financial Times granted IMD a third place worldwide in its Global Ranking of Executive Development, a first place in Europe for open-enrollment programs.

IMD has a very strong international focus: every year, some 5,500 executives, representing over 70 nationalities participate in IMD's Executive Development Programs and company-specific Partnership Programs. In addition, IMD's alumni network consists of over 45,000 alumni from 140 countries worldwide and 39 alumni clubs in 30 countries. The international factor also reveals itself by the international nature of the faculty composition, including 19 different nationalities. The Financial Times ranked IMD 1st worldwide on the set of criteria used to assess which school was the most 'international': IMD ranked 1st on international composition of its students, international composition of its faculty, international composition of its board, and international mobility of its graduates.

Many of the 54 full-time IMD faculty members, all professors, are recognized world authorities in their fields. They divide their time between teaching, carrying out research and acting as consultants to major companies in many industries, ensuring they remain on top of the latest developments in managerial practice. Drawing on these experiences, IMD's faculty aims at creating a particularly effective learning environment that is highly conducive to tackling critical issues facing businesses today.

IMD offers a range of management programs, which can be classified over a number of dimensions, like management level, stretch of programme time (for instance ranging from several days up to 16 months), and degree/non-degree programmes. An overview of IMD's offerings regarding open programmes is given in table 6.3.

Open programme	Description	Consisting of
Top Management Forums	An exclusive feature of the IMD portfolio – a series of short and intensive programmes bringing together executives at the very senior level of management. They come from widely different industries but have similar responsibilities and face similar issues	International Programme for Board Members Senior Executive Forum
General Management	Rigorous and comprehensive programmes that represent a major learning investment by the participants and their companies. They are designed for executives who have reached a decisive stage in their careers, preparing them to move forward. There is one programme for each level of management responsibility	Breakthrough Programme for Senior Executives Managing Corporate Resources Programme for Executive Development Building on Talent
Leadership & Strategy	Theme-based programmes examining the challenges of management in a range of specific contexts, e.g., managing across functions, through significant change, for international expansion, or in a family business. These programmes are particularly suitable for team participation	Orchestrating Winning Performance New Venture Booster e-Business Leading the Family Business Leading Corporate Renewal Mobilizing People Accelerating International Growth PRISM
Process & Functional Management	Each programme examines the challenges of managing a specific function, then helps participants expand their perspective from a narrow functional view to include the broader issues of contributing to the overall strategy of the company	Marketing in the Networked Economy Managing Manufacturing Managing the Innovation Process Strategic Finance
Degree Programs	IMD offers two routes to its MBA degree – the one-year full-time MBA programme and the Executive MBA which can be taken over 16 months or several years	Master of Business Administration Executive MBA
Joint Programs	These programs link IMD's expertise with the special strengths of other teaching organizations	Mastering the Technology Enterprise Job of the Chief Executive

Table 6.3. IMD's offerings.

In addition to these open enrolment programmes, IMD also organizes Partnership Programmes, which concentrate on company-specific learning programmes. The Partnership Programmes imply working with companies from IMD's Learning Network (which will be dealt with later on in this chapter) to develop programs that address the specific challenges these companies encounter. Themes of these company-specific programmes include strategy development and implementation, developing general management skills, leading change, and top management visioning.

Learning at IMD

Within the IMD learning environment, different modes of learning are deployed in order to provide a management learning experience that enables the participants to acquire knowledge, skills, and experiences that can be integrated into and applied to the managerial practice immediately. Next to learning through collaborative techniques, case studies, presentations, and (discussion with) guest lecturers, the IMD learning process is generally underpinned by a three-stage learning process. First, students begin working on a subject by studying the material individually. Subsequently, students' views are discussed in a group of six or seven classmates whose different work experiences or cultural backgrounds may lead them to form different conclusions about the material. Finally, each group presents its ideas in the classroom where a faculty member addresses the issues and introduces any relevant new concepts and techniques.

As a modern learning environment behooves, e-learning is also part of IMD's courses. Based on a 'Real World, Real Learning' philosophy (learning rather than teaching, a global meeting place, a range of quality content resources, and a commitment to real learning), the pedagogical fundamentals relate to a personalized and technology-enabled mode of action learning.

Complementary to the elements of the traditional learning environment, the benefits offered by the use of e-learning technology are capitalized upon in the form of extended global communication networks, through which learners can discuss and collaborate with peers around the world. E-learning enables learners to apply on-campus learning on the job, see how it works, maintaining the connection with both peers and IMD. In addition, according to IMD, e-learning allows deeper learning in the sense of more time (flexibility) and more reflection on complex topics and how they apply, personalization of the learning agenda, optimizing time away from the office, quality, and learning capture through central repository of learning information and new learning created by contributions of participants. Peter Lorange, president of IMD, adds:

> *"From a marketing point of view e-learning offers the possibility to communicate the real thing. It also enables the administrative management activities to be organized more efficient and enhanced network communication. However, in terms of learning, e-learning is an integral part of learning instead of a substitute. You should think of e-learning and learning in a hybrid sense. Online modules can be part of classical programmes. E-learning does fit executive learning, in modules"* (adapted from interview).

IMD as a networked business school

IMD can be considered as a true networked business school. Not only does it use learning methods that reflect network learning, and learning through communities, it also deploys advanced learning technologies. Next to learning, IMD organizational structure and its organizational arrangements clearly reflect network structures. These networks include IMD's Learning Network, networking with corporate universities, research networks, IMD faculty and department networks, and IMD's Alumni Network.

The Learning Network is a vehicle to facilitate organizational learning and invoke transfer of cutting-edge knowledge between IMD and its network members for the benefit of management development. By now, it includes over 130 international corporations (as Partner or Associate). The central objective of the Learning Network is to stimulate dialogue between network members themselves and between network members and IMD faculty on a range of topical management issues, so that new ideas are generated to foster innovation and to have access to the latest management knowledge. Another objective of IMD's Learning Network is to generate a cooperative climate between line executives and IMD faculty by encouraging active participation in IMD research projects of common interest. To realize this, IMD organizes 15 so-called Discovery Events every year. Discovery Events can be seen as short workshops in which IMD faculty present their latest thinking and research on specific management issues and members of the Network review and discuss the findings particularly in relation to their own businesses ('live benchmarking').

Through its Corporate Development Team, IMD currently supports the corporate universities and learning centres of many of the organizations participating in the Learning Network. The Corporate Development Team works closely with the network members in the design and delivery of corporate university and learning center strategies. This task force contributes to the development of corporations organizational learning arrangements by reviewing the corporate university curricula, conducting corporate university audits, and facilitating discussions among non-competing network members regarding their approach to corporate universities.

Within IMD's research networks, the participants (IMD and corporate partners) are enabled to conduct relevant and applicable research resulting in state-of-the-art knowledge about particular management themes. An example of a theme-based research network is MIBE, Managing the International Business Environment, in which 17 companies participate. The MIBE project is IMD's innovative and successful corporate social and environmental sustainability project. MIBE works with 17 members (major corporations and financial institutions) on cutting-edge research issues in the field of corporate sustainability. All MIBE research initiatives are based on what the companies define as being on their 'radar screens' when it comes to important corporate sustainability trends. This is what makes MIBE research so relevant to today's thinking within corporations and financial institutions. As is the case with the Learning Network, sub-networks have been formed spontaneously in which companies that have a common interest, or companies that think they can learn from each other, have gathered.

Though management experts with their own functional expertise work at IMD, IMD has no separate academic departments – all organizational members are expected to exert themselves for the overarching network purpose. Consequently, there's no hierarchy within the organization, though IMD's president functions as the *primus inter pares*, i.e., the general network manager. IMD faculty has no fixed tenure and it has established a performance-based compensation system in which almost half of the income is variable. Performance and output management of faculty occurs by reviewing the combination of practice-oriented research, theory-driven research, case study research, and original research. In this network environment staff, in fact, manages itself by, for instance, establishing its own research agenda.

The IMD Alumni Network, finally, consists of over 45,000 executives worldwide. Its main objective is to establish, maintain and strengthen the relationship among former participants in IMD programmes. The network is structured into 39 Alumni Clubs run by and for members in close association with IMD. Each Alumni Club organizes a series of learning events featuring speakers from industry, government, the media, and also with the participation of the IMD faculty. The IMD Alumni Office keeps the Alumni worldwide informed and involved through regular communications and events.

These networks can be organized in order to get IMD in position to capture benefits, respond to opportunities in the environment, compete with other business schools, and perform the operations as efficiently and effectively as possible. The absence of academic departments, for instance, contributes to IMD's capability to develop and transfer knowledge in a flexible and quick way. It's tight relationship with the corporate sector and it's offerings (solely focused at executive education) ensure that IMD keeps up with what the corporate sector deems relevant and is enabled to customize its offerings to the demands of its customers. A close connection with its alumni enables IMD to approach them with IMD's executive courses and establish a culture of engagement and interaction.

FINAL THOUGHTS

In both the previous chapter and this chapter, a picture has been painted illustrating contemporary trends, developments, and dynamics in the landscape of education in general and management education in particular. A myriad of prominent and powerful developments and dynamics has come to the fore, confronting traditional organizational and institutional arrangements with large-scaled and fast-paced change and new opportunities and threats. By now, a fierce debate about the desirability of virtual business schools, the value of online MBAs, the applicability and effectiveness of educational technology for management education, and the future of the educational sector in general as society knows it today, has emerged. No final answers have been formulated yet and no definitive directions have been taken. In fact, it seems that there *is* no single answer or direction. Different approaches to providing education have proven to be successful and formerly inconceivable markets, competitors, and organizational arrangements have emerged. In addition, especially regarding management education, the number of relevant variables – like the heterogeneity of the student body, structure and content of the curriculum, the use of technology, and the importance of branding – enables the development of different approaches that can co-exist.

The topic of management education and business schools in the network economy has proven to be an interesting venue of research, since it is situated at the interfaces of different contexts, with diverging themes and incorporates many stakeholders. The issues that have been addressed in this chapter particularly clearly illustrate that this topic is subjected to continuous change and new dynamics. The landscape of management education and business schools is being reshaped: the nature and structure of competition has altered significantly, incorporating non-traditional suppliers and customers, and has moved the venue to an international stage. New strategies are needed for business schools to survive. It seems implausible that the landscape of management education and business schools will take some 'definite' form. After all, it hasn't been that way in past either and the social, technological, economical, political, and educational transformations that are taking place today will contribute to its future shapes. The fact that the reshaping of this field and the development of new forms to adapt to this changing situation is still in an embryonic stage ensures that it will undoubtedly continue to be an, at least, equally intriguing venue for investigation in the 21st century network economy.

Some scholars have predicted the demise of traditional educational institutions in the 21st century network economy – which they have been doing for valid reasons without solely relying on rhetorics. A new landscape with new dynamics, new players, and which is to be governed by new 'rules' demands new organizational forms. Traditional arrangements do not seem to fit the new dynamics and demands of the network economy and, hence, are susceptible to decay. As Ives & Jarvenpaa have put it:

> *"Business schools (...) are vulnerable. Surviving institutions will likely to have the strongest brand names, be able to provide both scale and scope, and have the most flexible faculty. (...) The inflexibility of traditional universities, however, suggests that nontraditional educational suppliers may be best positioned to exploit the lucrative market for business education (...)"* (Ives & Jarvenpaa, 1996: 40).

In order to avert a possible demise and to anticipate a radically transforming market and future reshaping of the landscape of management education, organizations have to transform themselves according to the dynamics and demands of the network economy. Different authors have proposed the concept of a virtual university or business school as a possible way of surviving in the network economy, while others have suggested hybrid organizational forms. The concept of the networked business school has been put forward in this chapter to explore an organizational form that strongly reflects the organizational logic of the network economy. The networked business school capitalizes upon general network principles and, hence, is positioned to encounter the current challenges in the field of management education. The network logic can extend from the organization of personnel, educational processes and learning environments, the business school's strategy formulation and implementation, to ICT-facilitated arrangements. It enables business schools to be organized in a flexible, effective, and even cost-efficient manner, seizing opportunities and warding off threats in the 21st century market for management education.

The concept of a networked business school seems well-suited to cope with the contemporary institutional changes occurring in the field of higher education. Business schools, in particular, are confronted so much the more with the impacts and consequences of these transformations, since they have been on the front line regarding anticipatory actions and directions to cope with these transformations. More than most of the disciplines in (social) science, they have been maintaining relationships with the corporate sector – some of them have been engaging extensively in partnerships, some of them less extensively. By developing and integrating relevant actors and networks into a concept of network organization, business schools are better equipped to cope with the demands and needs of their customers, preventing them from rapidly becoming relics, to use Drucker's words. In addition to the explosion of corporate universities that occurred over the last years, some powerful partnerships have already been established recently, which may be an indication of the prominent way in which management education may be organized in the 21st century. The networked business school could be well-positioned to effectively overcome some of the enduring criticism by the corporate sector. As was shown by Chapter 4, this criticism has largely been focusing on the shortcomings of the business school curriculum, particularly relating to the development of (interpersonal and leadership) competencies and skills. Network organization of management education can stimulate and facilitate structural patterns of interaction between the business school and the corporate sector, thereby indulging to the need to transform as perceived by the corporate sector and exploiting the different and changing needs of business. The networked business school is also able to provide an integrated and rich learning experience to its students by means of availing itself of a pedagogy of network learning. Such a pedagogy flexibly integrates different relevant contexts into the business school curriculum enabling students to learn, develop and deploy skills and competencies, and experience at the same time and in the same place. This may be one of the domains that contains the challenge to transform management education in a way that encounters the demands of lifelong learning, the fading boundary between work and learning, just-in-time learning, and just-in-place learning put on education.

Of course, the idea of the networked business school leaves room for variation, its organizational form depending on the (strategic) choices made by the individual business schools – which is another inherent part of the flexibility it offers. The networked business school may rely heavily on ICT, opting for a particular model of virtualization to deliver its products. The networked business school may also capitalize on the mobility of its faculty, moving throughout the different contexts that are covered by the network, developing themselves, scanning the external environment, providing the opportunity for the business school to be sensitive and responsive to customer needs, and laying the building blocks for future markets or target groups of management education.

CHAPTER 7

EPILOGUE: THE NEED FOR STRATEGIC ACADEMIC LEADERSHIP

INTRODUCTION

Within the knowledge-based network era, education and learning have become crucial conditions for the development of nations, enterprises, and individuals. Traditionally being the purview of universities and business schools, the creation and transfer of knowledge should place institutions of higher education at a front line position of today's economy. However, fundamental transformational processes, economically, socially, politically, as well as technologically, and emerging non-traditional players are threatening education's monopoly in knowledge creation and transfer, creating shaking quaking soil in a traditional landscape. Perhaps higher education is not best positioned to serve the needs of the network economy alone. Put differently:

> *"The changes most important to higher education are those that are external to it. What is new is the use of societal demand – (...) market forces – to reshape the academy. The danger is that colleges and universities have become less relevant to society precisely because they have yet to understand the new demands being placed upon them"* (The Pew Higher Education Roundtable, 1994: 1).

In fact, business schools and other institutions of management education are experiencing the consequences of these transformations in a magnified way, making the challenge of survival even more critical. The business school's competitive reality is changing dramatically, now including new for-profit providers, a highly differentiated demand, and emerging global partnerships between content providers and technology service providers, urging it to become more sensitive to its external constituencies (Pfeffer, 1993). In addition, its internal constituencies, notably its faculty, may adopt roles that carry characteristics of free agents, since tenure will erode and there will be greater differentiation among business schools (Porter, 1997). The question then becomes: what should be done by business schools in order to endure the coming era? Business schools should take a more entrepreneurial stance (Hamilton, 1997), tapping new additional sources of funding, exploring and exploiting new markets, listening to market signals carefully, and seeking for partnerships to strengthen their competitive positions. Business schools should strengthen their competitiveness along three dimensions: closeness to the market and its needs, process efficiency optimization, and product differentiation. Entrepreneurship demands leaders with vision and the ability to think strategically and creatively.

STRATEGIC ACADEMIC LEADERSHIP

If there's one important topic that has not come clearly to the fore in this book yet, it's this need for strategic academic leadership to guide the networked business school through the 21st century playing field of management education. Though the art of strategic management is a relative alien subject within higher education, it is clear that it is becoming one of the quintessential conditions for survival of educational institutions – in particular for business schools. George Keller (1983) has developed an academic strategic planning model that focuses on the inside (organization) and the outside (environment) of an educational institution, which is presented in figure 7.1.

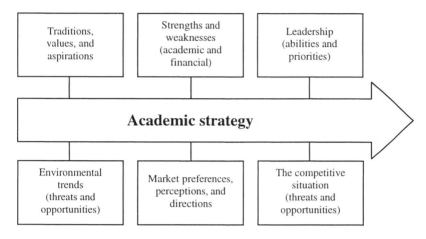

Figure 7.1. Academic strategy planning model.
Source: Keller (1983)

A recent and interesting approach to strategic leadership in business schools has been conceived by IMD's president Peter Lorange. Within the context of strategy setting, there is an important role for the academic leader. The focus of the academic leader, encompasses a directional dimension (adaptation versus proactivism), as well as an actor dimension (entrepreneurialism versus rational leadership), according to Lorange (2000). The strategy of the business school's research and teaching activities is set out by the directional dimension, while the actor dimension focuses on the deployment of human capital and leadership roles.

A focus on adaptation means that a business school engages in direction-setting and processes of adjustments according to changing needs of its students or clients. As both the magnitude of the demand for management education as well as the degree of differentiation of this demand have increased, this task is all but a sinecure. However, this task is fundamental to the business school's long-term profitability and, hence, survival. A proactive stance implies proactively exploring possible future directions of the business school's organizational development to lead change. These directional moves should be in line with the overall objectives of the business school.

The entrepreneurial dimension focuses on creating incentives and valuing bottom-up initiatives by faculty members. Such initiatives often are sources of new and creative solutions or ideas. This relates to both individual faculty members and to eclectic groups of faculty members. The dimension of rational leadership relates to the top-down management of a business school by a dean or president. This leadership role resembles a catalytic role "to try to improve the conditions of, and impact contexts for, how people work in a business school, so that clearer, more deliberate direction can be the result" (Lorange, 2000: 404).

Figure 7.2 displays these dimensions and their forces.

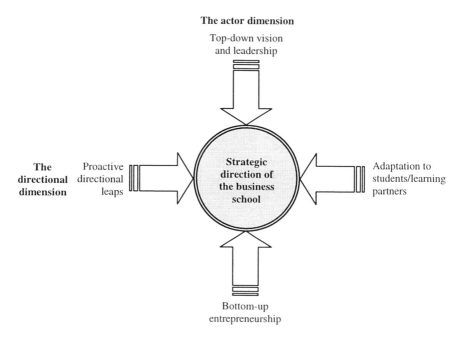

Figure 7.2. Forces with an impact on the strategic direction of the school.
Source: Lorange (2000: 405)

In order to realize an effective process of value creation, or in Lorange's terms a "dynamic business school", the four forces should be balanced. This means that the business school should respond to its customers' demands as well as capitalizing on faculty's interest in pioneering and rapidly expanding into new directions. It also means that there must be something that can be labeled as interactive management, i.e., having a strategic and visionary leader at the top of the business school next to using the contributions and visions coming from faculty.

MANAGING IMBALANCE: THE ART OF NETWORK MANAGEMENT

Only when these forces are slightly out of balance, the business school will be able to move in a particular strategic direction. The term slightly is a crucial qualification here, since it implies what Lorange calls 'controlled dynamics' – i.e., a state of change that can be managed. The management of this state of imbalance is an important task concerning the role of the business school's dean, the person that plays a central role in strategic academic leadership. The imbalance is created by choosing a strategic option or a particular strategic direction. With respect to the strategy formulation process, the dean has to model the interaction between strategic outcomes, defined in terms of projects and processes, and the involved actors, defined in terms of people and partners.

In order to create and cope with the controlled dynamics, a range of questions relating to the strategic direction of the business school emerges. Examples of relevant questions (adapted from Lorange, 2000: 410-411) the dean should ask him- or herself from the perspective of the involved actor dimension are:

–   What are the types of people who need to be attracted to the business school to enhance the strategy? (*people*);
–   Are there some areas of competence that would be especially desirable to look for in new professors to enhance the strategy? (*people*);
–   Which are the learning partners that should be involved that can have the most impact on the business school when working with them and learning from them? (*partners*);
–   Can companies be involved that see the business school as a learning partner as opposed to a subcontractor? (*partners*).

Examples of relevant questions the dean asks him- or herself from the perspective of the outcome dimension are:

–   What guiding principles do the people in the organization follow in order to create the academic work, and how can these be modified if dysfunctional, relative to the desired strategic direction? (*processes*);
–   Should academic departments be consolidated to more readily facilitate cross-disciplinary learning input? (*processes*);
–   What are projects are being chosen and what should the business school focus on? (*projects*);
–   What portfolio of activities should be aimed for? (*projects*).

A clear and focused strategy for the business school can be formulated by asking such questions concerning the domains of people, partners, processes, and projects. The fate of strategic academic leadership inextricably implies, however, that the dean's vision will always be subjected to a process of choosing and ruling out the (combination of) option(s) that is deemed right for the business school. After all, strategy means choice. A choice for network organization, however, implies the integration of imbalance in the sense that network organizations encounter diverging forces of stability against flexibility, specialization against generalization, and centralization against decentralization (Van Alstyne, 1997), as has been illustrated by Chapter 3. This emphasizes the importance of adequate leadership and management once again. The business school's dean, then, has to adopt the role of a network manager by integrating different characteristics of the network manager as an architect, a lead operator, and a caretaker: the essential characteristics attributed to these managerial roles have to meet in the role of the business school's dean. Sometimes the role of the architect prevails, while in other situations the dean primarily has to act as a caretaker.

One principal task within strategic academic leadership regarding the networked business school will be to establish a sense collective purpose within the business school's network. The business school, then, has to align its objectives and strategies with other network members, aiming for shared goals and interests. Perhaps this means succumbing to a limited loss of control of the business school in favor of the overarching goals of the network as a whole. This overarching goal entails the advantages of network organization of management education, providing the opportunity to flexibilize the organization of people, partners, projects, and processes, hence positioning the business school to survive in the 21st century network economy.

References

Alavi, M., Y. Yoo & D. Vogel (1997): Using information technology to add value to management education. *Academy of Management Journal*, 40(6), pp. 1310-1333.

Allred, B.B., R.E. Miles & C.C Snow (1996): Characteristics of managerial careers in the 21st century. *Academy of Management Executive*, 10(4), pp. 17-27.

Alstyne, van M. (1997): State of the network organization. *Journal of Organizational Computing & Electronic Commerce*, 7(3), pp. 83-151.

Angehrn, A.A. & T. Nabeth (1997): Leveraging emerging technologies in management education: research and experiences. *European Management Journal*, 15(3), pp. 275-285.

Apple Computer (1995): *Teaching and learning with technology: a report on 10 years of ACOT*. Cupertino, CA. Found at: http://www.apple.com/education/k12/leadership/acot/pdf/10yr.pdf.

Araujo, L. (1998): Knowing and learning as networking. *Management Learning*, 29(3), pp. 317-336.

Arthur, W.B. (1996): Increasing returns and the new world of business. *Harvard Business Review*, 74(4), July-August, pp. 100-109.

Atkinson, R.D. & R.H. Court (2000): *The new economy index: understanding America's transformation*. Found at http://www.neweconomyindex.org.

Baalen, van P. (Ed., 1995): *New challenges for the business schools*. Eburon.

Baalen, van P. & F. Leijnse (1995): Beyond the discipline: inserting interdisciplinarity in business and management education. In: P. van Baalen (Ed., 1995): *New challenges for the business schools*. Eburon.

Baer, W. (2000): Competition and collaboration in online distance learning. *Information, Communication & Society*, 3(4), pp. 457-473.

Baets, W. & G. van der Linden (2000): *The hybrid business school: developing knowledge management through management learning*. Prentice Hall.

Bagdikian, B. (1997): *The Media Monopoly*. Beacon Press (5th edition).

Baker, W.E. (1993): The network organization in theory and practice. In: N. Nohria & R.G. Eccles (Eds., 1993): *Networks and Organizations*. Harvard Business School Press, Boston, MA, pp. 397-429.

Barlow, R. (2000): The Net upends tenets of loyalty marketing. *Advertising Age*, April 17th.

Bates, A.W. (1995): *Technology, open learning and distance education*. Routledge, London.

Bedeian, A.G., D.A. Wren (2001): Most influential management books of the 20th century. Organizational Dynamics, 29(3), pp. 221-225.

Bednar, A.K., D. Cunningham, T.M. Duffy & J.D. Perry (1992): Theory into practice: How do we link? In: T.M. Duffy & D.H. Jonassen (Eds., 1992): *Constructivism and the technology of instruction*, Lawrence Earlbaum & Associates, Hillsdale, NJ, pp. 17-33.

Bertelsmann Foundation (1998): *The potential of media across the curriculum: the finding from the 1996-1997 evaluation at Athens Academy*. Gutersloh, Germany.

Black, S.E. & L.M. Lynch (1997*): How to compete: the impact of workplace practices and information technology on productivity.* NBER Working paper, no. 6120, August.

Black, S.E. & L.M. Lynch (2000): *What's driving the new economy? The benefits of workplace innovation.* NBER Working paper, no. 7479, January.

Blurton, C. (1999): *New directions of ICT-use in education.* World Communication and Information Report, UNESCO. Found at: http://www.unesco.org/education/educprog/lwf/dl/edict.pdf.

Boisot, M. (1998): *Knowledge assets: securing competitive advantage in the information economy.* Oxford University Press, Oxford.

Bolhuis, van H. & V. Colom (1995): *Cyberspace reflections.* VUB University Press, Brussels.

Bowers, C. (1988): *The cultural dimensions of educational computing: understanding the non-neutrality of technology.* Teachers College Press, New York.

Bresnahan, T.F., E. Brynjolfsson & L.M. Hitt (1999): *Information technology workplace organization and the demand for skilled labor: firm-level evidence.* NBER Working paper, no. 7136, May.

Brickell, G. (1993): Navigation and learning style. *Australian Journal of Educational Technology,* 9(2), pp. 103-114.

Brown, J.S. & P. Duguid (1995): *Universities in the digital age.* Found at: http://www.parc.xerox.com/ops/members/brown/papers/university.html.

Brown, J.S. & P. Duguid (2000): *The social life of information.* Harvard Business School Press, Boston, MA.

Brynjolfsson, E. & L.M. Hitt (1997): *Computing productivity: are computers pulling their weight?* mimeo, MIT and Wharton. Found at: http://ccs.mit.edu/erik/cpg.

Brynjolfsson, E., L.M. Hitt & S. Yang (1998): *Intangible assets: how the interaction of information systems and organizational structure affects stock market valuations.* Proceedings of the International Conference in Information Systems, Helsinki, Finland.

Brynjolfsson, E. & S. Yang (1998): *The intangible benefits and costs of computer investments: evidence from the financial markets.* mimeo. Found at: http://ccs.mit.edu/erik/.

Burgoyne, J. (1994): Managing by learning. *Management Learning,* 25(1), pp. 35-55.

Burt, R. (1992): *Structural holes: the social structure of competition.* Harvard Business School Press, Boston, MA.

Burton-Jones, A. (1999): *Knowledge capitalism: business, work, and learning in the new economy.* Oxford University Press, Oxford.

Business Week (2000): *The virtual MBA: a work in progress.* October 2nd.

Business Week (2001): *An international marriage of b-school giants.* March 29th.

Byrkjeflot, H. (2001): *E-learning alliances. The new partnerships in business education.* LOS-senter Notat 0102.

California.edu website. Found at: http://www.california.edu.

Cambre, M.A. (1991): The state of the art in instructional television. In: G.J. Anglin (Ed., 1991): *Instructional technology, past, present, and future.* Libraries Unlimited, Englewood, CO.

Cap Gemini Ernst & Young website. Found at: http://www.cgey.com.

Cardean University website. Found at: http://www.cardean.com.

Castells, M. (1996): *The rise of the network society*. Blackwell Publishers, Cambridge, MA.

Ciborra, C.U. (1996): *Teams, markets and systems: business innovation and information technology*. Cambridge University Press, Cambridge.

Clarke, S. & T. Clegg (1998): *Changing paradigms: the transformation of management knowledge for the 21st century*. HarperCollins Business, London.

Collins, J.C. & J.I. Porras (1994): *Built to last: successful habits of visionary companies*. HarperBusiness, New York.

Conklin, J. (1987): Hypertext: an introduction and survey. *IEEE Computer*, 20, pp. 17-41.

Contractor, F.J. (2000): What 'international' subtopics are crucial to business education? A survey of management school professors. *Journal of International Management*, 6, pp. 61-70.

CPB (Centraal Planbureau/Dutch Central Bureau of Planning) (2000*): ICT en de Nederlandse economie: een historisch en internationaal perspectief*. Werkdocument no. 125, CPB.

Cunningham, S., S. Tapsall, Y. Ryan, L. Stedman, K. Bagdon & T. Flew (1998): *New media and borderless education: a review of the convergence between global media networks and higher education provision*. Australian Government, Department of Employment, Education, Training and Youth Affairs. Evaluations and Investigations Programme, Higher Education Division. Found at: http://www.detya.gov.au/archive/highered/eippubs/eip97-22/eip9722.pdf.

Curry, J. (1997): The dialectic of knowledge-in-production: value creation in late capitalism and the rise of knowledge-centered production. *Electronic Journal of Sociology*, 2(3). Found at: http://www.sociology.org/content/vol002.003/curry.html.

Daniel, J.S. (1996): *Mega-universities and the knowledge media: technology strategies for higher education*. Kogan Page, London.

David, P.A. (1991): Computer and dynamo: the modern productivity paradox in a not-too-distant mirror. In: OECD (1991): *Technology and productivity*. OECD, Paris.

David, P.A. & G. Wright (1999): General purpose technologies and surges in productivity: historical reflections on the future of the ICT revolution. *Discussion papers in economic and social history*, 31, September.

Davidow, W.H. & M.S. Malone (1992): *The virtual corporation*. HarperCollins, New York.

Davis, N. (1996): *Cost-benefit analysis of integrated services digital network in education and training*. Working paper, University of Exeter, School of Education.

Davis, S. & J. Botkin (1994): The coming of knowledge-based business. *Harvard Business Review*, 72(5), September-October, pp. 165-170.

Davis, S. & C. Meyer (1997): An economy turned on its head: why you must be 'knowledge-based' to compete in today's world (and what that means). *Strategy & Leadership*, 25(6), November-December.

Davis, S. & C. Meyer (1998): *Blur: the speed of change in the connected economy*. Addison-Wesley, Reading, MA.

DeLong, J.B. (1998): *Book review of Information Rules: A Strategic Guide to the Network Economy* (by C. Shapiro & H. Varian). Found at http://www.j-bradford-delong.net/Econ_Articles/Reviews/Information_Rules.html.

DeLong, B. (1998): *Attack of the neo-luddites!* Found at: http://www.j-bradford-delong.net/Teaching_Folder/Digital_Diploma_Mills.html.

Dijk, van J.A.G.M. (1999): *The network society*. Sage, London.

Dillemans, R., J. Lowyck, G. van der Perre, C. Claeys & J. Elen (1998): *New technologies for learning: contribution of ICT to innovation in education*. Leuven University Press, Leuven.

Drucker, P.F. (1999): *Management challenges for the 21st century*. Butterworth-Heinemann, Oxford.

Duffy, T. and D. Jonassen (Eds., 1992): *Constructivism and instructional design*. Lawrence Erlbaum, Hillsdale, NJ.

Dumort, A. (2000): New media and distance education. An EU-US perspective. *Information, Communication & Society*, 3(4), pp. 546-556.

Elfring, T. & F. van Raaij (1995): Research in management science; the challenge of double integration. In: P. van Baalen (Ed., 1995): *New challenges for the business schools*. Eburon.

European Roundtable of Industrialists (ERT) (1997): *Investing in knowledge: the integration of technology in European education*. ERT, Brussels.

Evans, P. & T.S. Wurster (2000): *Blown to bits: how the new economics of information transforms strategy*. Harvard Business School Press, Boston, MA.

Farrell, C. (2000): The case for optimism. *Business Week*, October 9th, pp. 52-53.

Fernback, J. & B. Thompson (1995): *Virtual communities: abort, retry, failure?* Found at: http://www.well.com/user/hlr/texts/VCcivil.html.

Forbes Magazine (1997): *Seeing things as they really are*. March 10th.

Frank, R. & J. Porter (1997): The inspiration of experience. *Management Review*, 86(1), pp. 33-36.

Fraser, A. (1999): *Virtual communities*. Project discussion paper. Found at: http://create.suffolk.ac.uk/teaching/_disc1/00000010.htm.

Frazer, J. & Oppenheim, J. (1997): What's new about globalization. *The McKinsey Quarterly*, 2, p. 172.

FT.com (1999): *Schools drawn into new webs*. October 11th.

FT.com (2000a): *The case for corporate universities: savvy e-learners drive revolution in education*. April 3rd.

FT.com (2000b): *ABB Academy: a vehicle designed to bring about change*. April 3rd.

FT.com (2001a): *A future of promising alliances: London business School/Columbia, New York*. March 12th.

FT.com (2001b): *A combination to be reckoned with*. April 2nd.

Gastel, van L., A. Heck, S. Tobias & C. van Weert (1997): *Developing a vision of 21st century Math/Science classroom*. University of Amsterdam, Amsterdam.

Gibb, A. (1991): *Entrepreneurship and small business management: can we afford to neglect them in the twenty-first century business school?* Durham University Business School, Durham.

Gibbons, M., H. Nowotny, C. Limoges, S. Schwartzman, P. Scott & M. Trow (1994): *The new production of knowledge: the dynamics of science and research in contemporary societies*. Sage, London.

Gilder, G. (1989): *Microcosm: the quantum revolution in economics and technology*. Touchstone, New York.

Glennan, T.K. & A. Melmed (1995): *Fostering the use of educational technology: elements of a national strategy*. RAND Report, RAND, Washington DC. Found at: http://www.rand.org/publications/MR/MR682/contents.html.

Goldhaber, M.H. (1997a): *The attention economy and the web*. Presented at the conference on Economics of Digital Information Cambridge, MA, January 23rd-26th, 1997. Found at: http://www.well.com/user/mgoldh/AtEcandNet.html.

Goldhaber, M.H. (1997b): The attention economy and the net. *First Monday*, 2(4), April 7th.

Green, K.C. & S.W. Gilbert (1995): *Great expectations*. Found at: http://www.usask.ca/computers-in-teaching/Great_expectations.htm.

Hamilton, J. (1997): Stanford: eggheads and entrepreneurs. *Business week*, June 23rd.

Handy, C.B. (1995): *Beyond certainty: the changing worlds of organizations*. Hutchinson, London.

Harris, M. (2000): Virtual learning and the network society. *Information, Communication & Society*, 3(4), pp. 580-596.

Haug, G. (1999): *Trends in learning structures in higher education*. Project report. Found at: http://www.rks.dk/rapport/Trends/trends3.htm.

Herman, J. (1994): Evaluating the effects of technology in school reform. In: B. Means (Ed., 1994): *Technology and education reform: the reality behind the promise*. Jossey-Bass Publishers, San Francisco.

Het Financieele Dagblad (2000a): *US economic growth slows down, Euro increases* (orig. Economische groei VS vertraagt, euro hoger). October 27th.

Het Financieele Dagblad (2000b): *Europe catches up with the internet* (orig. Europa maakt inhaalslag met internet). October 27th.

Hiemstra, R., & R.G. Brockett (1996): From behaviorism to humanism: Incorporating self-direction in learning concepts into the instructional design process. In: H.B. Long & Associates (1996*): New ideas about self-directed learning*. Oklahoma Research Center for Continuing Professional and Higher Education, University of Oklahoma, Norman, OK.

Hilmer, F.G. & L. Donaldson (1996): *Management redeemed: debunking the fads that undermine our corporations*. The Free Press, New York.

Hitt, M.A. (1998): Twenty-first-century organizations: business firms, business schools, and the academy. *Academy of Management Review*, 23(2), pp. 218-224.

Hitt, L. & E. Brynjolfsson (1997): Information technology and internal firm organization: an exploratory analysis. *Journal of Management Information Sysytems*, 14(2), pp. 81-101.

Hoogeveen, M. (1995): Towards a new multimedia paradigm: is multimedia assisted instruction really effective?, In: H. Maurer (Ed., 1995): *Educational multimedia and hypermedia*. Proceedings of ED-MEDIA 95, World Conference on Educational Multimedia and Hypermedia, Graz, Austria, 1995, pp. 348-353, AACE, Charlottesville, VA.

Huey, J. (1994): Waking up to the new economy. *Fortune*, June 27th.

Hutchins, E. (1995): *Cognition in the wild*. MIT Press, Cambridge, MA.

Ives, B. (1992): Education: a sustainable national competitive advantage. *Management Information Systems Quarterly*, 16(3), September.

Ives, B. & S. Jarvenpaa (1996): Will the internet revolutionize business education and research? *Sloan Management Review*, 37(3), Spring, pp. 33-41.

Jacobson, M.J. & J.A. Levin (1993): *Network learning environments and hypertext: constructing personal and shared knowledge spaces*. Paper presented at the Tel-Ed '93 Conference, Dallas, Texas.

Jarillo, C. (1988): On strategic networks. *Strategic Management Journal*, 9(1), pp. 31-41.

Jarvenpaa, S.L. & B. Ives (1994): The global network organization of the future: information management opportunities and challenges. *Journal of Management Information Systems*, 10(4), pp. 25-57.

Johnston, J. S. & R.J. Edelstein (1993): *Beyond borders: profiles in international education*. Association of American Colleges, Washington, D.C.

Kanter, R.M. (1994): *When giants learn to dance: mastering the challenge of strategy, management, and careers in the 1990s*. Routledge, London (reprint).

Keller, G. (1983): *Academic strategy*. Johns Hopkins University Press, Baltimore.

Kelly, K. (1998): *New rules for the new economy: 10 ways the network economy is changing everything*. Fourth Estate, London.

Kirkpatrick, D.D. (2000): As publishers perish, libraries feel the pain. *New York Times*, November 3rd.

Knapper, C.K. & A.J. Cropley (1985): Lifelong learning and higher education. Croom Helm, London.

Krogt, van der F.J. (1995): *Learning in networks: organizing learning networks versatile considering humanity and labor relevance*. (orig. Leren in netwerken: veelzijdig organiseren van leernetwerken met het oog op humaniteit en arbeidsrelevantie). Lemma, Utrecht.

Krogt, van der (1998): Learrning network theory: the tension between learning systems and work systems in organizations. *Human Resource Development Quarterly*, 9(2), pp. 157-177.

Kulik, J.A. (1994): Meta-analytic studies of findings on computer-based instruction. In: E.L. Baker & H.F. O'Neil (Eds., 1994): *Technology assessment in education and training*. Erlbaum, Hillsdale, NJ.

Lankard, (1995): *New ways of learning in the workplace*. ERIC Digest, no. 161. Found at: http://www.ed.gov/databases/ERIC_Digests/ed385778.html.

Lauzon, A.C. & G.A.B. Moore (1992): A fourth generation distance education systems: integrating computer-assisted learning and computer conferencing, In: M.G. Moore (Ed., 1992): *Readings in distance education: 3. Distance education for corporate and military training*, Pennsylvania State University, American Center for the Study of Distance Education, University Park, PA, pp. 26-37.

Lave, J. & E. Wenger (1991): *Situated Learning. Legitimate Peripheral Participation*. Cambridge University Press, Cambridge, MA.

Leidner, D & S. Jarvenpaa (1995): The use of information technology to enhance management school education: a theoretical view. *Management Information Systems Quarterly*, 19(3), pp. 265-291.

Lichtenberg, F.R. (1995): The output contributions of computer equipment and personnel: a firm level analysis. *Economics of Innovation and New Technology*, 3.

Lorange, P. (2000): Setting strategic direction in academic institutions: the case of the business school. *Higher Education Policy*, 13(4), pp. 399-413.

Luthans, F. (1988): Successful vs effective real managers. *Academy of Management Executive*, 2(2), pp. 127-132.

MACIS Project (1999): *Development of a Management Curriculum for the Information Society*. Esprit, no. 22560, Athens.

Mandel, M.J. (2000): *The next downturn*. Business Week, October 9th, pp. 45-50.

Mandel, M.J. (2001): *The coming internet depression: why the high-tech boom will go bust, why the crash will be worse than you think, and how to prosper afterwards*. Basic Books, New York.

Marsick, V.J. & J. O'Neil (1999): The many faces of action learning. *Management Learning*, 30(2), pp. 159-176.

Martin, P. (1998): Gorging on Mergers. *Financial Times*, December 22nd, p. 15.

Massy, W.F. & R. Zemsky (1996): *Using information technology to enhance academic productivity*. Found at: http://www.educause.edu/nlii/keydocs/massy.htm

McGeehan, P. (1999): UNext.com signs course deal with four more universities. *The Wall Street Journal*, June 23rd.

Means, B. & K. Olson (1995): *Technology's role within constructivist classrooms*. Paper presented at the Annual Meeting of the AERA, San Francisco.

Meister, J.C. (1998): *Corporate universities: lessons in building a world-class work force*. McGraw-Hill, New York.

Miles, R.E. & C.C. Snow (1986): Organizations: new concepts for new forms. *California Management Review*, 28(3), pp. 62-73.

Miles, R.E. & C.C. Snow (1992): Causes of failure in network organization. *California Management Review*, 34(4), Summer, pp. 53-72.

Miles, R.E. & C.C. Snow (1995) The new network firm. A spherical structure based on a human investment philosophy. *Organizational Dynamics*, 23(4), pp. 5-18.

Miles, R.E., C.C. Snow, J.A. Mathews, G. Miles & H.J. Coleman (1997): Organizing in the knowledge age: anticipating the cellular form. *Academy of Management Executive*, 11(4), pp. 7-24.

Mintzberg, H. (1973): *The nature of managerial work*. Harper & Row, New York.

Mintzberg, H. (1979): *The structuring of organizations: a synthesis of the research*. Prentice-Hall, Englewood Cliffs.

Mintzberg, H. (1989): *Mintzberg on management: inside our strange world of organizations*. The Free Press, New York.

Mintzberg, H. (1994): Rounding out the manager's job. *Sloan Management Review*, 36(1), pp. 11-26.

Möller, K. & A. Halinen (1999): Business relationships and networks: managerial challenge of network era. *Industrial Marketing Management*, 28, pp. 413-427.

Moonen, J. (1994): How to do more with less? In: K. Beattie, C. McNaught & S. Wills (Eds., 1994): *Interactive multimedia in university education: designing for change in teaching and learning.* Elsevier Science, North-Holland.

Moor, de. C. (2000): *Entrepreneurship in the (new) economy.* (orig. Ondernemerschap in de (nieuwe) economie.) Doctoral thesis, Faculty of Business Administration, Erasmus University Rotterdam.

Multimedia Instruction Committee (1995): *Development of technology integrated learning environments.* Multimedia Instruction Committee Report, University of Texas at Austin.

Murphy, M. (1998): *Every investor's guide to high-tech stocks and mutual funds.* Broadway Books, New York.

Nadler, D.A. & M.L. Tushman (1997): *Competing by design: the power of organizational architecture.* Oxford University Press, New York.

Nettles, K., C. Dziuban, D. Cioffi, P. Moskal & P. Moskal (1999): *Technology and learning: the no significant difference phenomenon. A structural analysis on technology enhanced instruction.* Unpublished paper.

Newman, R. & F. Johnson (1999): Sites of power and knowledge? Towards a critique of the virtual university. *British Journal of Sociology of Education,* 20(1), pp. 79-88.

Noble, D. (1998): Digital diploma mills: the automation of higher education. *First Monday,* 3(1).

Nonaka, I. & H. Takeuchi (1995): *The knowledge-creating company: how Japanese companies create the dynamics of innovation.* Oxford University Press, New York.

Norton, R.D. (1999): *The geography of the new economy.* The Web Book of Regional Science. Found at: http://www.rri.wvu.edu/WebBook/Norton/contents.htm.

OECD (1996): Recent trends in foreign direct investment. *Financial Market trends,* 64, OECD, Paris.

OECD (2000): *A new economy? The changing role of innovation and information technology in growth.* OECD, Paris.

Papert, S. (1997): *Papert describes his philosophy of education.* MIT News Office, July 3rd.

Pasmore, W.A. (1994): *Creating strategic change: designing the flexible, high-performing organization.* Wiley, New York.

Pedler, M. (Ed., 1991): *Action Learning in Practice.* Gower, Brookfield, VT (2nd edition).

Pensare website. Found at: http:// www.pensare.com.

Perre, van der G., Roosendaal & Van den Branden (2000): The distributed virtual university. In: A. Rocha Trindade (Ed., 2000): *New Learning.* Universidade Aberta, pp. 419-436.

Peters, T. (1997): *The circle of innovation: you can't shrink your way to greatness.* Hodder & Stoughton, London.

Pfeffer, J. (1993): Barriers to the advance of organizational science: paradigm development as a dependent variable. *Academy of Management Journal,* 18(4), pp. 599-620.

Pilot, A. (1999): *The student as junior co-worker?* (orig. De student als junior medewerker?) Universiteit Utrecht. Found at: http://onderwijs.cs.utwente.nl/Kwaliteit/pers_medewerker.htm.

PIM website. Found at: http://www.stern.nyu.edu/PIM.

Pine, B.J. & J.H. Gilmore (1999): *The experience economy: work is theatre & every business a stage.* Harvard Business School Press, Boston, MA.

Poell, R.F., G.E. Chivers, F.J. van der Krogt & D.A. Wildemeersch (2000): Learning-network theory. Organizing the dynamic relationship between learning and work. *Management Learning,* 31(1), pp. 25-49.

Porter, L.W. (1997): A decade of change in the business school: from complacency to tomorrow. *Selections,* Winter, pp. 1-8.

Porter, L. & L. McKibbin (1988): *Management education and development: drift or thrust into the 21st century?* McGraw-Hill, New York.

Potashnik, M. & J. Capper (1998): Distance education: growth and diversity. *Finance and Development,* March. Found at: http://www.worldbank.org/fandd/english/pdfs/0398/0110398.pdf.

Pournelle, J. (1994): An educational trip. *Byte,* July, pp. 197-210.

Quinn, J.B. (1992): *Intelligent enterprise: a knowledge and service based paradigm for industry.* The Free Press, New York.

Rajan, A. (1996): *Leading people.* CREATE publications.

Ramondt, L. & C. Chapman (1998): *Online learning communities.* Found at: http://www.ultralab.ac.uk/papers/online_learning_communities/.

Reinhart, A. & P. Burrows (2000): The outlook for tech. *Business Week,* October 9th, pp. 38-43.

Revans, R.W. (1982): *The origin and growth of action learning.* Chartwell Bratt, London.

Rheingold, H. (1993): *The virtual community: homesteading on the electronic frontier.* Addison-Wesley, New York.

Rifkin, J. (2000): *The Age of Access.* Penguin Books, London.

Rimanoczy, I. (1999): *Action reflection learning: application for individual learning process.* Found at: http://www.mcb.co.uk/imc/al-inter/ali-news/ALI_paper2.html.

Rohlin, et al. (1996): *What do we mean by action reflection learning.* MiL Concepts.

Rothstein, R. & L. McKnight (1994): *Technology and cost models of connecting K-12 schools to the national information infrastructure.* Working paper, MIT Research Programme on Communications Policy, MIT.

Russell, T.L. (1999): *No significant difference phenomenon (NSDP).* North Carolina State University, Raleigh, NC.

Sabel, C. (1991): Moebius strip organizations and open labor markets: some consequences of the reintegration of conception and execution in a volatile economy. In: P. Bourdieu & J. Coleman (Eds., 1991): *Social theory for a changing society.* Westview, Boulder.

Sailer, L.D. (1978): Structural equivalence: meaning and definition, computation and application. *Social Networks,* 1(1), pp. 73-90.

Salancik, G. (1995): Wanted: a good network theory of organization. *Administrative Science Quarterly,* 40(2), pp. 345-349.

Salomon, G. (Ed., 1997): *Distributed cognitions. Psychological and educational considerations.* Cambridge University Press, Cambridge, MA.

Slaughter, S. & L. Leslie (1997): *Academic capitalism: politics, policies, and the entrepreneurial university*. The Johns Hopkins University Press, Baltimore, MA.

Schein, E.H. (1992): The role of the CEO in the management of change: the case of information technology. In: T.A. Kochan & M. Useem (Eds., 1992): *Transforming organizations*, Oxford University Press, New York, pp. 80-95.

Schieman, E., S. Taire & J. McLaren (1992): Towards a course development model for graduate level distance education. *The American Journal of Distance Education*, 7(2), pp. 51-65.

Schreyer, P. (2000): *The contribution of information and communication technologies to output growth*. STI Working paper 2000/2, OECD, Paris.

Shapiro, R.J. (2000): Thoughts on growth in the new economy. *Magazine on Information Impacts*, September 22nd. Found at http://www.cisp.org/imp/september_2000/09_00shapiro.htm.

Shapiro, C. & H. Varian (1999): *Information rules: a strategic guide to the network economy*. Harvard Business School Press, Boston, MA.

Shuell, T.J. (1992): Designing instructional computing systems for meaningful learning. In: M. Jones & P.H. Winne (Eds., 1992): *Adaptive learning environments. Foundations and frontiers*. NATO-ASI Series, Series F: Computer and Systems Sciences 85, pp. 19-54. Springer-Verlag, Berlin.

Simons, P.R.J. (1993): Constructive learning: the role of the learner. In: T.M. Duffy, J. Lowyck & D.H. Jonassen (Eds., 1993): *Designing environments for constructive learning*. Springer-Verlag, Berlin, pp. 291-313.

Snow, C.C., R.E. Miles & H.J. Coleman (1992): Managing 21st Century Network Organizations. *Organizational Dynamics*, 20(3), pp. 5-20.

Software Publishers Association (1996): *Report on the effectiveness of technology in schools, 95-96*. Software Publishers Associations, Washington DC.

Special Issue on Educational Technologies: Current Trends and Future Directions (1994): *Machine-Mediated Learning*, 4(2&3).

Spoun, S. (1998): *Internationalisierung von Universitäten. Eine Studie am Beispiel der Community of European Management Schools*. Dissertation no. 2179. Difo-Druck, Bamberg.

Star, S.L. (1992): The Trojan door. Organizations, work, and the open black box. *Systems Practice*, 5(4), pp. 395-410.

Stevens, G.E. (2000): The art of running a business school in the new millennium: a dean's perspective. *SAM Advanced Management Journal*, 65(3), Summer, pp. 21-28.

Stewart, R. (1970): *Managers and their jobs*. Pan, London.

Stewart, T.A. (1999): Have you got what it takes? *Fortune*, October 11th.

Strommen, E.F. (1992): *Constructivism, technology and the future of classroom learning*. Found at: http://www.ilt.columbia.edu/ilt/papers/construct.htm.

Summit (2001): April. Found at: http://www.henleymc.ac.uk.

Tapscott, D. (1999): *Creating value in the network economy*. Harvard Business School Press, Boston, MA.

The Chronicle of Higher Education (2000a): *Rupert Murdoch Joins with 18 universities in distance-education venture*. May 17th.

The Chronicle of Higher Education (2000b): *3 elite business schools to offer online instruction*. June 21st.

The New Economy Index website. Found at http://www.neweconomyindex.org.

The Pew Higher Education Roundtable (1994): To dance with change. *Policy Perspectives*, 5(3), pp. 1-12.

Thurow, L.C. (1999): *Building wealth*. Nicholas Brealey Publishing, London.

Torino Group (1998): *Re-designing management development in the new Europe*. European Training Foundation, Italy.

UNext website. Found at: http://www.unext.com.

Universitas 21 website. Found at: http:// www.universitas.edu.au.

Van de Velde, M.E.G., P.G.W. Jansen & C.J. Vinkenburg (1999): Managerial activities among top and middle managers: self versus other perceptions. *Journal of Applied Management Studies*, 8(2), pp. 161-174.

Vince, R. & L. Martin (1993): Inside action learning: an exploration of the psychology and politics of the action learning model. *Management education and development*, 24(3), pp. 205-215.

Volberda, H.W. (1997): *Building the flexible firm: how to remain competitive*. Oxford University Press, Oxford.

Vygotsky, L.S. (1976): The role of play in the mental development of the child. In: J. Bruner (Ed., 1976): *Play: its role in development and evolution*. Penguin.

Webber, A.M. (1993): What's so new about the new economy? *Harvard Business Review*, 71(1), January-February, pp. 24-42.

Webster, F. (1995): *Theories of the information society*. Routledge, London.

Weinstein, B.L. (1997): Welcome to the New Economy. *Perspectives*, 12(2), December, pp. 1-4.

Weinstein, K. (1995): *Action learning: a journey in discovery and development*. HarperCollins, London.

Wenger, E. (1998): *Communities of practice*. Cambridge University Press, Cambridge MA.

White, F. (1999): Digital diploma mills: a dissenting voice. *First Monday*, 4(7).

Wildemann, H. (1996): Management von Produktions- und Zuliefernetzwerken. In: H. Wildemann (Ed., 1996): *Produktions- und Zuliefernetzwerke*. München, pp. 13-45.

Williams, R.L. (1992): Social advocates and action learning: the discontent dancing with hope. *New Directions for Adult and Continuing Education*, 53, pp. 37-50.

Wired's Encyclopedia of the New Economy. Found at http://hotwired.lycos.com/special/ene/.

Woodall, P. (2000): Untangling e-conomics. *The Economist*, September 23rd.

Wüthrich, H.A., A.F. Philipp & M.H. Frentz (1997): *Head start through virtualization: learning from virtual pioneering enterprises* (orig. Vorsprung durch Virtualisierung: lernen von virtuellen Pionierunternehmen). Wiesbaden.

INDEX

A

Accountability 3, 57, 72, 157
Accreditation 7, 121-123, 126, 145, 146
Action learning 81, 83, 87, 88
Action reflection learning 88
Active learning 83, 97, 107
Administrators 5, 148
Alliance 32, 37, 45,47, 48, 50, 75, 125, 127, 128, 130, 131, 132, 135, 136, 137, 144, 149
Alumni 122, 132, 140, 141, 156, 158, 159, 162, 163
Architect 65, 66, 132, 154, 158, 170
Attention economy 25, 28, 30-31

B

Bologna Declaration 122
Boundary between work and learning 2, 6, 165
Branding 7, 122, 125, 130, 131, 135, 156, 164
Brand value 121-123, 130
Broker 49, 60, 65-66, 77, 92, 125, 146, 158
Business network 35, 49, 50, 67
Business school curriculum 54, 56, 68-74, 76, 77, 165

C

Caretaker 65, 66, 158, 170
Certification 121, 125, 137
Coach 47, 59, 81, 82, 86, 87, 88, 116, 136, 151, 156, 157
Community 3, 30, 76, 127, 128, 136, 140, 141, 158
Community of practice 90
Competencies 2, 4, 6, 25, 35, 43, 44, 45, 51, 52, 55, 57, 60-63, 64, 68, 77, 78, 85, 92, 96, 122, 133, 152, 154, 165
Competitive advantage 9, 30, 33, 41, 42, 43, 44, 45, 47, 52, 53, 60, 71, 72, 79, 80, 119, 132, 133, 145, 155
Competitiveness 35, 42, 48, 60, 80, 121, 122, 166
Conditional knowledge 6, 108
Connectedness 12, 31, 34, 35, 50, 102, 124
Connectivity 40, 41, 47, 102
Construction 41, 42, 81, 82, 83, 109
Constructivist perspective 108-109
Content provider 7, 127, 138, 158, 166
Context 1, 7, 34, 40, 44, 56, 57, 61, 63, 64, 73, 74, 79, 81, 83, 85, 86, 88, 89, 92, 95, 109, 110, 112, 114, 134, 154, 155, 156, 157, 164, 165, 167, 168
Continuous learning 25, 86, 111, 119, 133, 135, 151, 158